Educated Ta

Library of Congress Cataloging-in-Publication Data
Educated tastes: food, drink, and connoisseur culture
/ edited and with an introduction by Jeremy Strong.
p. cm.— (At table)
Includes bibliographical references.
ISBN 978-0-8032-1935-9 (pbk.: alk. paper)
1. Food habits. 2. Drinking customs. 3. Taste—Social
aspects. 4. Gourmets. 5. Food—Social aspects. 6. Beverages—Social aspects. I. Strong, Jeremy.
GT2855.E38 2011
394.1'2—dc23
2011015953

Set in Garmond Premier Pro by Bob Reitz.
Designed by Annie Shahan.

For my parents,
who first taught
me to taste

Contents

....

*Part Two: Theorizing and
Contextualizing Taste*

Introduction

··

JEREMY STRONG

This book is about taste. As such, its principal focus is one of the more slippery terms in the English language. Although our interest here is taste as it relates to food and drink, an important starting point is to recognize that the terminology of taste is frequently used in domains other than the gustatory. In the arts, design, architecture, fashion, and in countless other forms of visual and verbal communication, ideas and particularly judgments may be couched in terms of taste. Such expressions and assessments as "good taste," "bad taste," "tasteful," and "in poor taste" may be applied to matters as diverse as wallpaper, gardens, remarks, movies, the layout of a store, advertising, the wording of an invitation, wristwatches, timing in general, furniture, jokes, and flower arrangements. Questions of taste intrude into almost every act of selecting, combining, and positioning that we perform, particularly in a consumer society where we are as likely to be defined by what we wear, drive, eat, and drink as by our politics, beliefs, and jobs. (Equally, the separation of such realms is problematic; several of the essays in this volume insist upon the profound connection between our consumption and its political, ethical, and social ramifications.) Hence, although gustatory taste as one of the five senses does have a distinct meaning, a crucial theme of this book is how this narrowly defined physiological process spins out to meet the broader usage of taste described above—how taste encompasses those other dimensions of food, drink, and associated experience.

Even when limited to our engagement with foodstuffs, the meaning of taste still resists closure, for it signifies not only our physical/chemical responses to objects and combinations but also the elemental qualities of those objects that provoke our taste response. In terms of usage we routinely encounter the term *taste* describing either, or simultaneously, an essential property or a received experience—taste signifying both the "message" and its "reception," a cause and an effect. By way of comparison, we do not think of cutting or pain as being intrinsic properties of a knife; rather, they are outcomes that the knife may be used to bring about because it has other relevant properties such as sharpness and hardness. Those latter properties are not understood as transferred or otherwise mirrored when the knife is used. The joint of meat being carved does not acquire the property of sharpness. Yet as regards foodstuffs and the physiological sensations they bring about, we think of taste as being a property of the object and a property of the experience of its consumption; and, furthermore, we use a largely undifferentiated language of taste to describe both categories. An apple can meaningfully be described as *being* sharp, even when uneaten, and it can also be understood as giving rise to a sharp *taste*.

Taste may also mean discrimination pertaining to foods, and their tastes, on a wider social and cultural plane; that is, a taste for certain tastes signifying the possession, or not, of good taste. Physiologically, taste tells us if a thing is salty, sweet, sour, or bitter; and, though we need to exercise this aspect of the faculty less often than did our hunter-gatherer forebears, taste can, with our other senses, tell us whether it is safe to eat.[1] Yet such purely sensory factors are largely eclipsed when the language of taste is used to express the difference between, say, a meal of fried chicken from a cardboard bucket versus supper at a Michelin-starred restaurant. This difference exists, generating meanings and provoking ideas whether or not one has direct previous experience of either meal. To suggest but a few: the welfare and culinary quality of factory-reared poultry, the health and social effects of a diet based on take-out food, the expense of high-end dining, and the ever-changing trends in what constitutes fashionable food, could all be taste topics set in train by such a comparison. So when discussing food and drink, a seemingly foundational aspect of taste in such a context—that intersection of substance and mouth—may as often as not be absent from interpretive figures and discourses that invoke it. One can indeed understand a substantial aspect of the taste meanings and values that agglomerate around a Big Mac or a glass of Château d'Yquem without having tasted either.

Of course, a significant part of the mystique and skill of connoisseurship *is* vested in the capacity to discern attributes, origin, and "quality" through sensory means alone, as for example in the "blind tasting" of wines. Yet the very fact that such other cues as names and labels are excluded from these tests indicates that there prevails a complex register of values and expectations that, while it connects to potential sensory experience, also enjoys an independent existence as knowledge, as "taste collateral." To know that Chardonnay is the grape variety of the famous white wines of Burgundy while Pinot Noir is the variety of its reds is to possess a nugget of wine knowledge. To know that Gruyère is not only a village in Switzerland but also, as agreed at the Stresa Convention of 1951, a term that may describe three related but different French cheeses—Comté, Beaufort, and Emmental—is to possess a decidedly more abstruse fragment of food lore.[2] (And, of course, one could also know these things without being able to physically taste the differences, or taste them at all!) This is a facet of what Pierre Bourdieu describes as "cultural capital," that socio-intellectual resource of "cultivation" and familiarity with texts, institutions, media, and materials upon which individuals and groups draw to secure or maintain power and social standing.[3] A part of taste, or, in some formulations, the possession of "good taste," is to know and be able to negotiate this web of names, places, products, and dishes. In his essay for this collection John Ducker describes how some of those he tutors in wine tasting are seeking such knowledge—in particular of food and wine matching, and of the potential pitfalls of the restaurant wine list—to afford themselves cultural capital, often as a means of career enhancement.

Contributors Lisa Harper and Tim Waterman also describe, with considerable candor and humor, their own endeavors in the field of teaching and learning taste. Harper's essay concerns the foods she prepared and offered her infant son, Finn, charting her successes and failures in inculcating preferences for varied and sophisticated foodstuffs. Her offerings are selected with a view to such principles as healthy living and sustainability but also, as she cheerily confesses, to the development of a nuanced, educated palate that will afford him competitive social advantage as well as enhanced gustatory pleasure. Although Waterman's focus is on the landscape and lambic beers of Belgium's Payottenland—themselves an acquired taste—in a frank aside he relates his campaign to teach himself to appreciate and differentiate between single malt whiskies. Although ultimately successful, it was an autodidactic program that began with simply learning even to like a taste experience that he initially found far from pleasant. As he describes, it is a taste that he felt he *should* cultivate, an element missing from a range of preferences that he felt was otherwise proper to his sense of self. To "remedy" this, notwithstanding an undeniable sense of ironic detachment, was to participate in an act of self-improvement.

A theme that recurs in several of the essays assembled for this volume is the relationship between knowledge and taste, in particular the idea that taste experiences are, or should be, shaped by our knowledge of the food and drink we consume. In his book *The Omnivore's Dilemma* Michael Pollan charts the industrial food chain in the United States, observing how most consumers are now "eating in ignorance"; that is, comprehensively distanced from primary food production. In contrast to what has become, he argues, the norm, he sets out to prepare a meal that reverses this trend—to hunt, gather, grow, and prepare the materials for a meal in which as many elements as possible will be imbued with personal knowledge and experience.

In eating and sharing this meal, Pollan describes experiencing "the kinds of pleasure that are only deepened by knowing."[4] Joanna Blythman, in her book *Bad Food Britain*, describes a mainstream culinary culture largely analogous to that observed by Pollan in the United States, one in which consumers' "collective stock of food skills, knowledge and expertise" is severely attenuated, particularly any familiarity with food in its basic unprocessed forms.[5] For Blythman, it is only in the fantasy world of food television and publishing that the "ultra-literate in food and gastronomy" are to be found, "beautiful people" with a "great interest in foodie arcana, soaking up articles on items such as shade-grown peppercorns and salted, sun-dried Sardinian tuna roe." Outside this substitute realm of food pornography, in which watching others cook and eat has replaced doing it properly oneself, these people simply "don't exist," or rather, "they account for a vanishingly small percentage of the British population."[6] Although contemporary British and American food culture does form an important dimension of *Educated Tastes*, and the bleak assessment reached *inter alia* by Pollan and Blythman is recognized as essentially accurate, this collection of essays engages with a broader historical and geographical range of taste experience. Observing the culinary landscape of other countries, regions, and times, as well as charting intersections between food, drink, literature, and music, several of the essays that comprise *Educated Tastes* offer a more optimistic view of our gustatory situation and future.

Contributor Lisa Heldke argues for an "extensive pleasure" of eating—an appreciation of food that draws upon ethical, social, and political values. Borrowing and developing this term from Wendell Berry, she makes the case for culinary experience as an aesthetic realm, but one that should operate differently to such a realm as understood by "food loyalists."[7] In her essay such a position is represented by Christopher Kimball, editor of *Cook's Illustrated*, for whom it is the sensory aspects of food alone that justify any aesthetic claim, not to be clouded by extra-aesthetic elements such as ethical and political dimensions. For Heldke, it is precisely these elements, and our knowledge of them, that add richness, structure, and savor to our culinary lives.

In his essay, Roger Haden traces the historical origins of gastronomic connoisseurship, examining the relationships between taste, knowledge, and experience. Observing the long-standing philosophical tendency for sensory taste to be figured merely as an "effect," he sees this reductive logic at work in the scientific engineering of many modern food products that are created and marketed as vehicles for particular taste intensities, often touted as "maximum" or "max" taste. Against this background, in which taste has been denigrated and dumbed down, he examines approaches to food and eating that have sought to integrate taste and culinary thinking into broader social systems and ways of living, including those of the utopian philosopher Charles Fourier. Haden endeavors, like Fourier, to propose an "ecology of taste" as "a lived art of engagement with the world" in which knowledge about what we consume forms a vital part of pleasure.

Jeremy Strong takes this theme in a quite different direction. Sharing the perspective that knowledge about our food, its origins, conditions of production, and its multifaceted cost has a profound influence upon resulting taste experiences, he examines a range of foods that can be considered "cruel." Observing that the ethical credentials or environmental *bona fides* of certain foodstuffs may contribute to the gustatory pleasures of their consumers, he makes the controversial argument that, in a similar fashion, knowledge that certain foods and dishes have been produced through cruel means has been and continues to be a vital aspect of some consumers' expectations and pleasure. A key strategy for campaigners seeking to redress wrongs in fields such as animal rights and fair trade has been to expose to purchasers those unpleasant facts and conditions that producers would prefer to keep obscure—an approach that has enjoyed considerable success in influencing both consumers' habits and producers' methods. Yet Strong's essay suggests that not all food cruelties arise from consumer ignorance, that there is also a long and continuing tradition of connoisseur experience in which the full knowledge of deliberate cruelty serves to sharpen the appetite and enhance pleasure.

If knowledge as pleasure is a recurring theme in this volume, another is the significance of place to gustatory experience and, in particular, how a sense of foodstuffs in terms of place can comprise a major aspect of gustatory pleasure. A key concept in understanding the relationship between places and tastes, and indeed the master term for asserting that place has an influence upon taste, is *terroir*. Originally used in the context of winegrowing, where it signifies "the total natural environment of any viticultural site," the word has come to denote the range of local factors (primarily climatic, topographical, and geological, but also location-specific methods) that imbue a product with particular characteristics, particular tastes.[8] The French cru system of wine nomenclature and labeling, in which strictly bounded regional appellations and individual vineyards are the principal means by which wines are differentiated and valued, is underpinned by the concept of terroir. Historically, New World winemakers have sought to diminish the supposed importance of a terroir-based scheme of expressing a wine's characteristics to a purchaser and of determining quality and value. An emphasis on grape varieties, including the idea that a wine can be an expression or realization not of a place but of a varietal, and a focus on modern scientific production techniques have been among the principal features of New World winemaking. Yet in the early twenty-first century, it would be impossible to maintain that such a neat divide continues to inhere. Flying winemakers, mostly trained in the New World, have had a major impact on winemaking practices in France, Italy, Iberia, and Germany. Many Old World wines are now grown and marketed in styles associated with Australian and U.S. winemakers. And, crucially, many New World winemakers are making, selling, and understanding their wines in ways that acknowledge the contribution of place to the characteristics of their product. While many of these developments have been positive, albeit that the general result has been supermarket shelves full of wines that are cleanly made but somewhat homogeneous, one depressing effect has been the suggestion or invention of terroir where none exists. Several successful, mass-market wines from California and Australia have, through their branding, sought to convey the impression that their wines are the product, even the expression, of a particular place—this "Hill," that "Creek," and so on—when in fact such huge volumes are only achieved by bringing together the output of a vast and varied area of vineyards and ensuring that the resulting wine meets the brand's consistent taste formula. As such, the product owes as much, or rather as little, to terroir as Coca-Cola.

Recent years have seen a proliferation of "terroir-ed" foodstuffs, an ever-growing emphasis on the "niche" geographical status of products as part of the justification of their cost, and as part of the marketing proposition that they will taste better than alternatives with a more anodyne provenance. In addition to foods and drinks with a long-standing association with areas of permitted production such as Stilton, Parma Ham, Parmesan, Bourbon, and Champagne, consumers are now offered a bewildering diversity of choice and geographical information about products that have hitherto not been understood in terms of terroir. Chocolate is an interesting case in point. For many years manufacturers of high-quality chocolates in such countries as France, Belgium, and Switzerland—where, of course, cacao does not grow—established highly successful brand names without reference to the origin of their key raw material. Yet, since the 1990s, there has been a growing trend in the luxury end of the chocolate business to describe and market the product in terms of specific flavors associated with beans grown in different parts of South America and Africa. In part this has been a consequence of fair trade pressure, with a stratum of consumers expecting ethical assurances regarding a product that has historically been murky about its production conditions. Equally, it may also be argued that any luxury consumable that did not already foreground exclusivities of taste deriving from geographical origin was ripe to do so in a terroir-oriented marketplace. Susan Terrio observes how French chocolatiers endeavored to associate their work and products with the well-understood cru system of French wine:

"[C]hocolatiers invoke a system for blending cacao beans that closely parallels that of the highest quality officially classified growths or estates (*les grands crus*) in the Bordeaux winegrowing region. While no such classification or regulation of cacao bean plantations exists, French chocolatiers nevertheless assure consumers that they select only the best vintages from renowned domains in South America."[9]

The concept of terroir may evidently be traduced, and it is all too tempting to scoff at a food media and advertising enterprise that seems obsessed with provenance—every simple noun embellished with such guarantees of authenticity as "handmade," "farm-assured," "corn-fed," and "sun-ripened." Yet most would acknowledge an underlying truth beneath the marketing fatuity—that things may taste of places, and that there is pleasure to be found in this tasting and knowing. A corollary to this truth—and one that has found increasingly fervent expression in countless books, television programs, and editorials for at least the last two decades—is that cultures that lose this connection between taste and place are eroded in terms of their identity, that to accept a globalized diet of brand-name tastes is to imperil our health and cultural vitality.

Several of the contributors to *Educated Tastes* address food and drink in terms of place. Waterman argues that the flat, tart, lambic beers of Payottenland owe their distinctive, often challenging, characteristics to the specificities of the area and mode of production. A practicing landscape architect—well-attuned to reading the negotiation that occurs between people and spaces, between the social and the physical—his essay invites readers to learn to appreciate and enjoy that which at first may not be to their taste. Matthew Hibberd considers the development of Italy as a nation state alongside the emergence of a national food culture. The very idea of Italian food is, as he observes, a difficult and comparatively recent idea. Although non-Italians may have a concept of an Italian national cuisine—a sense commonly abetted by a diaspora of Italian restaurants that appear to offer a familiar roster of national foods such as pizza and pasta—most Italians continue to figure their identities and especially their culinary preferences with reference to region rather than country. Hibberd considers the role of leaders and regimes in promoting "Italian-ness" to Italians, including efforts to popularize certain dishes as national symbols. He also assesses the current situation in which regional traditions and foods—in tandem with enthusiasm for regional political autonomy—have enjoyed an upswing as part of a backlash against universalizing trends in food and the economic and political interests that coalesce in the media.

Contributors Jukka Gronow and Sergey Zhuravlev offer an essay linking food and place that addresses a topic mostly unknown to Western readers—the development of haute cuisine in the former Soviet Union. In particular they discuss the influence of a series of extraordinarily popular and long-lived state cookbooks that proved enormously influential in shaping the culinary aspirations of millions of Russians. The ideological difficulties attendant upon celebrating luxury in a command economy, and the place of regional and other national foods within a centralized, state apparatus, are among the topics they address. Perhaps unsurprisingly, with the expansion of influence of the Soviet Union we see the cuisines of "brotherly socialist countries" being incorporated into the dining opportunities offered to Soviet citizens. This gave rise to difficulties when Soviet-Chinese relations worsened and the "Peking" restaurant was obliged to cease serving Chinese fare, substituting it with dishes from the Russian Far East. As seen in Hibberd's analysis of Italian food culture, there is the effort by the state to inculcate a shared sense of taste, food preferences, and dining practices across a diverse citizenry. What distinguishes the Soviet example, however, is the added dimension that the cookbooks and other aspects of state-run food experience, such as work canteens and restaurants, were also expected to serve as proof of the success of the Soviet system. Variety, plenty, self-sufficiency, and evidence of the efficacy of modern industrial and agricultural modes were all to be evoked. One consequence of this heavy ideological burden was that the cookbooks, by foregrounding often inaccessible foods, echoed many of their counterparts in Western publishing and television—offering not so much a practical guide to dishes that will actually be prepared at home as providing a species of entertainment, of culinary escapism.

Robert Goodwin's essay offers an insight into the food of Spain at the start of the seventeenth century. His essay addresses the representation of food in Cervantes's *Don Quixote*; in particular he argues that food and eating are central concepts in this, arguably the world's first, novel. Goodwin observes that diet is shown to be a key to verisimilitude in *Don Quixote*, an often ironic work in which the boundaries of realism and fiction are frequently tested. His essay then compares this aspect of the novel to Diego Velazquez's naturalistic *bodegones*, or genre scenes, in order to highlight the moral dimension of realism in the context of the key intellectual concept of *desengaño*—disillusionment—which was prevalent in early seventeenth-century Spanish moral discourse.

The connections between nourishment and the (other) arts is a theme further developed in Colin Lawson's survey of the relationships between food, drink, and music. Noting that aspects of the sensory language used to describe the experiences of music and foodstuffs frequently overlap, he goes on to consider the place of food and drink in composers' and performers' lives as well as charting the great variety of ways in which eating and drinking figure in musical works. Although didactic treatises for performers invariably commend a moderate lifestyle, he charts the culinary excesses of numerous opera singers and musicians and discusses several of the instances where dishes are created for or named after musical figures. The linked traditions of music and feasting are also examined, from Greek and Roman references, through the Middle Ages, taking in the associated pleasures of table and music in the classical period, and concluding with discussion of the contemporary era.

In the early nineteenth century there were a number of attempts to move perceptions of food, cooking, eating, and taste—as dimensions of human experience and endeavor—into a similar discursive realm and level of esteem as that occupied by the arts and sciences.[10] Such figures as Jean Anthelme Brillat-Savarin (author of *The Physiology of Taste*), Grimod de La Reynière (writer of a guide to gourmet food shopping in Paris), and chef Antonin Carême (who proposed that his work was a branch of architecture) established some of the key ideas about gastronomy and connoisseurship that continue to circulate today. Although an outcome of their endeavors was that these realms came to be seen as the specialist purview of a bourgeois elite—a condition that (mostly) continues to prevail—they did provide an essential footing for arguments that taste is not merely a low sensory effect, that cooking and eating can be a thoughtful business, and that culinary matters merit intellectual enquiry.

The intervening years have seen some notable, if conflicting, developments. The invention of the discipline of food technology has brought the matter into the bailiwick of applied science, but its findings have essentially been in the service of a food-processing industry that has managed to diminish rather than grow our collective fund of food wisdom, offering us "meal solutions" that—as

Blythman astutely observes—necessarily construe mealtimes as problems.[11] For those of us living in the West, the availability and variety of food has increased dramatically; our supermarkets offer us the loot of the world while cookbooks and television programs show us how to prepare and enjoy this bounty. Yet in practice a majority of consumers do not bridge these domains. Indeed the prepared-food industry and the reliance its products engender make it ever more difficult for many people to reconnect with unprocessed foods, seasonal opportunities, and vernacular cuisine. However—and if only latterly—food, drink, and taste have become the subjects of a growing body of scholarship. The domain of food studies draws upon a range of disciplines, bringing their preoccupations and modes of enquiry to bear upon a field that spans—at least—questions of a social, cultural, ethical, political, and scientific nature. In its own way, and particularly by assembling a range of contributors from such diverse backgrounds, *Educated Tastes* aspires to make its own contribution to this once neglected, now thriving field.

Notes

1. The category of *umani*, or "deliciousness," may be added to this roster, a Japanese term designating the taste of glutamates. Also, in "An Abstract Art," from *The Chronicles of Bustos Domecq*, Jorge Luis Borges and Adolfo Bioy-Casares comically describe a fictional article in which the category of "insipid" is listed as one of the four basic tastes, sweetness being discovered later!

2. Len Deighton, *ABC of French Food* (New York: Bantam, 1989), 112.

3. Pierre Bourdieu, *Distinction: A Social Critique of the Judgment of Taste*, trans. Richard Nice (London: Routledge, 1989).

4. Michael Pollan, *The Omnivore's Dilemma: The Search for a Perfect Meal in a Fast-Food World* (London: Bloomsbury, 2006), 11.

5. Joanna Blythman, *Bad Food Britain: How a Nation Ruined Its Appetite* (London: Fourth Estate, 2006), 187.

6. Blythman, *Bad Food Britain*, 2–3.

7. Wendell Berry, "The Pleasures of Eating," in *What Are People For?* (New York: North Point, 1990).

8. Jancis Robinson, ed., *The Oxford Companion to Wine*, 3rd ed. (Oxford: Oxford University Press, 2006), 700.

9. Susan J. Terrio, "Crafting *Grand Cru* Chocolates in Contemporary France," in *The Cultural Politics of Food and Eating*, ed. James L. Watson and Melissa L. Caldwell (Malden MA: Blackwell, 2005), 154.

10. In his essay for this volume Haden offers an excellent summary.

11. Blythman, *Bad Food Britain*, 98.

Educated Tastes

Part One

Learning to Taste

Chapter One

Feeding Finn

LISA HARPER

I wanted to raise my children with taste—to have taste, that is, good taste in food. And unlike many stories of boy-meets-beet, the story begins well.

Like any perfectly reasonable child, my son, Finn, began to eat free from incident or trauma. From birth, there was nothing extraordinary about what or how he ate. Unlike his older sister, Ella, who ate desperately and heartily, then proceeded to spit up with gusto, Finn nursed contentedly until he was sated, then occupied himself with other important matters: sleeping, pooping, grabbing for his feet, gazing steadily at his spinning mobile, and so on. Food and feeding were necessary and rhythmical parts of his day—neither fraught nor especially craved.

In the general scheme of things, babies are offered so-called solid food somewhere around four to six months of age, and so, somewhere in this period, like most other Western mothers, I bought a small cardboard box of baby rice cereal. My box was organic and adorned with a pastoral picture of a babe in a wheat field, even though I had been raised contentedly on the more ubiquitous brand that came in a bright green box. I mixed the cereal into a thin gruel with a little warmed breast milk and offered it to my son. The runny goop dripped and drooled out of his mouth and generally baffled him (as it does many children), but he steadily mastered the task, and very soon he was opening his maw eagerly for the sustenance his three-year-old sister and I spooned into his mouth. Spoon, chair—those first real props of culinary culture—these became constant and stable elements in his life, as familiar as breast and lap. The gruel became a paste, then a porridge. He learned to eat, which at its most fundamental level involves basic physiology and no more.

But in the natural progression of things, as soon as the art of swallowing was a sure thing, we offered Finn his first "solid" food, and the fun began. In our house, this first food was a bowl of sweet lacinato kale, freshly steamed and pureed. This, too, went well enough. If he was not as gleeful and eager as his sister had been to confront a small bowl of bright green mush, he was still grateful for it and ate steadily, first the kale, then the spinach, then everything else I put in front of him. Some days I thickened the vegetables with more of the grain cereal, other days it was served straight up.

Over the coming months, Finn was introduced to the garden of produce eaten by his sister, his father, and me. He ate, without complaint, green beans, broccoli, freshly hulled peas, a colorful array of rainbow chard. He ate beans: smashed favas, white and black and cranberry. He ate a full range of root vegetables: carrots, beets, yams, potatoes. He ate butternut and delicata squashes. Corn was nearly as good as dessert to him, and when berries came into season, I couldn't keep enough in the house—golden and red raspberries, strawberries, blackberries, olallieberries, blueberries. The same could be said for any fruit: bananas, oranges, and apples, which he ate with such fervor they might as well have been candy. He progressed easily from purees, to mashes, to soft solid foods. Unlike many other children, he had no aversions to texture.

Our family food culture is a rich and healthy one, and our location in the world makes it almost embarrassingly easy to sustain.

We live in northern California, where the culture at large is mildly food obsessed. Every third person seems to write a food blog, or know someone who does, or reads one or two regularly. Many people cook regularly and well. Going to a restaurant can be an event, and we have as many excellent mom-and-pop joints as we do meccas of fine dining. It's possible to get all kinds of international ingredients in our big-box markets as well as in the specialty stores that proliferate in our area. It's not New York City, but within a fifteen-minute drive of our suburban home, we can easily source authentic Japanese, Indian, Arab, Mexican, Chinese, Latin, Hawaiian, and even the more obscure Mediterranean ingredients. And, most important to me, we have fresh, local produce all year round. Our local farmers market never shuts down, and the choices abound from one season to the next. Just when we're tired of apples, the citrus appears. Just when we think the oranges will never satisfy us through the long winter, we get a brief, spectacular burst of ruby red pomegranates and fragrant green pineapple guavas the exact shape of fat Christmas lights. When we're weary of winter root vegetables, the asparagus, artichokes, and fava beans emerge, followed quickly by berries, then stone fruit, then such a rainbow-colored abundance of heirloom tomatoes that it always seems like we've gotten away with something. But when crisp, cool Hachiya persimmons show up again in our favorite stalls, we're ready for them. We get our meat from small, organic, cattle- and pig-farming operations. We get our fish from Pietro, a fisherman who catches it himself, advocates in the political arena for sustainable fisheries, and sells his catch only at local farmers markets. We get gorgeous pastel Araucana eggs all spring and summer. Our kids know that leeks grow in dirt and that eggs can sometimes have straggly bits of nest stuck to them.

So that mantra of contemporary food culture—"local, sustainable, organic," (and now "real") food—has always been our own. Eating this way has been part of our family for so long that it's second nature. For instance, on family vacations, one of the first things we do is search out the local farmers markets, then build our meals around what the community has to offer. On another occasion, my husband actually came home excited one night because his company began offering local, organic produce and meats in their company canteen (which already had above-average food). By the time she was in kindergarten, my daughter already knew that a watermelon eaten in December would not taste like the watermelon she remembered from the summer. This is my children's food heritage and the bedrock of their food culture. It matters to me what they eat, not just in terms of health and politics, but also in terms of taste. I want them to know that food is tied to the earth and the seasons and that different times and different places will produce different foods with different pleasures. I want my children to enjoy their food and to know how really pleasurable it can be. I want them to have not just good taste, but a wide range of tastes.

And so it was no different for baby Finn who, like his sister before him, ate exactly what we ate, only mashed. All of his produce, just like the rest of our family's, was purchased at the farmers market, from farmers who I'd bought from for more than a decade. They knew us, they knew me pregnant, they knew Finn as a nursing baby, they sold us his first real food. Buying his food, like our own, was a highly personal, highly social affair. After the market, every Sunday afternoon, I steamed his portions in a three-tiered steamer, then cooled and froze them in an ice cube tray, producing instant, infant-sized portions. It was a technique I had perfected for his sister, and once issues of organization and planning were conquered, it proved an efficient, economical, and healthy way to feed both of them when they were babies. It was easy to give them fresh, organic food, and cheaper.

But as Pete Wells has written, I also thought it tasted better.[1] The food tasted like what it was and nothing else, and this mattered to me. From his earliest days, Finn would know what a beet tasted like. He would learn to like a wide variety of starches: rice and pasta and farro. He would learn that not all food has the same texture.

When his teeth came in, I gave him pomegranate seeds as well as Cheerios to practice his pincer grip. Snug in his high chair, with a pile of the red-jeweled fruit in front of him, he plucked one seed after another until his hands and chin were smeared with red juice. He looked like a cross between a sated vampire and a fruit bat. He ate eggs and yogurt, rice and pasta, bread in any form. He enjoyed any meat sufficiently well, especially sausages, and happily consumed tilapia, crab, shrimp, fried cod, poached halibut, baked trout, red snapper à la meunière, even the sand dabs, which I painstakingly deboned. There were days when we enjoyed a family lunch of white bean and tuna salad, drizzled with olive oil and sprinkled with sage. There were nights when we enjoyed sushi while Finn slurped a bowl of silken tofu with dancing fish flakes, then polished off everyone's rice. By his second Christmas (his being a November birthday), he ate a bowlful of chicken liver pâté with pure glee, something his sister had pioneered, and which—in spite of what came later—remains one of their most special eating skills. We had a really, really good family food life. My kids were the envy of my friends, whose own children ate much more reluctantly from a vastly more limited range of foods.

It is true that Finn's sister was always the more adventurous eater. Around her first birthday, she surprised the servers at our local Italian restaurant by eating an adult portion of pumpkin ravioli in sage brown butter. They had offered to bring her a small portion, one or two raviolis, but I demurred, and as those tender, sweet packets disappeared down her gullet, one server after another stopped by to shake his head in wonder. The performance earned her a free biscotti, on which she gnawed happily as we finished off the Vin Santo. Later she ate anchovies straight from the jar, all manner of goat and cow cheeses, and once slugged down a shot of vanilla when I turned my back. (Yes, I called poison control). And when she was five, she swooned at breakfast one morning over a vivid dream about a hamburger, layered with "sliced tomato and a little bit of salad," which would have been fine, except for the fact that she had never eaten one before. The only thing she ever flat-out rejected were mashed potatoes (it was the texture), but she eventually came around.

But if Finn lacked Ella's adventurous spirit at the table, he ate better than the average toddler. Although it sometimes took him longer to come around to a dish, he could in no way be called neophobic, one who is afraid of new foods. Like his sister, the quantity of food consumed was never a problem. He ate plenty, and I took pride not just in the range of my children's diet, but in their ability and eagerness to eat. Didn't such habits reflect well on the effort I put into feeding them? And on my impeccable knowledge of food sourcing? And on our family's generally excellent gastronomical taste? I didn't think these things, exactly, and I certainly never said them out loud, but these assumptions were as essential to my thinking as, well, the five varieties of salt are to my kitchen pantry.

And then one day, everything changed.

After a day that included eating cherry tomatoes off the vine for breakfast, I set Finn's dinner before him, and he refused to eat his green beans. Not a single bean was touched, sniffed, nibbled, or even pushed around his plate with a fork. He took one look at the plate and gave the green beans the cold shoulder. "Not I like green beans," he declared, before happily eating the rest of his food. I tried to make light of the situation, but from that day on, anything green was leprous to his taste.

Overnight, Finn had become a picky eater. I tried everything to change him. I offered him green beans for several days, because hadn't he eaten them happily for over a year? On every occasion they were rejected. Then I tried broccoli, which he had also once loved. Peas, sugar snap peas—both raw and stir-fried—steamed asparagus, grilled fennel. Nothing moved him. It was the height of summer, he was nearly two, and he should have been coming into the full pleasures of the table (so little did I know). "*Not* I like beans," he said adamantly. "Not I like *peas*." He clamped his mouth into a thin, red line, shook his head, and sat, immovable as Buddha and just as round. When he deemed the crisis passed, he shoveled more rice (or pasta or potato or white beans) down his throat.

For four long months, nothing green passed Finn's lips. No matter how much I tried, cajoled, bribed, or ate by example, he refused all things green. Not one nibble of lettuce. Not one solitary pea. One night when I was teaching, my husband declared that Finn had in fact eaten a plate of green beans that he had prepared, lightly salted with olive oil and red wine vinegar, but even though I hopefully prepared the same dish the following day, I had no such luck.

Then, things got worse.

Orange foods went the way of the green, and winter squash, carrots, and sweet potatoes fell from rotation. Then, finally, his beloved tomatoes were summarily rejected. True, it was the end of summer and the end of the season and we were all mostly ready to give them up. But he didn't really like them cooked, either. In my despair, I began to feed him vitamins. These, of course, he gobbled up because they tasted like candy. Then began the slow and steady rotation of white food. Milk. Rice. Potato. Bread. Pasta. And those candy-colored vitamins. To my gastronomic soul, it was a trial. And a tribulation.

Many, many young children are neophobic. We call them picky eaters in popular parlance, and they have always been with us. In fact, I was the pickiest of eaters, the bane of my mother's table. The pediatrician told her repeatedly, "When she's hungry, she'll eat." But I didn't, not really. For a year I ate peanut butter and jelly on something called "cocktail rye," bite-sized bread smattered with caraway seeds. I was tiny, and often sick. Eventually I came around, but not until I was well into my school years, and even then, only slowly.

My mother, however, is an excellent cook, so none of my behavior can be fairly blamed on her. We ate real food, sat down to balanced family meals every night, and we kids were never offered special choices. So, I should have known better when Finn mutinied. Some primitive, reptilian part of my food brain should have known that Finn's behavior was not extraordinary, that I had done exactly the same thing, and that I should not take it personally. But still, until Finn went on the Great Vegetable Strike, I assumed that neophobic children were children who, in large part, had never been given much variety to begin with.

For instance, I knew that my friends who had picky eaters were also not the most adventurous eaters themselves. One of my daughter's friends refused all fruits and vegetables until she was five, when she succumbed to frozen peas. Ella worried about her. But this friend's mother hated all fish, most vegetables, and even strawberries. In my limited experience, picky eaters were simply kids who hadn't been given an equal opportunity chance to learn about food.

And there is, in fact, some truth to this anecdotal evidence. Research has shown that the flavor of breast milk can vary with the mother's diet.[2] Eating fish will make your breast milk, well, a little fishy. Beer can make it taste fermented. Sugary food makes it sweeter. Eating garlic or chocolate can produce a strong indigestion in some breast-fed babies. It stands to reason—and the research of Julie Mennella has supported the claim—that if a nursing mother has a widely varied diet, her child will tend to be more accepting of new foods and will tend to eat a wider variety of foods.[3] Unlike formula, which always has the same flavor and contains the same composition of nutrients, breast milk reflects what the mother eats. The child of the omnivorous mother will learn that her food is varied, that there is a range of taste available in her particular food culture. Of course, this close connection between the mother's diet and the infant's gastronomic development has made many nursing mothers unusually vigilant about their food consumption—they might avoid chocolate or dairy or food with peppery heat or too much garlic or onions. And sometimes these things *do* cause aversions and indigestion and spit-up. But the opposite is also true—that since what you eat while you nurse is also what your baby eats, some mothers will go out of their way to eat sushi and stinky cheese and curry. It is never too early to cultivate taste. Such was my theory and practice at least.

But the new evidence is even more spectacular for anyone who considers the relationship between nature and nurture regarding taste in young children. There is significant evidence that babies can register smell and taste in the womb, and that flavors and smells from the mother's diet can infuse the amniotic fluid. Even general-use parenting sites report that by twenty weeks, a fetus's taste buds have developed.[4] Scientists have even shown that a fetus can differentiate between tastes before they are born.[5] Like breast milk, amniotic fluid, the liquid environment that bathes and sustains the fetus, absorbs the properties of food that the mother eats. But this absorption is not limited simply to the nutrients in the fluid. In fact, strong tastes from the mother's diet, like cumin or curry, garlic or onions, steep in the amniotic fluid, like a prenatal tea, which is regularly swallowed by the fetus in quantities up to a liter a day by the third trimester. Initially, scientist Julie Mennella theorized that such experiences served as a "flavor bridge" to breast milk and, ultimately, to solid food.[6] And in fact, fetuses do swallow more vigorously when surrounded by sweet tastes and less when surrounded by sour or bitter tastes.[7] Similarly, babies exposed repeatedly to anise in the womb turned toward that smell upon birth. Those who lacked such exposure turned away from the same.[8]

In this way, very young children, fetuses even, can be exposed to a range of smells and tastes, which can predispose them to eating a wide variety of foods and to developing, in fact, a broad sense of taste. For most of the population this bodes well for cultivating a taste for healthy food. Want your kid to eat his bok choy? Eat plenty of it yourself. Even more ambitious? Introduce the masala, nori, or lardo as soon as the morning sickness passes. Just as ambitious parents might mic a little Mozart into the womb, hoping to produce a musical prodigy, some gastrophiles will eat adventurously during pregnancy, hoping to preprogram a child for a lifetime of adventurous eating.

But Mennella's recent studies have shown that fetal exposure does much more than create a bridge in taste. It actually *creates* taste. Babies exposed to certain foods in utero—carrots, green beans, peaches—actually *prefer* such foods in their early months.[9] This research has profound implications for feeding children. If you want your kid to be a good eater, it helps if the pregnant and nursing mother is pretty adventurous herself. Is this nature? Is the baby hard-wired in utero to be a foodie (or not)? Or is it nurture? Is the mother responsible for yet one more aspect of cultural indoctrination? Must she really teach her kid to eat well by example—even before he sees her raise that spoon to his mouth?

And in either case, what had I done wrong?

After a few months of raising a girl and a boy, it was clear to me that my son differed from my daughter in more than his genitalia. One child differed, fundamentally and biologically from another, in personality, behavior, and preferences in play. My son was more addicted to the human touch, and although I had been warned of this fact—boys are more cuddly, more attached, more sensitive than girls—by the mothers of boys, I'm still not able to say the difference is gender inflected as much as it is my son's particular disposition and personality. Similarly, until Finn became a picky eater, I refused to believe that what kids were willing to eat was influenced by anything other than their earliest food culture. Hadn't Misty's half-Salvadoran children grown up on spicy salsa? Didn't Yoriko have a child who downed raw fish and rice and shunned most sugar? Didn't Michelle and Brandon, my most beloved farmers, have a child who ate any raw vegetable they put in front of him? And hadn't my own culinary adventure with my daughter produced a girl willing to try almost anything?

The answer was yes. And no. Because the truth is closer to what very many parents have long suspected: Being a neophobe is *not* simply a matter of nurture. It might be in your nature.

The most recent research into the science of taste has found that not only do we all taste differently (witness the phenomenon of "supertasters," uncovered in the 1990s, especially by researcher Linda Bartoshuk), but how and what we taste may be genetically coded.[10] The Human Genome Project has facilitated the identification of taste receptors, which are located all over the inside of the mouth, not simply on the tongue. And scientists have found further that there are many more than four basic tastes (sour, sweet, salty, bitter), more than four codes that are sent to the brain. To complicate further the new physiology of taste, how these receptors receive and send information to the brain differs from person to person, within families, and even, it seems, across cultures.[11] While it is true that most of these flavor chemists work for large multimillion-dollar corporations, whose job it is to advise the food industry about additives that will make your packaged, processed food taste better—by lowering sugar and sodium content without creating an aftertaste, by enhancing existing sweet flavors, by blocking bitter tastes in, say, cough medicine—the fundamental truth of their work is important for understanding how our kids eat.

If it is true that how we taste has a genetic foundation, this information has resonance for understanding how young children behave at the table, what children eat and reject, whether or not your child has good taste, and whether the parent has anything to do with it anyway. But while most of these sensory scientists would probably acknowledge that we *can* learn to like tastes that may initially be unpalatable, the evidence is mounting that a truly picky child is not simply a stubborn, willful one. He is not testing your patience because he is in the midst of his terrible twos (or threes). She does not reject broccoli because it is just a hard vegetable to like. He is not simply a child who hasn't had an equal opportunity in his food life. The rock-bottom truth may just be that your kid doesn't have good taste.

Somewhere in the middle of all the *sturm und drang* it dawned on me that Finn's inordinate love of sugar—in any form—was not simply a child's immature preference. Just as my husband will eat a bag of red licorice or a box of Girl Scout cookies in one sitting, Finn consumed pint after pint of berries, ate easily adult-sized helpings of pie, and lusted with uncommon fervor for chocolate. In fact, long before he could string together two words, before he had even twenty words in his vocabulary, "watermelon" and "chocolately" were uttered accurately, frequently, and with much passion.

There is other recent research, too, that takes the blame off the parent, concluding that picky eating is inherited and not a product of the child's environment. In the journal *Nutrition*, Dr. Lucy Cooke published her findings that 78 percent of neophobic behavior is genetically determined, and only 22 percent determined by a child's environment.[12] This suggests clearly that whether or not Finn tried that plate of chard in front of him, it was not my fault. When he took one look at a perfectly well-cooked piece of pork tenderloin and declared emphatically, *"Not* I like that chicken," there would be no way I could force, bribe, or cajole him into eating it. I shrugged my shoulders in attempted nonchalance. I let him eat rice. (And cake.) But it still bothered me.

It bothered me because feeding my kids was not simply about keeping them healthy, about giving them enough nutrition for them to develop strong, healthy bodies and agile brains. Feeding them well was partly about getting ahead of the curve of contemporary American food culture and showing them what is pleasurable about real food, cooked at home. It was about giving them a diverse food culture before they were old enough to be seduced by fast food and take-out and meals on the run and junk food. I thought my children needed a food culture that would help them make good, healthy choices when they went out on their own. I thought it was important to give them a foundation that would ground them for the rest of their lives. Teaching them to eat well was as important to me as teaching them to sleep, to walk, to talk, to read. It would certainly be as important.

There is a lot of conflicting information out there about how kids should be fed these days. On the one hand, there is a preponderance of food marketed to and for kids. Take a walk down any big-box supermarket aisle and observe the booty: prepackaged lunches, neon-colored crackers, cereal with all manner of flavorings, fluorescent yogurt, produce pureed and rolled into unrecognizable shapes then stamped with "tattoos," bars of grains pummeled into unrecognizable mash and bound with sweeteners, tarts that pop, and everything packaged in brightly colored boxes and promoted with popular cartoon characters. For a while, there was even green ketchup. Not far away are the drinks: sodas and juices in a rainbow of colors, loaded with high-fructose corn syrup, artificial flavorings, even aspartame and saccharine. Kids are sold "energy" bars and microwaveable snacks packaged in plastic. They watch advertisements promoting fried-chicken-in-a-tub as the ultimate family dinner. They are sold food that is meant to be thrown in the microwave and eaten in a paper towel on the way to school, or mixed with a little water and drunk on the way to soccer practice. They are repeatedly sent the message that conventional culinary culture—you know, actually cooking a meal and sitting down to eat it with some other people you like—is irrelevant. Food for kids has become, in lots of ways, something slick and fun and candy-colored, not a repository of labor or culture, of education, or even sensual pleasure. Eating is not something you do for fun; it can be cool in some kid circles to think new food is gross, to believe that family dinner is for squares. What's more, lots of so-called kid food has value-added vitamins, so parents actually believe it's healthy.

But kids' "taste" is catered to not only by big agro-business in big-box stores and on television, but also in restaurants, where the assumption is generally *not* that children will eat what adults eat, only less. Most children's menus pander to the familiar, the bland, the fried. I've been in Asian, Italian, and even Hawaiian restaurants where the offerings for kids bear no relation to the ingredients and techniques on the adult menu but are instead the predictable and ubiquitous pizza, peanut butter and jelly, a hamburger or hot dog, some version of grilled cheese, some sort of fried chicken nugget. These menus assume that children are picky eaters. They assume children won't eat their vegetables. They assume children prefer unhealthy, processed foods. There is, of course, something to be said about any dining establishment that welcomes children into their house, but David Kamp, author of *The United States of Arugula*, sums it up well, "My outlook on children's menus started to change at some point—probably around the 102nd or 103rd time my children ordered chicken fingers with French fries. Even if the chicken fingers were good ones, made from real breast meat rather than pulverized and remolded chik-a-bits, I was disturbed by their ubiquity and their hold on my kids, who are eleven and eight years old."[13] Kamp argues that the food on many children's menus is palate deadening and defines a food culture for children that is distinct and separate from that of adults. And he's right. Really, what is the difference between giving your kids that ubiquitous plate of mac 'n cheese or a prepackaged lunch tray? Kamp puts it this way, "I've concluded, the standard children's menu is regressive, encouraging children (and their misguided parents) to believe that there is a rigidly delineated 'kids' cuisine' that exists entirely apart from grown-up cuisine."[14]

While Finn would have dined happily on fries every day of the week, I was determined to resist. For a long time, we avoided restaurants.

On the other hand, there is a growing movement to teach children about healthy, organic, sustainable, real—and even sophisticated—food. Across the country, cooking schools for children have taken off, cookbooks aimed at children are the next wave of foodie-parent "must-haves," and even the adorable and competent Gerasole sisters of the Spatulatta.com have now become (deservedly) minicelebrities in the younger set's food culture. Jamie Oliver is hell bent on reforming school lunches and family food across the country, and even the ubiquitous Rachael Ray has expanded her empire to a nonprofit endeavor, Yum-O! Yum-O! isn't so much about forward-thinking food for kids as it is about combating hunger, providing education and—most germane to my concerns—getting families to cook and eat healthy food together, and knowing exactly where their food comes from. Yum-O's website offers some twists on the usual suspects, but it also provides recipes for less well-traveled foods like Waldorf salad, cashew chipotle chicken, and Middle Eastern rice bowls. In the world of the food business, it's more than a start.

And where we live, there are plenty of families who buck the popular trend, who do buy organic produce, who do cook family dinners from scratch, who choose vegetarianism for environmental as well as health reasons. At many fine-dining establishments it is not unusual to see a young child happily picking away at her child-sized portion of risotto or grilled fish. Our favorite pizzeria, the tiny Delfina Pizzeria—which serves house-cured salamis and fresh sardines to accompany their celestial pies—has happily seated us with our children even when a gaggle of regular-sized customers mingles impatiently on the sidewalk with their wine. Japanese restaurants host many young children (and not just Asian ones) happily eating sushi rolls. Often with chopsticks. And while our blonde-haired, blue-eyed kids are usually in the minority at our local shabu-shabu joint (Japanese hot pot), plenty of Asian kids tuck into their plates of noodles and Kobe beef the same way their peers scarf that mac 'n cheese down the street. Clearly, there is hope for moderation and diversity.

There are the extremes on this side of the spectrum, too, including those parents who assert bragging rights about what their children will eat, and where they have eaten, and what their culinary accomplishments have been to date. For this group of urban sophisticates, sushi *is* fast food, bento boxes are the only way to pack lunch, and a good Saturday morning involves not Nickelodeon but the latest TIVOed episode of *The Next Food Network Star*.

One food-sourcing professional in the ultrasophisticated San Francisco restaurant scene confided that his five-year-old was thrilled to discover that not one, but two, of the fine-dining establishments they frequent as part of his father's wholesale business offered butcher-block paper and crayons to young patrons. His son drops their names as casually as most of his peers mention McDonald's, and he has eaten at these places more times than I have. At a wedding that my husband and I attended in Sonoma wine country, I sat next to a two-year-old, who nibbled fairly effectively at her lamb tagine and ratatouille (even as she eyed the gorgeous series of pink-and-white wedding cakes displayed on the table next to hers). But then she asked her father, a wine consultant, for some wine to drink. Red wine. Her father replied, "I have white wine, honey. Do you want white wine?" The girl shook her head. "I want red wine," she proclaimed. So her father stood up and retrieved for her a glass of wine. "This is a Pinot," he said, in the very deliberate and conscious way one sometimes talks to a very young child, and presented her with a full glass of wine. He explained to me without irony that in fact she had a preference. Sitting on her mother's lap, the child took one small sip and was satisfied. Of course, such scenes are deeply unsettling, even for someone as gastronomically ambitious for her kids as I am, but they speak more generally to the kind of competitive mindset that can take hold of foodie parents. Successfully offering your two-and-a-half-year-old child escargot (and yes, I am guilty of this) is not so different from getting your child to read at three, or throw a double axel at four, or play a Chopin sonata at five. But really, what's the point? Why should we care? And why did I care if Finn was a picky eater? Was it because I wanted him to be healthy? Was it because I wanted him to be a fully participating member in our family food life? Was I simply a snob? Truly, Pete Wells spoke to me when he wrote that "a food snob is just a picky eater with an attitude."[15]

The answer is not simple. Had we had infinite amounts of disposable cash, I probably would take both my kids to really fancy restaurants. I just might enroll them in fancy cooking schools. I would definitely go on fancy vacations so my kids could taste truffles (and everything else) in Tuscany. As it is, I push our food culture where I can: Bistro Jeanty in the Napa Valley (where Ella ate those escargot) or Higuma Sushi House closer to home. We experiment with cutting pie crust or smashing up pesto or rolling fresh pasta; a themed, family movie night where an African turmeric-and-tomato chicken stew (to accompany *The Lion King*) was the sleeper hit of the year. We've had island vacations that expose our kids to a food culture more different from our own than one in Paris or Piedmont—think poi, and imu pig, a full range of seaweed, li hing mui, delicious fish unheard of in our local waters, and fruit that, to them, looks (and sometimes smells) more alien than earthly. But really, this is not my version of Pinot for the pre-K set. At bottom, we just like to eat this way, and feeding our kids well and widely is a way of exposing them to a range of pleasures, a range of cultures and histories and environments. It's a way of engaging them in a hands-on way to a vital aspect of human culture.

In the end, what I really wanted for Finn, and what Ella had already discovered, was to know that food is about pleasure. Food can bring you closer to people—to your family around a table, to your companion as you cook, to the people who grow your food. Food will teach you about the world—the natural world that it comes from, the vast aesthetic world of its preparation, the social and cultural world of habit and tradition. Food is political: think about workers' rights, environmental issues, issues of hunger and disease, scarcity and distribution. Food is about being human. It is about adventure and surprise, pleasure and openness, gratitude and love. It is about finding one more space in life for joy.

For two years, Finn and I struggled. Or rather, I struggled and he happily shoveled his rice. I didn't do anything fancy, or special, or especially innovative. I cooked what I cooked, and I offered him exactly what the rest of us ate. Since we do eat seasonally and locally, vegetables and fruits made frequent, repeat appearances, though they were often cooked or dressed slightly differently—seasoned in sea salt or herbed salt or soy sauce, for instance, dressed in butter or olive oil, sautéed or steamed, finished with balsamic or white balsamic or red wine vinegar, and so on. I followed the same staid, old-fashioned advice Dr. Spock had been giving since my childhood. It was my mother's advice, and probably my grandmother's, too. I didn't buy any fancy books. I didn't consult my friends, who had picky eaters themselves. I didn't bribe Finn with toys, or money, or even dessert. I didn't make him anything special. I didn't force him to eat. And I certainly didn't hide the food he didn't like in food he did. Deception never occurred to me as a way of making gross (to him) food delicious. Finn would eat regular food on its own terms, or he wouldn't eat at all. I seriously doubted he would get scurvy or rickets.

Slowly . . . oh, so very, very slowly, he began to relent. First, he ate a carrot. Then, come spring, a tomato or two seemed to please him. Chard and spinach still elicited the cabbage-patch face and a strongly voiced, "NOT . . . ," but with some homemade faux aioli (mayonnaise mashed with garlic, salt, and lemon juice), he discovered artichokes were sort of nifty. Then, one day the green beans appealed, and then it was shelling-pea season, and well . . . nothing pleased him so much as plucking one raw pea after another out of the cute little pod and popping them in his mouth like so many green treats.

We were by no means home free. There were still many days where all these things were rejected, weeks when no vegetable matter passed those little lips. But we still trudged to the farmers market, stuffed his face with berries and apples, and made sure that we gestured toward a modicum of dietary balance.

And then, when he was three and a half, we returned to Kauai. On our first full day, he spent six, or maybe eight, hours in the ocean. He snorkeled in the little protected lagoon on our beach. He dug big holes. He collected sea cucumbers and hermit crabs from tide pools. He figured out he could float, and sort of swim. He soldered himself to his boogie board and cried, "Surf's up!"

That night at dinner, I had purchased some ogo seaweed, which is used to garnish poke (a raw, seasoned dish of cubed fish), and dressed it with sesame oil, soy sauce, and a bit of rice wine vinegar. We grilled some ono, a sweet, mild white fish, and cooked a large pot of rice. The ogo was a little crunchy, with feathery-thin tentacles. I placed just a bite on his plate. "This is from the ocean you were swimming in today," I told him. His eyebrows shot up in surprise. His mouth was a round O of happy disbelief. "The ocean? Here? Wow!" he exclaimed, then popped the little green mound in his mouth. I watched, in stunned surprise as he threw his fork down, thrust both hands in front of him, and gave two thumbs up. "I *love* it," he exclaimed. I served him another spoonful.

After the ogo incident, our lives changed. On that vacation, Finn tried everything we put in front of him, including fiddlehead ferns (not a hit), papaya (big hit), a rather complicated-looking sushi roll stuffed with poke (moderate hit), and many plates of fried calamari (terrific hit, but also a terrific choking hazard). Since then, his sense of adventure has been maintained. I don't think he would eat an anchovy, and he still calls the little rounds of processed, prepackaged cheese "my favorite cheese," but he is generally willing to try a much wider range of foods than before, and even some things—like rapini or potstickers or that bright green chard—which he roundly rejected in the past.

I don't know what happened in his little taste receptors, or in his little brain, to make those taste messages welcome instead of frightening. Maybe it was finally connecting the food with its source, which he loved so intensely. Maybe it was all those years of perseverance on my part (one of us had to cave in the end, right?). Maybe he was just really hungry. Or just maybe it was some mysterious alchemy of nature and nurture; some combination of his genes and our family's food have finally conspired to bring him fully to the table. I'd like to think so.

Notes

1. Pete Wells, "Raising a Baby with a Four-Star Palate," *Food and Wine*, June 2005: 1, http://www.foodandwine.com/articles/raising-a -baby-with-a-four-star-palate-four-star-baby-food.

2. See, for instance, Helene Hausner, Wender L. P. Bredie, Christian Mølgaard, Mikael Agerlin Petersen, and Per Møller, "Differential Transfer of Dietary Flavor Compounds into Human Breast Milk," *Physiology and Behavior* 95, nos. 1–2 (September 3, 2008): 118–24.

3. The work of Julie Mennella has been instrumental in this field. See, for instance, Linda Bartoshuk, "Flavor Learning in Utero and Infancy: An Interview with Julie Mennella," *Observer* 23, no. 2 (February 2010), http://www.psychologicalscience.org/observer/getArticle .cfm?id=2613.

4. "Week 21 of Pregnancy: Baby's Taste Buds Develop," WhatTo Expect.com, http://www.whattoexpect.com/pregnancy/your-baby/ week-21/open-wide.aspx (accessed February 1, 2010).

5. Again, the work of Julie Mennella has been significant. See J. Mennella, C. P. Jagnow, and G. K. Beauchamp, "Prenatal and Postnatal Flavor Learning by Human Infants," *Pediatrics* 107, no. 6 (June 2001): E88; and P. G. Hepper, "Adaptive Fetal Learning: Prenatal Exposure to Garlic Affects Postnatal Preference," *Animal Behavior* 36 (1988): 935–36.

6. Julie Mennella, "A Cross-Cultural Perspective," *Nutrition Today* 32, no. 4 (July/August 1997): 144–51.

7. C. M. Mistretta and R. M. Bradley, "Taste and Swallowing in Utero: A Discussion of Fetal Sensory Function," *British Medical Bulletin* 31, no. 1 (January 1975): 80–84.

8. Benoist Schaal, Luc Marlier, and Robert Soussignan, "Human Foetuses Learn Odours From their Pregnant Mother's Diet," *Chemi-*

cal Senses 25 (2000): 729–37, http://chemse.oxfordjournals.org/cgi/content/full/25/6/729.

9. Catherine A. Forestell and Julie A. Mennella, "Early Determinants of Fruit and Vegetable Acceptance," *Pediatrics* 120, no. 6 (December 2007): 1247–54, http://www.pubmedcentral.nih.gov/articlerender.fcgi?artid=2268898.

10. See Thomas Levinson, "Accounting for Taste," *Sciences* 35, no. 1 (January 1995): 13; Bruce Feiler, "The Corrections," *Gourmet* July 2008, 47.

11. Feiler, "Corrections," 47.

12. Kim Severson, "Picky Eaters: They Get It From You," *New York Times*, October 10, 2007, http://www.nytimes.com/2007/10/10/dining/10pick.html?_r=1&scp=1&sq=picky%20eaters&st=cse&oref=slogin.

13. David Kamp, "Don't Point That Menu at My Child, Please," *New York Times*, May 30, 2007, 1, http://www.nytimes.com/2007/05/30/dining/30kids.html?scp=1&sq=kids%20menus&st=cse.

14. Kamp, "Don't Point That Menu," 1.

15. Wells, "Raising a Baby," 1.

Chapter Two

···

The Book of Tasty and Healthy Food

The Establishment of Soviet Haute Cuisine

JUKKA GRONOW AND SERGEY ZHURAVLEV

Cultural politics were an essential and important part of the building of socialism in the Soviet Union. Socialist society—and even more so the coming Communist society—demanded not only the industrialization of the country and high levels of economic and technical development, it also presumed the emergence of a new kind of citizen with new and greater needs and capabilities. This meant the overall cultivation of human needs. Food culture was no exception.

Culinary culture did not enjoy as prominent a profile as some other fields of "highbrow" culture, such as literature, film, and theater—which were the main targets of ideological and political interference from the Communist Party. The authorities and experts on nutrition did nonetheless codify a Soviet etiquette and actively influence the culinary habits, desires, and tastes of their citizens. To promote these goals they opened new exemplary restaurants, workplace canteens, and cafés, as well as propagating "proper" ways of eating and dietary manners. The Soviet case did not, after all, differ that much from many other rapidly industrialized and urbanized countries in Europe or North America. New socially mobile and urban classes had to be taught, and often were willing to learn, manners of eating more appropriate to their new social position and urban life styles. In addition to more formal school education—obligatory cooking classes for girls at school— books of etiquette and cookbooks as well as other popular instructions, such as recipes in the daily press and journals, served this purpose in the Soviet Union just as they did the capitalist West.

This chapter is based on a wide variety of sources from official documents and culinary publications to the authors' personal experiences and interviews. The Soviet cookbooks are, however, our main source. As historical evidence of the culinary culture, they undoubtedly have their limits. Using them as a source, however, we can analyze the culinary instructions and recipes as well as draw conclusions about the ideals of proper eating and table manners propagated in these publications. Less systematic evidence is available about how these instructions were received and used and how they might have, in fact, influenced both everyday and festive eating in the Soviet Union. No one has, to our knowledge, studied the reception of Soviet cookbooks and it would be almost impossible to reconstruct it in any comprehensive manner after so many decades. In this respect the Soviet Union is no exception: we have, in general, very little systematic information about how cookbooks are read, understood and used. In the capitalist West, cookbooks have belonged not only to the bestselling book genres but the number of individual titles has been on the increase for a long time as well. However, it is questionable whether this has had any remarkable and visible effect on the general cooking skills and eating habits of ordinary households. Equally, it is notable that, for example, products named by popular British TV cook Delia Smith have frequently sold in substantially increased quantities immediately after their media appearances. Cookbooks are clearly pleasurable to read, to look at, and think about, but assessing their impact on culinary and social practice is far from straightforward.

In the Soviet Union, which suffered from serious shortages of many quite basic food items long after the Second World War, the more festive cookbooks must have been to many readers real "dream worlds of eating," perhaps reminding them of their grandmothers' stories of the "good, old times." It is most likely that people used those recipes, for example from the different Soviet ethnic cuisines, which were relatively cheap, easy, and quick to cook. Recipes that were either too complicated or the ingredients of which were difficult or impossible to get, or too expensive to buy, were either simplified or not used at all. In many households the housewives experimented occasionally with the more complicated and new dishes or cooked them on some more festive occasions to celebrate a birthday or a national holiday. The advice of the general books on housekeeping on how to preserve fruit, vegetables, and mushrooms or how to cook jam was certainly highly appreciated and needed in the Soviet *dacha* or summer cottage culture.

In addition to cooking skills and new recipes, the cookbooks spread information about table manners. Since the 1930s, an increasing number of Soviet families used, for instance, knives and forks at the dinner table at home. The three-course lunches or dinners generally recommended in the culinary instructions and often even practiced in the workplace canteens became a Soviet standard quite early on. For most people, sharing a kitchen in a communal apartment with other families and enjoying their daily meals in the single room at their disposal, it would have been quite impossible in practice to follow any more refined, "aristocratic" manners of eating, with their complicated table settings, which the cookbooks also eagerly recommended.

There is, however, good reason to believe that these models of proper eating and table manners had a more direct impact on Soviet consumers than on their counterparts in the capitalist West. In the Soviet Union, the state had a total monopoly on the publication of all books and journals, and it regulated effectively and strictly all public catering organizations, from the modest canteens and beer bars to first-class restaurants. The alternatives on offer to the customers were therefore always more restricted and regulated than in the market economies. The enormous sales and multiple editions of the few Soviet standard cookbooks give further support to our own observations that they really belonged to the standard kitchen inventory of tens of millions of Soviet households.

The general institutional conditions under which Soviet culinary culture developed differed in crucial respects from those in the West. After the short period of New Economic Policy (1921–29), there were no longer any private restaurants or cafés in the country. The whole system of public service was centrally planned and directed. From the mid-1930s onward, all restaurants operated under the close guidance of the Central Administration of Restaurants and Cafés as a part of the Ministry of Trade. The menus of the restaurants, as well as all the dishes and drinks sold, were thus officially approved by the state. From the mid-1930s, the state apparatus controlled all the ingredients and even the number of meat dishes in the daily menus of the restaurants and canteens. Similarly, all culinary books and journals were published by a few state-owned publishing houses. Fortunately this did not mean that there could not be any variation and renewal due to the initiative of individuals and professional groups active in the field of gastronomy. After all, it was obvious that the basic doctrines of Marxism-Leninism did not offer much concrete or detailed advice in culinary matters or other debates concerning taste. To date, no one has tried to apply the doctrine of socialist realism, otherwise accepted as the final truth in aesthetic matters since the 1930s, to Soviet culinary culture. The general standards and ideals adopted in culinary art had, however, parallels in the Soviet fine arts, like music or literature: they presented a selectively "lighter" version of the bourgeois culture of the second part of the nineteenth century.[1]

In the late 1920s, new progressive and scientific ideas of nutrition dominated the Soviet discourse of proper eating. In 1929 a

Scientific Institute of Nutrition opened in Moscow. Soviet experts on nutrition expressed great confidence in developing new scientific-technical solutions to the problems of nourishment. They promoted huge, standardized, factory kitchens and canteens as ideal solutions to catering effectively for the basic nutritional needs of the working population. Similarly, they put great hope in developing new and industrially produced synthetic foodstuffs, such as protein substitutes derived from soybeans. The radical representatives of modern natural science challenged the traditional canons of nutrition and called for a new rational diet and for medically proven scientific rules of eating, based on new knowledge of the proper amounts of calories and vitamins needed to keep the human body in a healthy working condition. For them culinary art and the sensual pleasures of eating were an "anachronism of the bourgeois past." For instance, M. Dubyanskaya claimed in her book *Zdorovaya pishcha i kak yeyo gotovit* (Healthy Food and How to Cook It) that the use of spices and vinegar were unhealthy habits and remnants from the past that only led to overeating.[2]

In the culinary instructions in the popular press, the new science of nutrition, however, mostly joined forces with old gastronomy. Beginning in 1923, the Soviet working women's monthly journal *Rabotnitsa* started to publish regular food recipes under the general title *domovodstvo* (housekeeping). Despite the popularity of the new doctrine of rational nutrition, the journal also published rather fancy recipes from the "old-fashioned" aristocratic cuisine. It is quite remarkable that the new emphasis put on the good taste of food coincided with the collectivization of agriculture and the establishment of collective canteens in the *kolkhozes* (Soviet collective farms) in the late 1920s and early 1930s. For instance, in her cookbook aimed at professional cooks at the kolkhoz canteens, M. Zarina emphasized the need to pay special attention to the taste of food since good taste promoted both good appetite and better absorption of nutrients into the human body.[3] To pay attention to the taste of food and to culinary pleasure was not necessarily regarded as a sign of a reactionary bourgeois attitude. The new science of nutrition played an important but varying role in the ideology and politics of food throughout the Soviet era.

In 1936, Stalin coined his slogan "Life has become better, Life has become more joyous, Comrades." As he now announced, the Soviet Union had reached the stage of general abundance and its citizens could expect to enjoy general material well-being.[4] As the Soviet authorities and ideologists insisted upon repeating, the Soviet Union was not a "barrack society" where all the people lived alike and shared the same meager conditions. With increased material well-being, people's needs increased and developed too. New, higher and more cultivated needs emerged to supplant the old crude standard. At the same time, as was also officially stated, needs simultaneously became more individualized and differentiated. Consequently, Soviet people all had the right to expect that the Communist Party would see to it that the socialist state would satisfy their various expectations. However, not all needs or desires had a similar right to be satisfied. The promise of general abundance did not mean that every wish was equally acceptable. Only those needs that were rational and that contributed to the development of a harmonious and balanced personality, ones that could make valuable contributions to the building of socialism, were justified. In addition, all excessive desires were seen as harmful. One had to learn moderation and avoid extremes. And in the final instance, the Communist Party—or its representatives, the higher party functionaries (through the state planning institutions)—decided which needs and goods were proper and which excessive.

Nevertheless, a considerable gulf separated these general maxims and rules of behavior for Soviet citizens from their practical application in the different fields of everyday life, including eating and culinary art. The first modern Soviet cookbook intended for ordinary housewives, *Spravochnik po kulinarii*, was published in 1934. The book came out at the personal initiative of Anastas Mikoyan, the People's Commissar of the Food Industry (later a minister), at about the same time as the opening of new—and the reopening of some older—more luxurious restaurants in Moscow as a part of a major reorientation in Soviet cultural politics. According to the interpretation of Rothstein and Rothstein, we can notice a clear change of emphasis in the recommendations of the *Spravochnik po kulinarii* to Soviet housewives: "The book contains hardly any simple recipes that could be quickly prepared in a large kitchen: all recipes are complex and require special skills and equipment; they have to be individually cooked and garnished. Thus the ideal of public food service had changed. The communal table was now more like a bourgeois restaurant than a public cafeteria."[5]

Mikoyan was very active in this first Stalinist *perestroika* of the models and ideals of food consumption as well as consumption in general.[6] Just as the traditional signs of luxury—champagne, chocolates, and perfumes—became by the end of the 1930s an essential part of the Soviet culture of consumption, eating a three-course dinner in a fine restaurant with a big dance orchestra playing, or stopping at a "Viennese" café to enjoy a cup of coffee and a piece of cake, became models of proper Soviet eating and urban behavior. There were, however, some interesting tensions built into these now eagerly propagated ideals of the good life. In the first place, they should be available to everyone at the same time or at least to all decent and hard-working citizens of the Soviet Union and not, as under capitalism, only to the few members of the ruling class. In practice this meant that these better services were first—and in many cases only—available to the urban, industrial vanguard of the Soviet working class as well as to its self-nominated representatives, the Communist Party ruling elite—the *nomenklatura*—and other higher civil servants.[7] They were heavily centralized in Moscow and in a few other big cities. In the second place, and as a logical consequence of the first point, these luxuries should ideally be industrially mass-produced. There was of course a problem in servicing the laboring masses at the finer restaurants or cafés, but at least as far as the food products were concerned, there was no longer any contradiction between the aura of rarity or exclusivity, usually characteristic of "bourgeois" luxury, and mass-produced and cheap versions of such items. In socialism these luxuries would be available to everyone at a cheap price. In the official Soviet "commodity aesthetics," the fact that goods were industrially produced, according to the latest techniques, became an extra recommendation and a sign of socialist finesse rather than a marker of cultural and social inferiority.

Soviet "champagne" was probably the best example of this "value change." The mass production of Soviet champagne also started in the mid-1930s. Its promoters were wholly convinced that, owing to the modern technology used in its production, it was not only equal in quality to its French model but often even surpassed it in its excellent taste and other fine qualities.[8] In the service sector, in which technical rationalization was not as easily achieved by mechanization and standardization as in the food industry, the general tendency was to build big units, huge workplace canteens, large restaurant halls with hundreds of tables, and big cafés. After the Second World War, large local service centers opened everywhere with a variety of domestic services concentrated in one big building. In this sense, the ideals of industrial mass catering were never really relinquished. For instance, the Third Party Program of the Communist Party of the Soviet Union, adopted in 1961, promised that by the end of the 1970s various forms of "eating out"—or communal eating—would become more common than eating at home. What had changed, however, compared to the 1920s, was that the low-standard, large workplace canteens that had been the universal solution to all problems of nutrition, were now only the lowest level of Soviet catering. From the mid-1930s, they were accompanied by more expensive restaurants and cafés operating at a better standard. Some self-service snack bars and beer bars, where the customers enjoyed their food and drinks standing up, completed the list of Soviet eating facilities.[9] Their rapid turnover of customers compensated for their smaller size.

The concrete social and economic conditions under which the greatest part of the Soviet population lived were certainly as important, if not more so, than ideological goals in influencing Soviet culinary culture and practices. Most ordinary Soviet citizens did not visit a "real" restaurant many times in their life. As late as the 1960s the Soviet Union was still predominantly an agrarian country and the majority of its population lived in villages or small agricultural centers that did not have any restaurants at all. The urban population ate its main dishes either at home or in a workplace canteen. In the countryside, eating at home was even more common both because of the very low incomes of the village population and because workplace canteens existed as a rule only in the bigger regional centers of a state or collective farm. The quality of food in these canteens in the countryside could, however, be better than in their urban counterparts because the food was cooked from local products and the cooks were close neighbors and even relatives of their customers. In all canteens, both in the cities and in the countryside, the menus and the dishes were strictly standardized, and they had a limited number of alternatives on offer. Even in the bigger urban centers, real restaurants were much more limited in number than in the capitalist West. Ordinary people visited them, if at all, only on some special occasions, like weddings or other important celebrations. To many Soviet tourists and other visitors to Moscow, dining in a real restaurant was a part of "the obligatory cultural program" (alongside visits to the Kremlin, the Red Square, the Bolshoi Theater, and State Department Store). The relatively well-to-do intellectual Bohemians (artists, actors, composers, filmmakers, writers, models) comprised another growing group of customers in the elite Soviet restaurants in the postwar decades. But on the whole, home cooking, family lunches, and dinners preserved for many reasons their traditional status and role in the Soviet Union. Just as elsewhere in Europe, cooking was a predominantly female occupation, both at home, in the canteens and cafés, as well as in the finer restaurants. Men took part in it only rarely.

The state actively promoted eating out by increasing the chains of restaurants and cafés, making them easily available and more economically attractive, at least during the lunch hour. Through the distribution of cookbooks and recipes it promoted "Soviet culinary culture for the masses," propagating etiquette, values, and tastes as well as encouraging the development of home cooking skills. It recommended dishes that were somewhat delicate and complicated as well as espousing a more cultivated manner of serving food, an "aristocratic etiquette" of eating. This improved and refined culture of eating frequently presented a grotesque contrast with the hard, everyday reality of Soviet life, which was plagued with near-permanent shortages of basic foodstuffs in stores, with the dirtiness and low quality of food in the ordinary canteens, and with the crudeness of the service to be encountered in those venues.

Before the Second World War, the families of the nomenklatura often employed domestic servants for housekeeping and cooking. When great numbers of peasant women and girls moved into the cities, domestic work was relatively cheap and even the members of the new Soviet urban intelligentsia—engineers, teachers, doctors of medicine, and the like—could hire domestic help to do their cooking. They needed practical cooking instructions available in the cookbooks. The Soviet elite and the "new middle class," therefore enjoyed their lunches and dinners either at their workplace canteens or at home. After the war the situation changed. The numbers of the nomenklatura, as well as the scientific and cultural intelligentsia who had almost equal rights to such privileges, increased particularly rapidly from the 1960s. Some were able to order home ready-made dishes, while others had special access to hard-to-find foods. Visiting finer restaurants was not that popular among the older generation, partly for ideological constraints linked to the revolutionary era and partly because of the lack of time; they often worked long hours. Above all, they could get almost as good or even better food in their closed workplace canteens for a much cheaper price. They could also enjoy good food in the special sanatoriums in the south, at which they spent their vacations. Many were evidently satisfied that the state took care of their nutritional needs in exchange for their service to the country, an attitude that did not promote higher culinary interests among the ruling elite of the Soviet Union. Real gourmets were an exception among the Soviet political elite, though Anastas Mikoyan, a longtime, top-level party and political leader, had a reputation of being a gourmet. In the homes of the nomenklatura, cooking was not a necessity but—in some cases—a hobby. They most likely had the standard Soviet cookbook on their bookshelves but they used them only rarely. Their children, the Soviet "golden youth," who had grown up under the more normal social conditions of the late 1950s and 1960s, developed a more hedonistic attitude toward life. They were the citizens who were understood to frequent the finer restaurants in the Soviet capital and other big cities.

The lowest level of Soviet social catering consisted of the canteens, the *stolovaya*. They did not, as a rule, open in the evenings. They were divided into general canteens, open to all, and to canteens pertaining to certain work organizations. The canteens that catered exclusively for the workers of a certain organization had their beginnings in the early 1930s, an era of strict rationing of food, which was centrally distributed according to the importance of one's workplace and of that work in the Soviet economy.[10] This paternalistic organization of work and distribution of commodity goods continued to the very end of the Soviet Union.[11] Both the menus and the quality of food were usually better in those canteens that served the workers of a particular organization because many of these industrial and administrative organizations had their own farms that provided them with, for example, milk, eggs, and vegetables. In addition, the factories and institutions subsidized their workers' eating. In consequence, food was better, more varied, and cheaper in these than in the "open" regional canteens. The menus of the regional canteens were generally poor and highly standardized. From the 1930s, Thursday was declared a "fish day," when all the canteens across the country served only fish-based dishes. This was promoted as a healthy alternative but was also dictated by serious shortages in meat production.

Among the peculiarities of Soviet food policy was the strict regulation of recipes used in public catering as well as the amounts of ingredients that were needed to prepare a dish or product. State standards regulated everything to the smallest detail. The same standards were valid all over the Soviet Union, from Central Asia to the Baltic Republics, and they regulated everything from wines and chocolate to cabbage and sausages. These state standards were renewed periodically and the norms for the recipes used in restaurants and canteens were adjusted accordingly.

Food in a "real," first-class restaurant was, as a rule, somewhat better and tastier than in the canteens. It was made from better quality raw materials, many of which were never available in food stores but were only ever distributed to the first-class restaurants and a few highly privileged workplace canteens. However, despite the fact that the prices were much higher and therefore expensive for ordinary Soviet workers, the quality of both the food and service in many finer restaurants was not as substantially improved as might be supposed. Also, in the minds of many Soviet citizens, the image of a Soviet restaurant was connected with moneyed people and, consequently, with the Bohemian way of life and corruption. Their patrons were members of "the golden youth," children of the Soviet elite or black-market dealers. In particular, restaurants serving foreign tourists gathered black-market dealers, prostitutes, and illegal moneychangers.

A great proportion of the population did not have any alternative other than to rely on the services of public catering for at least some limited period of their lives. This was the case with millions of children and teenagers in "closed state institutions" (orphanages and boarding schools) as well as in the kindergartens and at ordinary schools, who all received at least their lunches and snacks in the canteens of their educational institutions.[12] Two other big population groups, those doing military service as well as the prisoners in various penitentiary institutions, from prisons to labor camps, were forced to rely more or less totally on the services of public catering for the satisfaction of their basic nutritional needs. Soviet military service was long, from two to three years—and even longer in the immediate postwar years. It was undertaken by the overwhelming majority of young men. Consequently, almost half the population acquired their formative experiences of Soviet culinary standards and manners of eating from army or navy canteens. The prison population, again consisting mainly of males, was also sizeable in the Soviet Union, even after the closing of the Gulag forced-labor camps in the 1950s. The food served and the standards of service in all these "closed" institutions were, as a rule, of a very poor quality. At best, it could be said that it guaranteed the bare minimum of one's nutritional needs. Manners were crude too. Canteens mostly lacked knives and forks, providing only aluminum spoons. Food was eaten fast and under a strict regime. The practical models of Soviet eating manners that these institutional canteens offered to their "customers" did not offer much in the way of culinary delights and were hardly conducive to the cultivation of a refined approach to eating. They formed a stark contrast to the ideals and models represented by the finer Soviet restaurants and official culinary guidebooks of the period.

There was also another interesting tension in the development of Soviet culinary culture. One of the main ideological pillars of socialism was the promise of liberating women from the slavery of housework.[13] Ideally, as victorious socialism advanced and the country became richer, it was envisioned that preparing food at home would become the exception and the main meals of the day would be enjoyed in various public catering services or, alternatively, high-class catering providers would deliver readymade dishes to the homes of Soviet families. Cooking in one's own kitchen for one's family would thus soon become obsolete. These, as well as many similar tasks of female, domestic work, would be best left to professional workers, like restaurant cooks or industrially organized factory kitchens and service centers. These utopian ideas, often with strong feminist overtones, flourished in particular in the late 1920s. They soon gave way to the promotion of more realistic practices of housework, even though they were never totally abandoned.[14] The reasons for the gradual de-emphasis of women's external roles were both practical and ideological. The unpaid domestic labor of millions of Soviet women was essentially the cheapest means of feeding the population. The wartime idealization of Soviet motherhood and of the family in the construction of socialism, in addition to the new emphasis on the role of woman in a proper socialist family, led to a revaluation of traditional female domestic skills, cooking and hosting included. This also meant that a need to elevate and develop the cooking skills of Soviet housewives emerged. What could be a more natural way to do this than by publishing cookbooks?

A real boom of culinary writing and publishing occurred in the mid-1950s. Many Soviet women's journals, *Rabotnitsa* (Working Woman), *Sovietskaya zhenshchina* (Soviet Woman), *Krest' yanka* (Peasant Woman), and so on, as well as newspapers, like the Moscow evening paper *Vecherniaya Moskva*, regularly published food recipes. Calendars, like the *Woman's Calendar* (1957–59) also included recipes dedicated to special days. Just as in many other countries, housewives and other home cooks eagerly collected these recipes and kept them either in special notebooks or amongst their cookbooks. But these years also saw a lively interest in the publication of cookbooks that was unprecedented in the history of the Soviet Union. In the beginning of the 1970s, many homes already had three or four big cookbooks on their bookshelves. But there were many reasons for this sudden demand for new and more interesting recipes. Firstly, strict wartime rationing finally ended in the second half of the 1950s. Now, for the first time since the war, Soviet food stores had better and more varied food on offer. Due to the general rise in wages and salaries, more people could also afford to buy them. People who had suffered from pure hunger during the war, and had been deprived of the most basic food items for a long time, were understandably obsessed with food and eagerly welcomed new opportunities to eat dishes that were at least fractionally more tasty and varied. Secondly, owing to an era of almost total deprivation, a whole generation had grown up in the Soviet Union who had had virtually no opportunities to experience real gustatory delight or to experiment with more varied styles of cooking and eating. Thirdly, since restaurants were relatively expensive and rare, scarcely accessible to the great majority of the population, and since the food in their local canteens was usually of a poor quality, cooking and eating at home was for many the only way to improve their often meager and dull diets. The Soviet state and its culinary and nutritional experts undertook great efforts to satisfy this demand by publishing new, comprehensive, and relatively advanced cookbooks. The education of taste and eating manners were regarded as an important part of the general cultural education of a cultivated Soviet man and woman.

The *Kniga o vkusnoi i zdorovoi pishche* (The Book of Tasty and Healthy Food)—later shortened to the *Kniga*—had a special position among the Soviet cookbooks.[15] It can be compared to the most popular prerevolutionary Russian culinary book, Elena Molokhovetz's *Podarok molodym khozyaikam* (A Present to Young Housewives), which her contemporaries called the culinary bible and which was first published in 1861. By 1917 it had reached its twenty-ninth edition.[16] The first edition of the *Book of Tasty and Healthy Food* came out in 1939, shortly before the war. It offered an unprecedented degree of luxury in its scale and style, with well over four hundred pages, all richly illustrated with pictures, including several color prints of the delicious dishes and foods it recommended. Further identical editions were issued in the last prewar years, 1940 and 1941. Its publication recommenced shortly after the war.

It was not the only Soviet cookbook of the 1930s; several other smaller and more specialist volumes were also published from the early 1950s. But in many ways this was the standard Soviet cookbook. It came out in numerous renewed editions throughout the Soviet era. In the immediate postwar years, several abridged, shorter, and smaller editions with no photographic illustrations were issued (1945–51) until the first postwar, full, large edition was published again in 1952, toward the end of Stalin's reign. After that, regular new editions appeared practically every year. The 1952, 1953, and 1954 editions each sold five hundred thousand copies. The 1955 edition sold one million copies. The fifth edition from 1952 was published altogether six times in an unaltered form, selling four million copies in total, the last being printed in 1964. A renewed edition came out in 1965, selling seven hundred thousand copies. The last three Soviet editions were published in 1971, 1981, and 1988 but the book was still printed a couple of times after the fall of the Soviet Union in the 1990s. All these complete and renewed editions were produced in the same opulent, large format with many illustrations, including color plates.

It was, however, not only its scale, ambition, and enormous readership that made this work the standard Soviet cookbook. Its editorial collective also had great scientific authority, which raised its status far above any ordinary cookbook written by a professional cook or other expert on nutrition. For it was published by the Institute of Nutrition at the Soviet Academy of Medical Science. Hence both its nutritional and culinary recommendations enjoyed the authority and imprimatur of official Soviet science.

Throughout its different editions the main contents and basic recipes of the book remained unaltered. However, some important changes also took place. In 1965, new chapters were added: The

Organization of Eating at Home, Kitchen and Food Service, The Festive Table, and Healing Food. The 1971 edition had an updated index. New scientific knowledge about the principles of nutrition had an impact on the contents too. To emphasize the scientific nature of the instructions of the book, from 1965 onward, two members of the Soviet Academy of Medical Science, A. I. Oparin and A. A. Pokrovskii, acted as its main editors. The previous long-term editor in chief, I. K. Sivolap, had come from the Soviet food industry.[17] Accordingly, the main emphasis gradually changed from tasty to healthy food, reflecting a more general tendency in Soviet food policy in the 1970s. For instance, the preface to the renewed edition of 1981 announced a shift toward recipes for healthier food—taste was afforded second place. The editors had also discussed changing the name of the book from "tasty and healthy" to "healthy and tasty" food, but gave up the idea because of the book's firmly established reputation.

This was a cookbook aimed at ordinary Soviet families and housewives. Millions of ordinary Soviet households had a copy on their bookshelves or in their kitchens. The instructions and the recipes of the *Kniga* were distributed at the same time in the more modest, slightly shorter and cheaper cookbook *Kulinarnye retsepty iz knigi o vkusnoi i zdorovoi pishche* (Culinary Recipes from the Book of Tasty and Healthy Food).[18] It was published by the same publishing house, had the same main editor, and was in practice a slightly abridged version of the *Kniga*. Issued in the years in between publications of the *Kniga* itself, the number of copies of each edition sold varied greatly, from one million in 1960 to "only" one hundred and thirty thousand in 1965.

The *Kniga o vkusnoi i zdorovoi pishche* was, however, not the only one of its kind. At about the same time as publication of the complete book reissued in the mid-1950s, another prestigious cookbook also emerged, the *Kulinariya* (1955), by the publishing house of the Ministry of Trade.[19] Its editor in chief was M. O. Lif-shits, who also figured among the editors of the *Kniga*. The readers of the *Kulinariya* were originally meant to be different from those of the *Kniga*. As its preface stated, the *Kulinariya* targeted professional cooks working in canteens and restaurants: "The book *Kulinariya* is written to the cook, in order to help him in his work, to improve his qualifications, to teach the basics of modern gastronomy, and to introduce useful habits and practices."[20]

The layout and size of the *Kulinariya* were as impressive as the *Kniga*'s. Its contents resembled those of the *Kniga* too. They both presented a rich assortment of all kinds of recipes as their main contents in the manner of similar, general-cum-aspirational cookbooks from other countries. But in addition, *Kulinariya* offered, for instance, more advanced technical instructions about cooking utensils, techniques, and kitchen equipment. Its recipes were also both more numerous and more technically advanced—a quality especially evident in the section on the sauces recommended for meat and fish. *Kulinariya* was also more straightforward and professional in its style of presentation. Each section included a large number of recipes after a lengthy, general discussion of the qualities and possible uses of each basic food category, like fish, meat, and poultry, as well as instructions on how to handle these raw materials in cooking; for example, how to cut up a chicken or bone a sturgeon. At first, the *Kulinariya* also had a lengthy, rather technical chapter on the instruments and machines of a large restaurant kitchen. However, its second edition, which came out in half a million copies in 1960, was revised and slightly abridged, better to suit the demands of ordinary home cooking. In 1963, under exactly the same title, *Kulinariya*, a book of practical instructions for professional cooking schools came out. Just as in many other countries, Soviet publishing houses distributed several cookbooks for cookery classes in secondary schools.

By the beginning of the 1960s, Soviet home cooks had two very impressive and comprehensive cookbooks from which to choose. Even though the *Kniga* was the more glamorous of the two and included more general information on culinary matters, the *Kulinariya*—which also enjoyed color plates as illustrations—was slightly more advanced and professional in terms of its recipes and cooking instructions. *Kulinariya* was also more matter of fact and did not include any general political or ideological statements. In addition, Soviet home cooks had one more important and widely disseminated source of culinary inspiration at their disposal. They could rely on a whole series of books called *Domovodstvo* (Housekeeping). Judging from their content and their publishers—either regional publishing houses or the Ministry of Agriculture—these books were aimed at rural housewives. They followed the long tradition of early European and Russian manuals on practical housekeeping, which, in fact, were the predecessors of "real" cookbooks.[21] In addition to a rich collection of practical recipes and cooking instructions, they included, for instance, advice on how to prepare, conserve, and preserve fruit, berries, and mushrooms; how to keep bees for honey; and how to brew ale. Some of these Soviet manuals evolved into pure cookbooks, which mainly featured recipes.

The first postwar Domovodstvo came out in Moscow in 1956, selling half a million copies. New, bigger editions were published in each of the following four years.[22] A similar Ukrainian book with the same title was published in 1965 in Kiev.[23] Other related but smaller practical manuals appeared during these years too. Among these practical cookbooks, N. V. Fedorova's *Domovodstvo: Kulinariya: 350 poleznykh retseptov* (Housekeeping: Culinary Art: 350 Useful Recipes) deserves special attention because of its great popularity and unusual, decentralized publishing history. Its main "competitors," *Kulinariya* and the *Kniga*, were strictly based in Moscow. The first edition of the Domovodstvo series was published in Leningrad in 1957.[24] Between 1958 and 1960, twelve new and partly revised editions of Fedorova's *Domovodstvo* came out all over the Soviet Union, in Magadan and Izhevsk, in Moscow and Alma-Ata, in Astrakhan and Kirov.

Kniga, *Kulinariya*, and *Domovodstvo* were not the only Soviet cookbooks published in the 1950s and early '60s, the era of the postwar establishment of "standard" Soviet restaurant cuisine and a new interest in home cooking. To take some typical examples, N. S. Aleshin published his *Kniga dlia povara* (Book for the Cook) in Moscow as early as 1952.[25] It was a concise and very practical, matter-of-fact collection of recipes with some general practical instructions on cooking aimed at professional cooks working in canteens. P. G. Kovalenko's very short cookbook *Kulinarnye sovety* (Culinary Instructions) came out shortly after the war in 1947 and was dedicated to cooking in the officers canteens—a reflection of the priorities of the times.[26] A. A. Ananiev's small cookbook from 1957 was dedicated to soups, typical of traditional Russian cuisine.[27] P. Ya. Grigor'yev's *Kholodnye bliuda i zakuski*, from 1957, was in its turn dedicated to cold starters and cold cuts, preferably enjoyed with a tumbler of vodka, comparable to soups in their importance in Russian culinary culture.[28] In the beginning of the 1970s, the publishing house Ekonomika started a very popular series of tightly focused, small cookbooks under the general title *Sovetuem prigotovit'* (We Recommend to Prepare). Each separate volume specialized in the recipes of a particular kind of food, such as pies or desserts.[29] These and similar books were both less ambitious and had much smaller editions than the two big standard cookbooks with their collective and authoritative editorship. Judging from the publication of these cookbooks, the end of the 1950s and the beginning of the 1960s appears to have been a very active time in the development and propagation of Soviet cuisine.[30] A. A. Pokrovskii's *Besedy o pitanii* (Discussions about Nutrition), from 1966, was not an ordinary cookbook but is a good postwar example of another popular genre of Soviet food writing, dietetics.[31] It offered general advice on "what to eat in order to preserve one's health, how to live without getting old."

While direct references to Stalin's speeches disappeared from the foreword of the *Kniga* soon after his death, the 1955 edition of the book still commenced with a well-known slogan (associated with Stalin in the 1930s): "Toward abundance!" Unlike its predecessor, the 1952 edition, it did not, however, continue to refer to Friedrich Engels's classic study of the working class in Britain a hundred years earlier in order to prove that Soviet workers lived in abundance compared to their comrades suffering under the yoke of capitalism. Such ideological arguments almost totally disappeared from later editions but they had by no means determined the tenor of those earlier editions either. As if to show that such statements were merely an obligatory gesture of political ritual, almost on the next page of its preface the book made a very practical and concrete recommendation, encouraging its readers to drink fruit and vegetable juices since they are rich in vitamins. In particular it recommended tomato juice.[32] That tomato juice was particularly, warmly, recommended might still be a late echo of Mikoyan, then the People's Commissar of the Food Industry, who gave an enthusiastic report on canned tomato juice, from his visit to the United States in 1936.[33] Fruit and vegetable juices were indeed widely available in the Soviet Union and sold, for instance, to customers in the Gastronom food stores in glasses filled from specially constructed juice bottles hanging upside down with taps.

The book, just like many of its "bourgeois" counterparts published in the West, consisted mainly of detailed recipes of various dishes ordered in a way typical of such general cookbooks, according to the order of the dishes (the first course, soups, second course, desserts, bread, and sweet bread), as well as according to the main ingredients of the dishes (egg, fish, meat, milk, vegetable, grain or flour). In addition, the book included a lengthy chapter on the basics of the science of nutrition, on the etiquette of eating, and how to serve food in a proper way, that is, how to place the crockery and cutlery and how to serve and bring food to the table. All this was done in the spirit of European bourgeois haute cuisine. Its numerous recipes followed the standard style of presentation common to many contemporary cookbooks with a short summary of the mode of preparation of the dish and a list of all the required ingredients in their proper quantities. In addition, almost every page of the book included on its margins small informative pieces of text on various culinary themes, from introducing all the fish species available in Soviet waters (from the polar seas to the lakes and rivers), to news on national culinary specialties now industrially produced in some parts of the Soviet Union, like the Tadzhik dish of steamed lamb, *bara-kabob*, or Russian bread filled with meat. These instructive texts even included historical and exotic recipes from old cookbooks, such as how to make a fermented drink from honey. Typically the *Kniga*, as well as many other Soviet cookbooks and gastronomic manuals, devoted much space to special dietetic dishes suitable for people with various health problems. A special dietetic cookbook for professional cooks was published in 1962 (*Dieticheskoe pitanie v stolovykh*). It classified its numerous recipes according to ten basic special diets suitable to people suffering from such diseases as diabetes, heart failure, liver disease, and kidney problems. The Soviet Union also had a big chain of regular food shops and canteens that catered for the needs of this special clientele.

Notwithstanding that many of the recipes of the *Kniga* were quite ordinary, in the sense that a housewife could well imagine regularly cooking and preparing such dishes for her family, the general impression one garners from the book is that it expresses a real Soviet haute cuisine. Compared to the first authorized Soviet cookbook from the 1930s, however, the recipes presented are already made more achievable to suit the practical resources and skills of its target readership of home cooks. For instance, the sauces recommended to accompany meat dishes are quite basic. Instead of the béarnaise, hollandaise, picante, or tartar sauces recommended in the earlier *Spravochnik* from the 1930s, the *Kniga* offers recipes for only a few simple brown and white gravies made of breadcrumbs or flour fried in butter with bouillon added: "Sauces are necessary for all meat dishes, in particular for fried and cooked ones. . . . In order to prepare sauces, use in most cases wheat flour fried in butter and add meat bouillon. For the white sauce, fry the flour only slightly to turn its color slightly yellow, and for the brown sauce into dark brown. In order to improve the taste of the sauce we recommend adding 1–2 spoonfuls of wine to each glass of sauce (to white sauce, white wine and to brown, Madeira or Port wine).[34]

In an almost paradoxical way, and in sharp contrast to its great culinary ambitions, the book's big, colorful pictures sometimes present simple items such as industrially canned peas or a can of sardines, a piece of wurst or a plateful of buckwheat porridge. These were obviously regarded as great delicacies or novelties in their time. As many Soviet people will testify, the book was appreciated by its readers and is still cherished by those who remember looking with great admiration and longing at its colorful pictures during their childhood. And yet most people never actually saw or tasted many of the foods in those pictures and recipes. The raw materials, even some of the more modest foodstuffs, were simply not to be found, or, if available, only irregularly so. Some others, like asparagus, were almost totally unknown to Soviet customers.[35] Many Soviet citizens could, however, order rare and delicious food products through their workplaces before big national celebrations, like the New Year, the First of May, or the anniversary of the October Revolution. This practice became widespread in the 1970s. Practically each factory and institution offered its workers a standard, limited selection of deficit food items, such as better wurst, cheese, caviar, and salmon. The price was the same as in an ordinary food store but access was guaranteed without having to spend a long time queuing. All one had to do was to place an order well ahead of time. These were food products that customers appreciated. They were not typical raw materials for home cooking but rather served as part of a festive buffet table. This common practice of special orders might well be one of the reasons why the first course, consisting of all kinds of cold cuts and salads, was often the real highlight of Soviet festive domestic eating.

The "proper" order of presentation of meals and dishes in the *Kniga* follows the French—or international restaurant style—of haute cuisine, which had become common in affluent urban circles in prerevolutionary Russia. However, it also features some important elements of sturdy peasant eating traditions, for instance heavy Russian soups (*borshch* or *solianka*) and porridges. Consider the recommended daily order of meals:

The morning breakfast should above all be nourishing: it should include either fish or meat, cooked or fried, eggs, cheese, bread, tea, coffee, and milk. It is useful to eat porridge made of cereals (tartar or wheat) with milk or butter, as well as fruit, in the morning. The second breakfast [early lunch]—three or four hours after work has started—can include one hot dish, preferably all made of vegetables (casserole, ragu, etc.), sandwiches, and tea (or coffee or milk). Sausages and sardines are also recommended for the second breakfast.

It is usually good to rest at least some time after finishing work in order for the metabolism to recuperate and to develop a good appetite. Dinner can consist of three dishes: First course—fish, meat, or vegetable soup; the second course a meat, fish, or vegetable dish, fried or stewed; and the third (sweet) course—compote, *kisel'* (fool), a sweet pie, or fruit. In order to increase one's appetite in the beginning of the dinner, we recommend hors d'oeuvres: a salad, herring, and so on.

The supper should always be rather light because one should not eat food later than two to three hours before going to sleep. A salad, sour milk, an omelet, vegetable pudding, milk, tea, vegetable and fruit juices are recommended for supper. . . . And last but not least: do remember to make your menu varied.[36]

The *Kniga o vkusnoi i zdorovoi pishche* also offered exemplary weekly menus for an ordinary family. These were different in each of the seasons in order to emphasize the need for variation in one's daily eating and to encourage the use of the seasonal specialties. For a Sunday in spring, the following was recommended:

"Spring" salad
White fish meat
Meat bouillon with a pie
Anglerfish soup

Fried chicken
Beef roast
Pancakes (*vareniki*) with quark

Rhubarb jelly
Éclair (*Vozdushnyi pirog*)[37]

The difference between a Sunday menu and an ordinary weekday menu was not that great. They both followed the same general order and were equally opulent and nourishing.

For a weekday (Wednesday) in the same season, the model menu looked like this:

Aubergine caviar
Sausage poltava

Chicken bouillon
Macaroni cooked in milk

Chicken plov
Cooked fish
Rice pudding

Compote made of frozen fruit
Biscuit Swiss roll with jam

To encourage its readers to try beverages other than vodka, the *Kniga* offered general advice on the selection of wines and other drinks to accompany various kinds of food. These instructions followed French etiquette with some minor local variations, for instance the recommendation to match Kakhetian (East Georgian) white wines to a *shashlyk* (grilled meat on a skewer).[38] According to the book, Russians have a bad reputation of drinking vodka in great quantities, but this was a remnant of the czarist past, when "people drank because of their miserable living conditions."[39] This was the standard and often-repeated explanation for the heavy drinking of many Russian citizens, which, together with all other social problems, should have disappeared under socialism.

Probably the most distinctive feature of this Soviet cookbook, compared with other standard, national cookbooks of the time in Western Europe, was its open admiration of industrially produced and canned dishes. It had, for instance, a short chapter of its own on canned food, proudly announcing that "the [Soviet] assortment of canned food includes over 350 titles, among them 120 for meat, 150 for fish, 70 for vegetables, 150 for fruit, 22 juices, and a few sorts of canned-milk food."[40]

Even though the recipes and the general classification of dishes resembled other European cookbooks of the time—many of the recipes are part of traditional European or, more precisely, central Eastern European cooking—it naturally had many recipes typical of the traditional Russian and Ukrainian peasant kitchen. These included soups (*borsch* and *solianka*), pancakes (*vareniki, blinis*), and various dishes made from Russian sour cream (*smetana*) and quark. Remarkably, some traditional and well-known Russian specialties were omitted from this collection, such as *paskha*, made of quark, or the Eastern cake, *kulich*—both of which belonged to traditional Eastern Orthodox celebrations and had obvious religious connotations. The book also included several examples of Soviet ethnic cuisine, most notably Caucasian and Georgian, but also some typically central Asian dishes of Turkish or Persian origin. Some of these dishes, such as *shashlyk, liulia kebab, tsyplata tabaka, kharcho*, soup, and aubergine with walnuts had already become an essential part of Russian restaurant cooking before the Soviet era.

In Soviet-Russian cooking, Caucasian, and in particular Georgian, cuisine played a role similar to Mediterranean cuisine in Western Europe, presenting a tasty, spicy, and somewhat exotic ethnic cuisine as a complement to European-Russian cooking. These dishes were served in finer Soviet restaurants too. Bigger Soviet cities often had one or two special Caucasian restaurants, which had a Caucasian menu as well as Georgian wines and Armenian brandies on their list, though this did not mean that they were always available for sale. Moscow had a whole chain of ethnic restaurants, one for almost every Soviet republic opened in the postwar decades, in addition to Georgian, Armenian, Azerbaidzhanian, Uzbek, Ukrainian, and Belorussian restaurants. It also had a chain of eateries dedicated to the cuisines of brotherly socialist countries, such as the restaurants Prag, Budapest, Havana, and Peking. This last became somewhat problematic after the schism between the Soviet Union and China deepened in the 1950s. It was not closed, but instead served food from the Russian Far East. Other Soviet cities, including such major centers as Leningrad and Kiev, had to satisfy themselves with one generic Caucasian restaurant; though Kiev could boast a German restaurant, called Leipzig, which in the 1960s and 1970s served, among other dishes, schnitzels accompanied with the Czech beer President.

At first these Soviet ethnic cuisines were not codified, nor was their culinary peculiarity emphasized in general Soviet cookbooks. Recipes with Caucasian influence were usually presented as ordinary alternatives among the various courses. Quite soon, however, Soviet gastronomic experts started to publish specific ethnic cookbooks dedicated to the kitchens of the different regions of the Soviet Union. Omel'chenko's *Kulinariya narodov severnogo Kavkaza* (The Culinary Culture of the Peoples of North Caucasus) appeared, for instance, in 1963 and presented recipes from the numerous North Caucasian national cuisines, such as Tchechenian, Ingushian, Ossetinian, and so on.[41] The delicacies of Lithuanian national cuisine were presented to a Russian readership in 1959, when *1000 vkusnikh bliud* (1000 Delicious Dishes) was published, comprising 588 pages and selling 325,000 copies.[42] Peterson and Pasona's *Povarnaya kniga* (The Cookbook) was translated from Latvian and published in Russian in 1960.[43] This Latvian cookbook sold two hundred thousand copies. These two are good, early examples of cookbooks wholly dedicated to the cuisine of one of the Soviet titular nations. Similar ethnic cookbooks addressing other Soviet national cuisines followed suit and became genuinely popular. At about the same time, Soviet home cooks could become acquainted with French cuisine as well as other types of international cooking by reading, for instance, *Retsepty frantsuzskoi kuhkni* (Recipes from the French Kitchen, 1967) or I. A. Fel'dman's work with the challenging title *Kulinarnaya mudrost'* (Culinary Wisdom or The Kitchen of the World's Nations, 1972).[44] Thus, the Soviet amateur and professional cook had, by the 1970s, quite an assortment of recipes and cuisines from which to choose: Soviet-Russian and Soviet "internal" ethnic, as well as various international styles. However, they most certainly faced the nearly impossible task of finding the necessary raw materials to cook many of these dishes.

The first comprehensive, Soviet ethnic cookbook came out in 1978, written by V. V. Pohklebkin, a well-known historian and commentator on gastronomy.[45] It presented the cuisines of all the Soviet republics, from the Baltic States to the Caucasus and Central Asia, with a short introduction describing what was typical of these national food cultures, as well as a short list of the recipes of their typical dishes. It also had a section on Jewish cooking. As such the cookbook itself, translated quite soon after its publication into various foreign languages, including Finnish, came to contribute to the codification of the image of typical Soviet national cuisines.[46]

On the other hand, the standard, general Soviet cookbook, the *Kniga o vkusnoi i zdorovoi pishche*, was translated quite early in the 1950s into other Soviet languages as well as into, for instance, Czech.[47] An Estonian edition came out as early as 1955.[48] Ukrainian culinary and nutritional experts, for their part, produced their own version of the book, *Ukrainski stravy* (Ukrainian Dishes), published in 1959 with one hundred thousand copies.[49] In its general outline, it closely followed its Russian predecessor but also included many typical Ukrainian recipes as well as general information on Ukrainian culinary culture and eating traditions.

Even though the Soviet cuisine codified and presented in the *Kniga o vkusnoi i zdorovoi pishche* and other major cookbooks mostly presented the traditional food and dishes of the three big Slavonic nations—Russia, Ukraine, and Belarus—Soviet experts never emphasized this fact. These were not books on Russian cuisine. On the contrary, their Russianness was downplayed because it could have led to the accusation of "Great Russian Chauvinism," something that was, most definitely, not politically acceptable in the Soviet Union. Therefore, culinary publications explicitly dedicated to Russian culinary culture were rare. Instead, Soviet experts emphasized that Soviet cuisine was a combination of all that was best in the culinary traditions of the various Soviet nations. However, one large cookbook dedicated exclusively to Russian cooking, *Russkaya kulinariya*, appeared in 1962. Compared with many cookbooks of the other titular Soviet nations, its edition of one hundred thousand copies was quite limited.[50] The recipes of this Russian cookbook had their origins both in the *Kniga o vkusnoi i zdorovoi pishche* and in its prerevolutionary predecessor, Molokhovetz's cookbook. But it also published the best recipes selected by a jury from an open competition conducted among cooks working in public catering. In this way, the editors could both disseminate some creative new recipes and share some traditional and possibly forgotten specialties that had been preserved in the memories of local professional cooks.

The intensive publication of general and national cookbooks in the 1950s and 1960s in Russian, as well as in the other languages spoken in the Soviet Union, undoubtedly contributed greatly to the unification of Soviet eating habits. These books offered a standard but also rich repertoire of cooking and eating to all interested Soviet citizens throughout the vast country, irrespective of their ethnic or national origins. It also contributed to the gradual diversification of Soviet cuisine by offering new, exotic, ethnic and international recipes. The professional cooks serving at workers' canteens, as well as in finer restaurants, also helped make them available to the wider public. The centralized nature of the Soviet system of food distribution and catering, with its limited amount of alternatives and its preference for industrially produced dishes, certainly restricted the innovative spirit of many amateur and professional cooks and led to a certain forced uniformity in Soviet eating habits. The alternatives to standard Soviet-Russian food were promoted and sold mostly in a few standardized "packages." The common image of other ethnic and international cuisines among ordinary Soviet consumers was probably at least as stereotypical as in the more commercial food markets of the capitalist West.[51]

Notes

1. R. Stites, *Russian Popular Culture: Entertainment and Society Since 1900* (Cambridge: Cambridge University Press, 1992), 65.

2. M. Dubyanskaya, *Zdorovaya pishcha i kak yeyo gotovit* (Leningrad: Izdatel'stvo Leningradskaya Pravda, 1927). The end of the 1920s witnessed a real boom in books dedicated to the propagation of the principles of the new science of dietology. In addition to Dubyanskaya's book, see M. Pevzner, ed., *Dieticheskoe i lechebnoe pitanie*, vol. 2—tomakh (Moscow and Leningrad: Izdatel'stvo Narkomzdrava RSFSR, 1927–30); P. Ignatieva-Aleksandrova, *Prakticheskie osnovy kulinarnogo iskusstva* (Leningrad: Izdatel'stvo Leningradskaya Pravda, 1927; first ed. published in 1908); E. and L. Izrael'yantz, *Zdorovaya kukhnya*

(Tiflis: Gosizdat, 1929); V. Kiselev, *Detskaya kukhnya* (Leningrad: Izdatel'stvo Narkomzdrava RSFSR, 1929); N. Miuller and S. Belotelov, *Osnovy kulinarnoi tekhniki* (Moscow: Pishchepromizdat, 1929); K. Noorden and G. Dornbliut, *Dieticheskaya povarnaya kniga* (Kharkov: Ukrgosizdat, 1929).

3. M. Zarina, *Za obshchim stolom: Kak organizovat' obshchestvennoe pitanie v kolkhoze* (Moscow and Leningrad, 1932).

4. Sheila Fitzpatrick, *Everyday Stalinism: Ordinary Life in Extraordinary Times: Soviet Russia in the 1930s* (New York and Oxford: Oxford University Press, 1999); and J. Gronow, *Caviar with Champagne* (London and New York: Berg, 2003).

5. H. Rothstein and R. A. Rothstein, "The Beginnings of Soviet Culinary Arts," in *Food in Russian History and Culture*, ed. M. Giants and J. Toomre, 162–76 (Bloomington and Indianapolis: Indiana University Press, 1991).

6. Gronow, *Caviar with Champagne.*

7. E. Osokina, *Our Daily Bread: Socialist Distribution and the Art of Survival in Stalin's Russia, 1927–1941* (Armonk NY: Sharpe, 2001).

8. One of the authors of this article remembers standing in Moscow one gray October morning in a long queue at the local food store shortly before its opening. The evening news on TV had advised that the Soviet government had decided to raise the price of vodka by 50 percent. The guys in the queue—often with shaky hands, suffering from a terrible hangover and in very bad need of their first drink of the day—were rather surprisingly quite understanding of their government's decision. They did not protest about the new higher prices since the vodka sold, with a new trademark, Ekstra, was to them yet another proof of the scientific technical progress of the Soviet Union. Soviet vodka was now totally synthetic, as they proudly declared!

9. Gronow, *Caviar with Champagne*; and J. Hessler, *A Social History of Soviet Trade: Trade Policy, Retail Practices, and Consumption, 1917–1953* (Princeton and Oxford: Princeton University Press, 2004).

10. Osokina, *Our Daily Bread.*

11. See, for example, S. V. Zhuravlev, M. R. Zezina, R. G. Pikhoia, and A. K. Sokolov, *AVTOVAZ mezhdu proshlym i budushchim: Istoriya Volzhskogo avtozavoda, 1966–2005* (Moscow: RAGS, 2006).

12. Unlike in Western countries, a great number of Soviet children grew up in state institutions, even in the peaceful 1960s through 1980s. About nutritional standards, culinary culture, and the menus in Soviet orphanages of the 1920s, see, for example, Tatiana Smirnova, "Deti likholetja:povsednevnaya zhizn' sovetskikh detdomovtsev: 1917-nach.1920-kh gg," in *Materinstvo i detstvo v Rossii XVIII–XXI* [Motherhood and Childhood in Russia in the Eighteenth to the Twenty-first Centuries], Part 1, 255–99(Moscow: Mosckovskiy gosudarstvennyi universitet servisa, 2006). According to Smirnova, in 1923 about 850,000 children lived in such "closed state institutions" on a permanent basis in the Russian part of the Soviet Union alone.

13. L. Attwood, *Creating the New Soviet Woman: Women's Magazines as Engineers of Female Identity, 1922–1953* (Basingstoke: Macmillan, 1999); and Yu. Gradskova, *Soviet People with Female Bodies: Performing Beauty and Maternity in Soviet Russia in the Mid-1930s–1960s* (Stockholm: Stockholm University, 2007).

14. As a matter of fact, as early as the 1930s a greater proportion of people in the Soviet Union enjoyed their main meals in workplace and school canteens than almost anywhere else in the world.

15. *Kniga o vkusnoi i zdorovoi pishche* (Moscow: Pishchepromizdat, 1952) and several later editions.

16. Elena Molokhovetz, *Podarok molodym khozyaikam, ili sredstvo k umensheniyu raskhodov v domashnem khozyaistve*, 1st ed. (Kursk, 1886). In all, the total number of copies published during half a century did not exceed three hundred thousand. The book was not forbidden during Soviet times but was not printed either. In 1932 the Russian emigrants printed a version of it in Berlin under the title *Malaya povarennaya kniga sostavlena po knige: E.N. Molokhovetz "Podarok molodym khozyaikam"* (A Little Cookbook Based on the Book: E. N. Molokovetz's *A Present to Young Housewives*).

17. Sivolap was one of the main directors of the Soviet food industry. He published several technical reports on food production. See, for instance, I. K. Sivolap, *Za sozdanie obiliya produktov pitaniya v SSSR: Stenogramma lektsii* (Moscow: Znanie, 1954); and I. K. Sivolap and A. S. Shakhtan, *Pishchevaya promyshlennost' SSR* (Moscow: Gospolitizdat, 1957).

18. *Kulinarnye retsepty iz knigi o vkusnoi i zdorovoi pishche* (Moscow: Gostorgizdat, 1955) and several later editions.

19. *Kulinariya* (Moscow: Gostorgizdat, 1955); the second edition appeared in 1960.

20. *Kulinariya*, np.

21. Compare, for instance, A. Nel'sina, *Molodaya khozyaika: Rukovodstvo k prakticheskoi podgotovke i vedeniyu doma* (Sankt-Peterburg: Tipografiya tovarishcheshtva A.S.Suvorova, 1913). For a history of European cookbooks, see, for instance, S. Mennell, *All Manners of Food: Eating and Taste in England and France from the Middle Ages to the Present* (Oxford and New York: Basil Blackwell, 1985).

22. This was A. A. Demezer's and M. L. Dziuba's comprehensive housekeeping book (the Domovodstvo series) with five hundred pages and a publication of half a million copies (Moscow: Sel'khozgiz, 1956).

23. *Domovodstvo* (Kiev: Izd. Urozhai, 1965).

24. N. V. Fedorova, *Domovodstvo: Kulinariya: 350 polezhnykh retseptov* (Leningrad, 1957).

25. N. S. Aleshin, *Kniga dlia povara* (Moscow: Gostorgizdat, 1952).

26. P. G. Kovalenko, *Kulinarnye sovety: Kratkoe rukovodstvo po prigotovleniyu pishchi v ofitserskikh stolovykh* (Moscow, 1947).

27. A. A. Anan'yev, *Supy* (Moscow: Gosudarstvennoe izdatel'stvo torgovoi literatury, 1957).

28. P. Ya Grigor'ev, *Kholodnyie bliuda i zakuski* (Moskva: Gostorgizdat, 1957).

29. See, for example, L. I. Timofeeva, *Sovetuem prigotovit': Vypusk 2: Sbornik retseptov prigotovleniya pirogov* (Moscow: Ekonomika, 1971).

30. This period, when Nikita Khrushchev was the leader of the Soviet Union, witnessed similar active professional engagement in many other fields of the consumer culture.

31. A. A. Pokrovskii, *Besedy o pitanii* (Moscow, 1966).

32. *Kniga o vkusnoi i zdorovoi pishche*, 1955, np.

33. Gronow, *Caviar with Champagne*, 73.

34. *Kniga o vkusnoi i zdorovoi pishche*, 1955, np.

35. In his autobiographical novel *Khoroshii Stalin* (Moscow, 2004), Viktor Yerofeyev, whose father was a high-ranking Soviet diplomat

and had access to the special system of distribution at the Kremlin, makes a joke that his family belonged to the few who, in fact, could have cooked at home following the recipes in the *Kniga o vkusnoi i zdorovoi pishche.*

36. *Kniga o vkusnoi i zdorovoi pishche,* 1955, 24–25.

37. *Kniga,* 43–44.

38. *Kniga,* 115.

39. *Kniga,* 79.

40. *Kniga,* 77.

41. E. S. Omel'chenko, *Kulinariya narodov Severnogo Kavkaza* (Makhachkala: Dagknigoizdat, 1963).

42. E. Drasutiene, O. Radaitiene, E. Starkiene, and A. Sliziene, *1000 vkusnykh bliud* (Vilnius: Gosudarstvennoe izdatel'stvo politicheskoi i nauchnoi literatury Litovskoi SSR, 1959).

43. Milda Peterson and Anita Pasona, *Povarnaya kniga* (Riga: Latgosizdat, 1960).

44. V. V. Petroshenko, *Retsepty frantsuzkoi kuhkni* (Moscow: Pishchevaya promyshlennost', 1967); I. A. Fel'dman, *Kulinarnaya mudrost': Kuhkni narodov mira* (Kiev, 1972).

45. V. V. Pohklebkin, *Natsional'nye kukhni nashikh narodov: Osnovnye kulinarnye napravleniya, ikh istoriya i osobennosti: retseptura* (Moscow: Pishchevaya promyshlennost', 1978).

46. V. V. *Pohklebkin, Neuvostoliion kansalliset keittiöt: Porvoo-Juva* (Helsinki: WSOY, 1983).

47. The Czech language edition from 1956 has totally and mysteriously disappeared and is not available in any library.

48. *Raamat maitsvast ja terveslikust toidust* (Tallinn: Eesti Riiklik kirjastus, 1955).

49. *Ukraiinski stravy* (Kiev: Derzhavne vidavnityztvo techliteratury Ukr SSR, 1959).

50. *Russkaya kulinariya,* ed. A. A. Kaganovich and V. A. Sidorov (Moscow: Gostorgizdat, 1962).

51. For an interesting account of the history of ethnic cuisines in postwar Britain, see P. Panayi, *Spicing Up Britain: The Multicultural History of British Food* (London: Reaktion Books, 2008).

....

Chapter Three

The Flavor of the Place

Eating and Drinking in Payottenland

TIM WATERMAN

In the time before the reign of products that are sorted, graded, carved, prepackaged, and packaged in an anonymous form where only the generic name attests their original nature, everything had flavour because everything was dangerous.

Michel de Certeau, Luce Giard, and Pierre Mayol

The beauty that we see in the vernacular landscape is the image of our common humanity: hard work, stubborn hope, and mutual forbearance striving to be love. I believe that a landscape which makes these qualities manifest is one that can be called beautiful.

John Brinckerhoff Jackson

Belgium: Flanders and Payottenland

The popular image of Flanders is of a flat and somewhat bland landscape. The north of Flanders does little to belie this stereotype. Driving south from Dunkirk, there is little topography, and what little exists is usually the result of human intervention rather than geology. The landscape also flattens out visually into the distance. Objects near and far are juxtaposed against one another without depth or perspective, like cut-out scenery sliding across a stage set. Flanders is famous for its towers and belfries, which gain some of their imposing nature through contrast with the low landscape. As one approaches Brussels, though, a more voluptuous landscape grows from little ripples into hills, with small towns grouped around churches, tree-lined roads, and tidy hedgerows. It is a cozy landscape with only the barest of hints that the dark forest of the Ardennes and the rusted heavy industry of Wallonia lies beyond. This area, to the west and southwest of Brussels, is an area known as Payottenland, and the coziness one sees in the approach is qualified, compromised by numerous tensions, psychological and political, that at times inscribe themselves onto the landscape.

Payottenland is part of the province of Flemish Brabant, and it is inhabited by both Flemish and Walloons. Belgium is not one nation, but two: Flanders to the north and francophone Wallonia to the south. Payottenland lies on the fault line between the two. This fracture is a tectonic divide of language and culture, and its extreme and constant pressure inevitably results in seismic events in politics and prejudice. The big earthquakes are felt across Belgium and in the halls of its government, while the tremors are much smaller and the damage local: shattered glass, a lick of flame, a shadow disappearing into night.

Payottenland also sits on another kind of divide, and one equally difficult to define, that of the urban fringe. It is the interface between urban and rural, a seemingly haphazard assemblage of housing, industry, and open fields. It is transected by infrastructure leading into Brussels: roads, railway tracks, power lines, canals, and the lugubrious River Senne. In this densely settled part of Europe—and Flanders has been incredibly dense since the Middle Ages—one urban fringe can often seem to blend seamlessly into the next. Despite, or perhaps because of all this, Belgians have made a virtue of the uneventful and ordinary. This is a landscape that is comfortable rather than inspirational, often pretty but rarely beautiful. Its deficits are measured mainly as pragmatic necessities, not as compromises or intrusions.

The historic village life in the area would have been much the same as in many areas of Europe: an agrarian existence, shaped by the relationship between fields, home, market, and church. Flemish villages, as so many elsewhere, were traditionally centered around a church, which usually sits even now just opposite a café. Roads and paths lead out radially from the church. The congregation was composed of those who lived within walking distance of the center, and thus was the community defined. The radial routes into the church would have passed farms, which, like miniature castles, formed a sort of defended enclave with the house, barn, and outbuilding ranged around a yard. Farm buildings looked inward to the courtyard rather than out to the landscape, with their backs resolutely set against winds, rains, and adversity. Belgian life is still very much an interior one, focused on the creature comforts of the home and the pleasures of the table.

It is still possible to find these patterns imprinted upon Payottenland. On a map, village cores are a dense knot of streets clustered around an often awkwardly, organically trapezoidal church square. Radial routes may still be traced. These routes, though, have become encrusted with structures, in the same way a string suspended in salt water collects crystals. It is often no longer possible to tell where one town leaves off and another takes up as the intervening space is filled with car dealerships, furniture showrooms, budget supermarkets, and all other such markers of the urban fringe. Passing through the area by car along certain routes, it might never be apparent that one was in the countryside at all. And countryside is just what the people who live there wish it to be. In Payottenland a new generation is attempting to imprint a rural ideal upon a stretch of land that for many years served only as a hinterland—a zone hitherto beneath notice registering only, if at all, as a mysterious realm of uncertain use and occupation beginning at the garbage cans behind the endless strip and extending to the back doors of the next strip. Perpendicular to this grain is a "gradient from urban core, to community urban fringe to urban fringe farmland to urban shadow."[1] It is perhaps this lack of definition, spiced with dereliction, that makes it possible to cast this productive area as a mysterious landscape that is perfectly capable of accepting romanticization. This area of exurban overspill is actually a tremendously valuable stretch of cultural landscape fertile with latent potential.

In the village of Eizeringen—just off the intersection of the busy road from Asse to Enghien (and eventually Mons) and the road from Brussels to Ninove (both so crisply straight that one can feel the bite of the cartographer's pen against the ruler)—is to be found a delightful traditional Payot café called In de Verzekering tegen de Grote Dorst (Insurance against Great Thirst). It is open only on Sundays "for those on their way to church, those on the way home from church, and those who say they are going to church, but don't make it."[2] It is run by the brothers Yves and Kurt Panneels, who took over as proprietors from its octogenarian landlady in 1999. Since their careful restoration of the café, a window opens into the past every Sunday.[3] It has become common for beer connoisseurs to make pilgrimages to the café, where they stock an exhaustive selection of traditional Payot beers. This is historic preservation as it should be. It preserves not just a building and the surrounding spaces, but the way of life that animates them. It is an urbanite's ideal of country living, but one that works with the place and its people rather than imposing a ludicrous fantasy.

It is a cliché that "everyone eats well in Belgium," though, as with all clichés, it is well-founded. The patterns of living that make it possible for the In de Verzekering tegen de Grote Dorst to continue to exist are still alive and well in the Belgian kitchen. The North Sea makes possible a mouthwatering range of seafood, particularly the sweet, plump mussels that have become emblematic of Belgian cuisine. They are at their best in the autumn and winter before their spawning season begins, and a giant pail of mussels steamed with cream and white beer is just the thing to take the chill off. Succulent "eel in the green" (*paling in 't groen* or *anguilles au vert*) is another favorite—thick slices of eel in a sauce of wine and green herbs such as sorrel, sage, and chervil. *Waterzooi* ("watery mess") is either a chicken or seafood stew made with leeks, potatoes, eggs, and cream. The seafood version may contain eel, pike, or carp, and possibly also shellfish.

The influence from the south, the Ardennes, contributes a love of game. Rabbit is served grilled or cooked slowly and sauced richly with its own blood. Wild boar, partridge, and venison make regular appearances at table in a myriad of forms from roasts to stews to patés and sausages (sausages are often served with *stoemp*—mashed potatoes and vegetables). Every menu also features beef, and always *stoofvlees* (*carbonnade Flamande*), the quintessential Belgian stew of beef and sweet brown beer. Belgium, though a fraction of the size of France, produces roughly as many different types of cheese. Few but the formidable, perhaps notorious Limburger cheese, are known outside Belgium, though, as most are produced locally by small producers. It can be a challenge, even, to find Belgian cheeses in Belgian supermarkets.

While the Belgian diet is almost always anchored by meat, vegetables also receive more than their due. The princeliest of vegetables are at their best here, many raised in the dark, secret earth and plucked in tender youth—it is the illicit air of decadence that lends them their cachet. The delightfully bitter Belgian endive or chicory (*witloof/chicon*) features in many typical dishes. They are almost always cooked, whereas elsewhere in the world they may appear more commonly as a salad vegetable. Asparagus, either green or white, is consumed with gratitude in season. A specialty that has experienced a resurgence lately comprises the shoots of the hop plant (*jets d'houblon*). These are harvested like asparagus, but in February and March, and are commonly served with a mousseline sauce (hollandaise folded with whipped cream just before serving) and poached eggs.

It is no surprise that the hop plant should make an appearance in cuisine, as everyone drinks well in Belgium too. This is the cool, damp north, though, and few wine grapes are found here. Belgium's extraordinary range of local cheese is matched or outmatched by a dizzying variety of exquisite, hand-crafted beers. Even the mass-produced lagers are a cut above, and the run-of-the-mill such as Bel, Maes, or Stella Artois are flavorful and stimulating. At the other end of the spectrum are the six world-famous and highly alcoholic beers produced by Trappist monks: Westvleteren, Westmalle, Rochefort, Orval, Achel, and Chimay. These are usually "double" and "triple" beers—rich, sweet brown beers. There are many other styles as well, the most common being blonde or golden ales, the most famous of which is Duvel, and white beers—fruity, cloudy light beers typified by Hoegaarden. Every beer in Belgium is meant to be served in its own distinctively shaped glass, and the best cafés will ensure that they have the correct glass on hand for every beer they serve. Many of the beers I have mentioned (with the notable exception of Westvleteren, which is available only at the abbey in limited quantities or by reservation) have international brand profiles, but most of the rest are distinctly local products, produced on a small scale locally by people who brew as a labor of love on a marginal wage.

The people of Payottenland, and Belgium as a whole, are often fiercely (though not exclusively) loyal to their local producers, and it is this characteristic that both allows these producers to exist and yet limits their range and commercial viability. It also, presumably, has the effect of ensuring a continuing market despite incursions from the big supermarkets. In turn, it keeps the pressure on supermarkets to provide quality products. It helps to ensure that the average food consumed in Belgium is not merely adequate, but delicious too.

The *Terroir* of Lambic

Terroir is a French term that is most often used in relation to oenology, the study of wine.[4] In this sense it refers to the effect of soils, geology, topography, and climate upon the flavor of wine from a given region. The French *appellation d'origine contrôlée* (aoc) system defines and protects agricultural products such as wines and cheeses from specific regions. Other countries as well as the European Union as a whole also protect the names of foods and beverages based on their origins. These products are held to possess character and qualities that can only be produced by certain methods in a certain region. While terroir certainly refers to this, it also refers to the patterns of habitation and the practices of daily life that have evolved in an area as a complex interrelationship between a landscape and its inhabitants. In this sense, the idea of terroir is not too terribly different from the definition of cultural landscape. The unesco World Heritage Commission defines cultural landscapes as those "that are representative of the different regions of the world. Combined works of nature and humankind, they express a long and intimate relationship between peoples and their natural environment."[5] The implication is that, while the flavors of some agricultural products are deeply dependent upon a region and upon human practice in a certain area, these products also exert a strong influence upon the personality and cultural identity of people in that same area. You are what you eat. And what one eats, at least ideally, is an indelible connection to one's environment.

The French aoc system is very specific about certain products, such as wines and cheeses. Elsewhere, though, and for other products there is less or no emphasis on terroir. Beer is one such product, and possibly this is because of a long-standing association of wine with the cultured upper classes and beer as a drink of the masses. With wine prices being pushed ever downward, the premium prices of many top-quality beers would seem to reverse that social order, especially with restaurant markups. Still, the question must be asked whether the term *terroir* can apply to beer. I believe so. A few years ago, when I had first moved back to England, I was riding on one of the last "slam-door" trains through the area around Faversham, what is now possibly the last remnant of the

Kentish hop-growing landscape. I was drinking a bottle of Spitfire, a bitter beer brewed in Faversham. When fresh, the beer has a most stimulating spicy, fiery hop character, and it could just as well be this, as well as the British fighter plane, for which it is named. As I drank, the train passed farm workers loading freshly harvested hops into a truck. The sharp perfume of the hops filled the train through the open windows. The hops being loaded were probably destined for the brewery in Faversham, and the experience of tasting the beer and smelling the fresh hops simultaneously was both electrifying and somehow chthonic. It was like being plugged into the landscape and, literally, grounded.

Many readers will be familiar with English bitter beers, but far fewer will have ever tasted, or even be aware of the existence of lambic and gueuze beers. Lambic is particular to Payottenland and Brussels, and its production is now limited to a handful of brewers. Lembeek, which is the home of the Boon Brewery, is the source of the name "lambic." Lambic beers are produced in what must be the original method of brewing beer around the world. "In traditional lambic fermentation, freshly brewed wort [the liquid extracted from cooked grains in the brewing process] is left in an open shallow vat to cool, usually overnight. Naturally occurring yeast land on and drop into the sweet mixture. When properly cooled the next day this wort is drained into large oak casks, where it ferments slowly for between six months and three years."[6] The wild yeasts that settle into the wort are a mix specific to the Senne Valley, and they include the yeast *Brettanomyces bruxellensis*, which is named for Brussels. Most if not all other brewing processes, at least in Europe, are highly controlled and sanitary. Lambic breweries, in striking contrast, exhibit exposed wooden beams draped with spider webs (the spiders control the fruit flies) and an overall atmosphere that can only be described as, well, yeasty.[7] The enjoyment of lambic is definitely an acquired taste. It is a flat beer, served fresh at cellar temperature in earthenware jugs. It packs an attack of tartness at the front of a whole range of earthy, antediluvian flavors that may invoke leather, mildew, or mud. The flavor of lambic lifts and separates the taste buds in the same way that fresh, unsweetened grapefruit juice does. It is a down-home drink that is as macho as bourbon.

I met with Chris Pollard, an expert on Belgian beers who coauthored the book *Lambicland*. He told me that lambic is the taste of Payottenland, and associated with country life and labor in the fields. Gueuze, on the other hand, is the taste of cosmopolitan Brussels and "the Champagne of Belgium." Gueuze (the name of which may be from the Norman word for wheat, which is a common ingredient along with barley) is a sexed-up, blended lambic that undergoes a secondary fermentation in champagne bottles and is topped with a wired-on cork. The second fermentation makes it a sparkling beverage. Gueuze is produced from the output of various lambic breweries and of various vintages, in much the same way that blended scotch is handled. The blending adds complexity and depth, and the natural carbonation satisfies more effervescent urban tastes. Fruit is also added to lambics, the most traditional being sour cherries, which produce a drink called *kriek*. Raspberries and blackcurrants often make an appearance, and occasionally sugar or caramel is added to make *faro*. A range of Belgian malt beverages flavored with fruit syrups are currently causing confusion with the more traditional beers, but these are tailored to juvenile tastes, and have little character other than as sweet/fruit pablum. The flavor of real lambic beers is stamped with the moist air of the Senne Valley and it is a palpable link to a whole history of inhabitation of the area. To taste it in Payottenland is to experience the same sort of chthonic connection to place that I felt drinking bitter in Kent.

The complex and earthy flavors of lambic and gueuze beers make them the perfect complement to much of Belgian cuisine, from the gamey flavors of boar and rabbit to the decadent spears of asparagus and jets d'houblon as well as fat, bitter little chicories. The sharp, citrusy flavors of gueuze also cleanse the palate between bites of what is often rich and creamy food. They may even help to curtail the appetite somewhat, helping to reduce the damage done by all that saturated fat, though this may be wishful thinking. To acquire a taste for lambic and gueuze is to gain entrance to a spectrum of sensation and a way of life that is peculiar, and special, to Payottenland.

Acquired Taste, Discovered Taste, Accrued Taste

Taste, though it can be defined as a single sense, is never truly autonomous. The boundaries between taste and olfaction are blurred. Those without the sense of smell find it difficult to taste anything as a result. Taste also involves touch—the way a food or drink feels in the mouth has a distinct influence on its flavor. In fact, the boundaries of the sense of taste continue to swell ever outward to include all the human senses and numerous variables such as color and composition in the presentation of food, positive or negative associations, and so on. Taste, ultimately, has psychosocial and cultural meaning that is not altogether inseparable from the five senses at any time.

Babies rely early on their sense of taste to explore the world around them and make meaning of it. If possible, every object is inspected, felt, and tasted. Through these encounters, the infant pieces together a composite portrait of the surrounding environment and landscape that is the basis for taste preference and has a strong influence on personality, identity, and character. In this way, even if children are not consuming the produce of their immediate landscape, which is likely the case for first-world children who may eat a largely processed diet sourced from supermarkets and franchised restaurants, they are probably still responding to taste stimuli that are rooted in their native landscape. Local preferences, even in a globalized market, may still be the result not just of local acculturation (nurture), but of a direct relationship with soil, air, climate, and vegetation of a place (nature). Many discovered basic tastes, then, may not be completely universal, but may be tempered to one degree or another by the landscape of place.

Discovered tastes are those that might be considered to be innate. Bland, salty, and sweet foods—"comfort foods"—have instant appeal to infantile tastes. Some tastes may well be nearly universal. There are probably only a handful of people of any age, anywhere in the world, who wouldn't be seduced by a plate of perfectly golden-fried Belgian *frites*, for example (though some might object to the Belgian preference for serving them crowned with mayonnaise. I myself can't fathom the practice of eating them with ketchup). Because of the instant rewards of comfort foods, products are engineered for the market to pander to and encourage these basic tastes, which can often be quite addictive. The food industry probably has much to gain from playing to childish or "kidult" tastes and from actively infantilizing the consumer. Unfortunately, the consumer has little to gain from this market dynamic except weight.

In a healthy environment where the development of taste is not inhibited, taste is slowly developed. The more we learn to like, the broader our range of choices and combinations becomes, and the more open we become to further taste possibilities. I will call this *accrued taste*. Accrued taste is acquired taste that is learned, constructed and additive, contextual and associative, but not necessarily intentional. It may be the discovery that a food is pleasing because it is sauced with hunger, or it may simply be that repetition has bestowed familiarity, which has grown into fondness.

Educated taste I shall define as acquired taste derived from intentional taste explorations. If a people come to believe, wish to believe, or are coerced into believing that learning to like something will enrich their lives, then they will undertake to do so, even though the process may be unpleasant. It is the taste equivalent of "working out" or "reading up." Scotch whisky is the sterling example of this. I have slowly grown to find single malt whisky quite indispensable, though at first only the gentler brands were acceptable. The first time I brought home a whisky from the Isle of Islay, I was horrified at the taste that assaulted me. It was as though I had uncorked a Molotov cocktail. The bouquet was of tar pit, and the flavor was of diesel. I don't believe I finished the glass, and the offending bottle remained at the back of the cabinet for some months. A visit from an American friend, though, prompted a tasting of the various scotches I had on hand. Tentatively, I retrieved the bottle, brushing off the dust, and, warning my companion about the violence I was about to do to his palate, poured some. This time, however, I was more prepared for its flavor. I found it challenging, but not altogether unpleasant. It was only a matter of weeks before I tried it again, and by the time the bottle was finished, I was quite enjoying it and looking forward to trying more Islay whiskies. Now a couple of the Islay malts rank among my great favorites, profound comforts.

Educating taste is usually quite rewarding in this way. There is the satisfaction of having overcome an obstacle, the pleasure of adding a new experience to a repertoire of experiences, and the lift of knowing that one's tastes are now a marker of difference, perhaps even superiority. Further, the acquisition of tastes through intention leads to the possibility of more innocently accrued tastes building upon a new framework and expanded context. To complicate matters, though, educating taste is also a process of elimination. Often, in acquiring new tastes, we leave others behind as an act of casting aside the training wheels, perhaps, or as a conscious step up the class ladder, and this expression can be quite violent in its refusal. Pierre Bourdieu, in his landmark study *Distinction: A Social Critique of the Judgment of Taste* states: "Tastes (i.e., manifested preferences) are the practical affirmation of an inevitable difference. It is no accident that, when they have to be justified, they are asserted purely negatively, by the refusal of other tastes. In matters of taste, more than anywhere else, all determination is negation; and tastes are perhaps first and foremost distastes, disgust provoked by horror or visceral intolerance ('sick-making') of the tastes of others."[8]

Fitting in to a social and physical environment involves both accrued and educated acquired tastes, in the process of the accumulation of Bourdieu's "cultural capital." We first become attuned to the landscape in which we are raised, beginning with the infant's explorations. Geophagy, the consumption of soil, is common among children, and is one quite vivid and literal way in which the landscape might be internalized, understood, ingested, digested. Later in life, acquired taste will be a way to identify with a certain group, whether this is acquiring upwardly mobile tastes for champagne and truffles, or simply a liking for lager to facilitate and lubricate conviviality at the local watering hole. Bourdieu again, this time at some length:

> Taste classifies, and it classifies the classifier. Social subjects, classified by their classifications, distinguish themselves by the distinctions they make, between the beautiful and the ugly, the distinguished and the vulgar, in which their position in the objective classifications is expressed or betrayed. And statistical analysis does indeed show that oppositions similar in structure to those found in cultural practices also appear in eating habits. The antithesis between quantity and quality, substance and form, corresponds to the opposition—linked to different distances from necessity—between the taste of necessity, which favors the most "filling" and most economical foods, and the taste of liberty—or luxury—which shifts the emphasis to the manner (of presenting, serving, eating, etc.) and tends to use stylized forms to deny function.[9]

The larger issues of identity can be descried in these taste ambitions (or lack thereof), and the elements of personality both drive those ambitions and are informed and shaped by them. It is possible that acquired tastes have little to do with basic needs, but rather could be seen as practices or tactics to enable us to discriminate and navigate through everyday life. They may well be essential, though, to making a home in a community. Michel de Certeau, Luce Giard, and Pierre Mayol, in volume 2 of *The Practice of Everyday Life*, point out that "the practice of the neighborhood introduces gratuitousness instead of necessity; it favors a use of urban space whose end is not only functional."[10] It also favors a deployment of taste whose end is not only functional—a fact reinforced by the tendency of the wealthy and privileged to be distinguished by being thin—a perverse reversal in which the existence of plenty is displayed through the appearance of scarcity. Less signifies more. Educating taste, in this case, becomes not only *like* working out, but the appearance of it actually *requires* working out.

The Agony of Taste

Agony and ecstasy dwell in close proximity to one another. Agony is a sensation not only allied with pain, but with competition, with striving and aspiration. It's not unusual for the most satisfying emotions to have both a dark and a light side. The bittersweet and the melancholy, for example, are experiences with a piquancy derived from a mixture of pleasure and pain. It is also a measure of the emotional content of taste that terms relating to taste, such as "bittersweet" and "piquant," should so aptly describe a state of being.[11] In all its aspects, life is a jumble of emotions that are always queerly juxtaposed, and the ability to savor the mix is the ability to apprehend all of life and to draw nourishment from it. Chocolate, dark chocolate, perfectly contains this delightful opposition—and Belgian chocolate is without argument the best in the world. Without the sweetness (and light) of sugar, chocolate is too intense for most tastes. It is almost black, the color of oblivion, but the mild euphoria it delivers is elevating. Cocoa grows in messy, fetid conditions necessitated by the habitat of its pollinators, but the best chocolate is sold in immaculate, light-filled boutiques like Pierre Marcolini in the Place du Grand Sablon in Brussels. Marcolini's exquisite chocolates certainly walk the razor's edge of agony and ecstasy, a taste that can only be delivered on a small and exclusive scale by producers with passion.

Payottenland has its own producer with the same sort of passion as Pierre Marcolini. Armand Debelder is the owner and brewmaster at the Drie Fonteinen Brewery in Beersel, a tidy, intimate town with a small but well-formed castle and pleasant, composed views over Payottenland. He is an elegant, confident, and well-spoken man who is a proselytizing believer in lambic beers and who produces some of the very finest. I spoke with him in the "Lambik-o-Droom" tasting room at his brewery, and he underscored many of the themes that have been appearing increasingly, and for good reason, in the media: the importance of the small producer, the virtues of sourcing goods locally, the need to maintain patrimony and tradition for future generations, and shedding empty consumerist ambitions in favor of those things that are "free."

He has lived his life in Payottenland, and he told me that there are two moments of that life that stand out as possessing singular beauty. The first was the birth of his granddaughter, and the second was the death of his mother. His mother died in winter, a season she loved. As the family gathered around in the last moments of her life, they threw open the shutters into the yard, where the light picked out the flakes of falling snow. Why these two moments? Because they contain agony and joy; sorrow, pain, and hope. Because they are about the continuity of life in a landscape, belonging in family, community, place. As I listened and sipped an astounding gueuze, it seemed that the flavors presented in that drink held all the richness and depth of such a story. Tart like tears and brash like laughter and with undertones of sweat and soil, longing and belonging. If a drink can be a true reflection of a place and a people, of terroir, then Armand Debelder's gueuze is a textbook example.

It is, of course, difficult to discern how much of the intensity of this taste experience is held within the beverage itself. Does it, in fact, intrinsically contain all this information? The question could well be metaphysical, and it is delightful to contemplate that the flavor could tap into an ancestral collective consciousness. More pragmatically, as a cultural construct, educated taste is the product of foreknowledge and context that shape the experience. The story thus influences and enhances the taste, though it would be unpoetic and unnecessary to rule out metaphysical factors. Indeed, beliefs and spirituality are integral to the formation of place through practice. Bourdieu notes: "But one cannot fully understand cultural practices unless 'culture,' in the restricted, normative sense of ordinary usage, is brought back into 'culture' in the anthropological sense, and the elaborated taste for the most refined objects is reconnected with the elementary taste for the flavors of food."[12] And the elaborated taste for the most refined places, for homeland, for landscape are inextricably tied to culture in the anthropological sense and the flavors of food in a way that is basic to identity and is fundamentally both ideological and spiritual. Terroir implies that taste is much more than simply aesthetic judgment, but is (or at its best can be) part of the total framework of identity that is a construct not only of human associations, but of the full matrix of associations across home, work, and community that are bound together by modes of occupation and daily practice in the landscape.

The Tower of Babel

The Tower of Babel has somehow haunted me the whole time I have been in the process of writing this essay, appearing in conversation and print and image, though I doubt I have heard the story mentioned in years. Armand Debelder spoke of it when he talked about the appreciation of those things that are "free," like bluebells in the spring, rather than those that are accorded value due to supposed rarity or exclusiveness. Indeed, many things are accorded value simply because they are expensive. Debelder's brewing is an attempt to find a better way of operating in the world, a more authentic mode. He sees society as building a new Tower of Babel, one that is surely destined to collapse.

The story of the Tower of Babel is the classic tale of hubris. It ends with the fall of the tower and the fragmentation of a great, unified society that is undone by its own arrogance. The punishment for attempting an ascent to heaven from the mortal earth is the dispersion of the people across the lands and the appearance of myriad different languages. Thus the groundwork is laid for misunderstanding and misinterpretation, the drawing and redrawing of boundaries, fractiousness, skirmishes, battles, wars, ethnic cleansing, and all-out genocide. Ironically, the linguistic and geographic distance between people is also the foundation of exotic difference, of the allure of the foreign. It is this other that draws us but also is thrown into relief to remind us of the comforts of home. Linguistic and cultural differences are interlinked with geography, producing terroir. Producing the taste *of* the place, informing the taste *for* the place.

Our most enduring images of the Tower of Babel come from the Flemish painters. That of Pieter Bruegel the Elder, in particular, shows a tower possibly modeled on the Colosseum in Rome, but placed in a landscape that is ineffably Flemish; tall, pointy houses fill a lowland landscape that merges effortlessly with the sea. In the castle at Gaasbeek, which looks out over the Payot landscape, there hangs a large rendition of the same scene by another, later Flemish painter. The lesson of the Tower of Babel seems to have been taken to heart in Belgium and is taught with the same gravity in a very secular society that it once was in a rigidly Catholic medieval Flanders. The tale, after all, has resonance for a society that is so starkly separated by language. The popularity of the story may also reflect the Belgian respect, even love, for the ordinary or quotidian. The popularity of the story in Belgium also reflects the divide in language and culture that so bedevils the country.

In the current economic collapse, we are once again being punished for heedlessness and hubris. We have become further fractured, not just nationally or regionally, but into single solitary individuals who are losing the ability to communicate and cooperate. We have become tiny islands of greed whose actions may be justified solely by invoking the rights of the sovereign individual or the privilege bestowed by the status of wealth. Yeast, even the noble *Brettanomyces bruxellensis*, will eat sugars voraciously, dividing and increasing as they sate themselves. In the process, though, they produce alcohol, which in sufficient quantity paralyzes the mass of them. People are not so unlike yeast. We keep eating, consuming, producing waste until the environment is toxic, until the tower falls. In these times it is ever more crucial to seek out the cultural ties that bind, to reach out to one another to rebuild community and to begin to live in and use the landscape once more. We look at landscape through a frame, at a distance, and it is landscape that puts food on the table, that provides open spaces for meeting and greeting, that provides air and light and health. It is a good time to reconnect, and Payottenland provides some compelling possibilities.

The New Payot Landscape

For much of Western Europe, the legacy of the Industrial Revolution seems to have receded impossibly far into the past. The economy is now often based upon retail and services, especially financial services. The frustration and disorientation that people may have felt leaving behind meaningful trades and well-defined roles and struggling to make a way in a world without any definitions except rich and poor, laborer and master of industry, are hard to fathom today. And yet, one of the characteristics of the Industrial Revolution was the "struggle to maintain wages, material welfare, and moral values against the exploitive and alienating implications of the new form of social organization being forged in the factories and cities."[13] This struggle seems suddenly, desperately pertinent again, despite the fact that the shifting ground of social organization is utterly different. We may now be moving into an age when people will once again define themselves in terms of trades and activities rather than simply wage, class, and branded lifestyle.

Characteristic of the struggle during the Industrial Revolution were the actions of the Luddites and the *saboteurs*, but their actions have come to be seen as merely antiprogress or antiindustry, rather than defensive of a *moral economy*, one "founded on custom and attributed status as the dominant conditions of human relationships." The emergence of a *political economy* (italics mine), one "founded upon contract and the status provided by access to capital and the means of production," during the Industrial Revolution affected not only the cities, but colonized the countryside with mines and mills while it consolidated the means of agricultural production and distribution.[14] The emergent relationship between city and countryside was less clear than it had been in the Middle Ages, where dense cities were separated from the surrounding territory by a strong demarcated boundary. Now cities displayed a dense core and a diffuse boundary where agricultural production, noxious industry, waste, and transport corridors interwove. The haphazard nature of the resulting landscape was so disorganized as to be apparently placeless. Carolyn Steel, in her book *Hungry City*, which manages to be simultaneously delightful and ominous, says, "As civilization is city-centric, it is hardly surprising that we have inherited a lopsided view of the urban-rural relationship. Visual representations of cities have tended to ignore their rural hinterlands, somehow managing to give the impression that their subjects were autonomous, while narrative history has relegated the countryside to a neutral green backdrop, good for fighting battles in, but little else."[15] The geographer Yi-Fu Tuan had earlier noted similar trends, but emphasized the ideal of the country as pleasure ground: "In modern life physical contact with one's natural environment is increasingly indirect and limited to special occasions. Apart from the dwindling farm population, technological man's involvement with nature is recreational rather than vocational."[16]

The creeping desecration of and separation from the rural landscape was accompanied by a conflicting set of attitudes toward the country in city dwellers: the first an Arcadian idyll, and the second of a forgotten and forlorn, muddy, dusty place inhabited by inbred and ill-educated country bumpkins. While there may be an element of truth to both, city life contains the same sorts of extremes (and stereotypes) from the cosmopolitan high life to Skid Row. Country life has now changed so drastically that there is hardly anyone left in it to apply any stereotypes to. Steel goes on to say,

> Meanwhile, the countryside we like to imagine just beyond our urban borders is a carefully sustained fantasy. For centuries, city-dwellers have seen nature through a one-way telescope, molding its image to fit their urban sensibilities. The pastoral tradition, with its hedgerows and its meadows full of fluffy sheep, is part of that tendency, as is the Romantic vision of nature, all soaring peaks, noble firs and plunging gorges. Neither bears any relation to the sort of landscape capable of feeding a modern metropolis. Fields of corn and soya stretching as far as the eye can see, plastic polytunnels so vast they can be seen from space, industrial sheds and feed lots full of factory-farmed animals—these are the rural hinterlands of modernity.[17]

Preindustrial cities depended heavily upon their hinterlands, often in a virtuous cycle in which fruits and vegetables were cultivated in soil enriched by human waste collected in the cities as "night soil." This loop has been broken, with waste pushed ever further away and produce shipped from the four corners of the earth. The rural hinterland that Steel speaks of is at a significant remove from most of our cities. Thus a rural hinterland is no longer synonymous with an urban hinterland. The urban hinterland has ceased to be a landscape whose importance is primarily production and is now cast in the same role as an Arcadian landscape, as a landscape of leisure, consumption, and recreation. In many European countries, as in America, the countryside is now the setting for luxury second homes, often in a rustic style or in reinhabited farm buildings (homes as well as barns and other outbuildings) as seen in the French *fermette*. What is missing is a romanticized notion of what might constitute a life in such a setting. These places are often not truly inhabited in the fullest sense. They are commuter dwellings in bedroom communities, weekend country bolt-holes or holiday homes that may only function seasonally. These dwellings could, though, begin to form the basis for a new style of settlement in the urban fringe and shadow, following the Jeffersonian model of the gentleman farmer and his smallholding, though the ranks of servants may need to be replaced by technology.

It is vital to find a way of inhabiting the urban fringe, a way that people like Armand Debelder and Yves and Kurt Panneels seem to be, that values the association between people, place, food, drink, and landscape, that is based in a moral economy and a delight in the miraculous and spiritual act of dwelling in a mundane and quotidian world. We need to come to live in a multisensual landscape once again. Dolores Hayden compellingly highlights this association between the senses and our inhabitation of the landscape:

> If place does provide an overload of possible meanings for the researcher, it is place's very assault on all ways of knowing (sight, sound, smell, touch, and taste) that makes it powerful as a source of memory, as a weave where one strand ties in another. Place needs to be at the heart of urban landscape history, not on the margins, because the aesthetic qualities of the natural and built environments, positive and negative, are just as important as the political struggles over space often dealt with by urban historians and social scientists.[18]

Key to imagining a sustainable future for the urban fringe is the reinhabitation of the landscape with people who do so out of volition or earnest vocation, in the same way that the ideal inhabitation of the city is by people who aspire to city life, rather than those who see it as drudgery. Why not envision a future in which all people do what they love? This may sound utopian, but perhaps only because it is an idea that is at odds with the present industrial and agricultural complex. It also may be queried because it is a dangerous oversimplification to romanticize the nature of life on the land. Nathaniel Hawthorne had his spirit nearly broken shoveling manure on George Ripley's transcendentalist (and later Fourierist) utopian community at Brook Farm, and countless hippies returned from "getting back to nature" to a very earnest "getting back to civilization." To "simplify" or "get back to nature" shows a profound misunderstanding of the relationship between soil, climate, place. It's complex. It's very hard work. There is still value to romanticizing the life of the small farmer or small producer, though, especially if visionaries like Armand Debelder are around to show us what an earnest and satisfying life can be made in a newly reinvented hinterland. It is possible to learn to savor the agony and ecstasy of a textured and flavorful life in the countryside as part of a vibrant community that might show the reemergence of a moral economy. Perhaps all that is needed is that we acquire a taste for it, an educated taste.

Notes

Michel de Certeau, Luce Giard, and Pierre Mayol, *The Practice of Everyday Life*, vol. 2, *Living and Cooking*, trans. Timothy J. Tomasik (Minneapolis: University of Minnesota Press, 1998), 205.

John Brinckerhoff Jackson, *Discovering the Vernacular Landscape* (New Haven and London: Yale University Press, 1984), xii.

1. R. Wood and J. Ravetz, "Recasting the Urban Fringe," *Landscape Design*, October 2000.

2. Tim Webb, Chris Pollard, and Joris Pattyn, *Lambicland: The World's Most Complex Beers and Simplest Cafes* (Cambridge: Cogan and Mater, 2004), 62.

3. In de Verzekering tegen de Grote Dorst has a website at http://www.dorst.be/en/ that gives directions and their opening hours. It is well worth a visit.

4. Oenology also refers to the making of wine, a field separate from, but related to, viticulture—the science, study, and growing of grapes.

5. UNESCO World Heritage Commission, "Cultural Landscape, History, and Terminology," http://whc.unesco.org/en/culturalland scape/ (accessed January 17, 2009).

6. Webb, Pollard, and Pattyn, *Lambicland*, 6.

7. This atmosphere may be savored at the Cantillon Brewery in Brussels, which is not far from the Gare du Midi. It offers self-guided tours and tastings and it refers to itself as Le Musée Bruxellois de la Gueuze/Het Brussels Museum van de Geuze. It is well worth a visit and their beers are first-rate.

8. Pierre Bourdieu, *Distinction: A Social Critique of the Judgment of Taste*, trans. Richard Nice (New York and London: Routledge, 1979), 56.

9. Bourdieu, *Distinction*, 6.

10. De Certeau, Giard, and Mayol, *Practice of Everyday Life*, vol. 2, *Living and Cooking*, 13.

11. To "bittersweet" and "piquant," we might add sour, sweet, salty, spicy, and so on, as emotions, moods, or descriptors of personality.

12. Bourdieu, *Distinction*, 1.

13. Denis Cosgrove, *Social Formation and Symbolic Landscape* (Madison: University of Wisconsin Press, 1984, 1998), 224.

14. Cosgrove, *Social Formation*, 224.

15. Carolyn Steel, *Hungry City: How Food Shapes Our Lives* (London: Chatto and Windus, 2008), 7.

16. Yi-Fu Tuan, *Topophilia: A Study of Environmental Perceptions, Attitudes, and Values* (New York: Columbia University Press, 1990), 95–96.

17. Steel, *Hungry City*, 8.

18. Dolores Hayden, "Urban Landscape History: The Sense of Place and the Politics of Space," in *Understanding Ordinary Landscapes*, ed. Paul Groth and Todd W. Bressi, 114 (New Haven and London: Yale University Press, 1997).

....

Chapter Four

National Tastes

Italy and Food Culture

MATTHEW HIBBERD

Few would doubt the importance of food to Italian national and cultural identity. Food is widely recognized to be a fundamental part of what it means to be Italian. National signature dishes—which actually originated in the Italian cities, regions, or localities—provide many proud Italians with a cause for national celebration. Italian food also constitutes a key feature of global food culture. The development of international food chains selling pizza or pasta ensures that people across the globe recognize Italy as one of the world's great food nations. But as much as we recognize the importance of Italian cuisine in today's globalized world, food has not always held such importance to Italians, and for many years after the birth of the Italian nation-state, in 1861, food was not considered an essential feature of Italian cultural life. In this essay, I will look at the development of the Italian nation-state, linking this to the key advances in Italian food cuisine. Only in the past sixty years has Italy developed a fully-fledged national food cuisine aided by a period of sustained economic growth in the post Second World War years. The so-called economic miracle of the 1950s and 1960s, especially, saw mass migration from south to north; a rapid increase in infrastructure, such as motorways; and allowed Italians more conspicuous wealth, allowing them to buy "white" goods, such as fridges, and to eat out in restaurants and bars more. However, Italian national cuisine sits rather uneasily between global versions of popular Italian dishes and more autonomist demands that place emphasis on regional or local cuisines.

The lineaments of Italy's *cucina regionale* are distinctive. Although, for example, pasta might be understood as a staple shared by much of the nation, a broad subdivision also inheres in which the south relies upon dried pasta whereas many of the famous dishes of the center use fresh. Northern Italy, mountainous in many parts, is notable for the alpine cheeses of the Valle d'Aosta, the *pesto alla genovese* of Liguria, and, in Piedmonte, the Alba truffle. In the Alto Adige, the influence of neighboring Austria may be found in a regional repertoire that includes *speck* and dumplings. In the north, rice and polenta have tended to serve the staple function taken by pasta across the rest of the country. Italy's center includes the celebrated culinary regions of Tuscany— famous for its olive oil, bean dishes, and Chianti—and Emilia-Romagna—home of *prosciutto di Parma, parmigiano-reggiano*, and *ragù*—the latter now produced (and traduced) worldwide as spaghetti bolognese. Southern Italy includes the hearty food of Lazio in which meat and offal frequently figure, but also the vegetable-focused fare of Basilicata, historically one of Italy's poorest regions. The islands of Sicily and Sardinia have distinctively different foodways. The former is notable for its many sweet dishes, seafood, and citrus fruit, while Sardinian cuisine has traditionally looked to its hilly interior with a cuisine centered on lamb, sucking pig, breads, and pecorino cheese. It is in the food of Naples and Campania, however, that many visitors would recognize the foods that have come to be regarded as quintessentially Italian: pizza, spaghetti with tomato sauce, aubergine parmigiana.[1]

The argument of this essay is that the rise of nationalist sentiment led to the formation of an Italian food culture. The link between food and territory, however, predates this development and the subject of food, like that of the nation-state, requires study over the *longue durée*. It was with the arrival of the Renaissance in the thirteenth and fourteenth centuries that Italian cuisine and dishes, such as *torta bolognese, pizza napolitano*, were associated with geographical places, namely cities. It was in the prosperous Italian cities—Bologna, Ferrara, Florence, Milan, Parma, Palermo and Rome—where food was celebrated most in Renaissance Italy. This is contrasted with the Roman Empire, for example, where local produce was likely to be found sold side-by-side with produce drawn from across the empire, so that the geographical dimension or origin of food was downplayed; rather Rome was identified as a "grand food emporium."[2] Similarly, the ancient food markets in Bologna or Milan were seen as gastronomic marketplaces for produce from different regions and countries.[3] It was only in the later Middle Ages, with the publication of books like Ortensio Lando's *Commentario delle più notabili e mostruose cose d'Italia e d'altri luoghi* (A Guide to the Most Notable and Monstrous Things of Italy, 1548), who documented the variety of food and wines across the Italian peninsula, that the link between geography and food took on further emphasis.[4] In France, La Varenne's 1651 book *Le Cuisinier François*, played a similar role, although food historians such as Jean-Louis Flandrin argue that a distinctive French cuisine emerged prior to this date.[5] The association of food with geography developed further with the rise of nationalist sentiment that linked regional cuisine to Italian cultural identity. This coincided with other changes in collective gastronomic habits and tastes in Europe, for example, where *service à la française* gave way to *service à la russe*, which resulted in a trend toward greater uniformity in food among all social classes at a national level.[6] So rather than being in any way innate or God-given, culinary tastes in Italy have developed in line with broader social, political, and economic changes and are closely aligned to cultural changes brought about as a result of these historical trends.

Nation-States, Globalization, and Food Culture

The development of national cuisines is also intimately tied in to the wider economic, political, and cultural transformations of the past two and a half centuries. The rise of European nationalism in the late eighteenth century constituted a key period when the processes of nation building, along with industrialization and urbanization, brought about the reconfiguration of social classes and traditional economic ties. The emergence of new urbanized social classes and the growth of educational systems and cultural institutions also brought about changes in how societies viewed cuisine. New importance was placed on food to help ensure a healthy workforce, so food took on increased material and political importance. In 1826, for example, the Italian writer Giacomo Leopardi wrote that the subject of food was very interesting, stating, "It is important that we eat well since with good digestion comes the improved general physical, mental, and moral well-being of man."[7] But national cuisines spread in an irregular fashion in line with waves of nationalism. And, as we shall see in Italy's case, food played little part in its nationalist movement with many of its key figureheads little interested in culinary matters.

The key features of European nationalism are a unitary political authority (the state) and a national culture. Nationhood has also favored those societies that have evolved similar cultural habits through the slow sedimentation of multiculturalism and by the emergence of a single political authority.[8] If the nation-state is a political configuration of modernity, the advent of a "postmodern condition" has also warranted an urgent rethinking of how citizenship and consumerism can be hypothesized without the nation-state, especially in relation to cuisine. Anthony Giddens argues that in the period of modernity—defined broadly as the age of industrial capitalism—the concept of time-space distanciation has occurred: the separation of time and space through the intensification of worldwide social relations. Social relationships have to an extent become disembedded and disconnected from traditional face-to-face interactions. Instead, social relationships via communications and the mass media have become re-embedded across different social places and physical places.[9]

The jump to a "postmodern condition" has occurred through the acceleration in the globalizing and unifying tendencies of monopoly capitalism. The rapid expansion of global capital accumulation, aided by instant telecommunications, and a supply of cheap, international labor, has resulted in a further distribution of social relationships across time and space. This has created conditions in which a new social order can emerge. The postmodernist claim is that this new economic, social, and technological revolution has affected how culture is made and remade, with the explicit assumption that the old concept of a "high" or national culture has been in part superseded by global cultures and a vast multiplicity of localized cultural identities. It is this pressure from above (global) and below (local) that has threatened the stability of the nation-state. Some theorists have emphasized the increasing economic and political importance of multinational companies and special interest movements, effectively bypassing the nation-state: environmentalists, peace campaigners, and so on, as evidence that political activism is moving away from the sphere of traditional institutions of the nation-state and political parties to new nongovernmental movements that best reflect the emergence of global issues: the nuclear threat, climate change, and so on.[10] The development of giant, global food-and-beverage companies highlights the congruence of financial muscle with cultural hegemony. Although many such companies are American owned or franchised—McDonald's and Coca-Cola, for example—one can trace the importance of Italian food and drink, exported to the United States in the great migratory rush of the late nineteenth and twentieth centuries, to key global food companies. Cappuccinos or pizzas, for example, are enjoyed every day of the year by millions of people around the world, and Italian identity in the wider world is strongly shaped by culinary associations.

Perhaps nothing shows the link between cuisine and American cultural hegemony better than the depiction of Italian food in Hollywood cinema—for example, in the American Mafia films from the 1970s onward, such as Coppola's *Godfather* trilogy or Scorsese's *Goodfellas*. As Marlisa Santos argues:

> Food is one of the most obvious elements in this later depiction of the Italian-American culture world, through meals themselves and preparation. The addition of such scenes provides a clear sign in modern American Mafia films of the cultural foundation that informs the seeming dichotomy of life in such "families." Food highlights the power structure of the "family" as a military structure, but also highlights the family as the foundation of home and tradition. The depiction of food in these films is the glue that binds together the often-contradictory elements of the American Mafia way of life—the seeming incongruities of family, tradition, and religion joined with murder, bloodshed, and brutality. Food becomes the emblem of what it means to be civilized, the reinforcement of whatever cultural rules or aspirations Italian-American Mafia families live by.[11]

In some ways, food acts as the glue that binds together the often-contradictory aspects of global culture. Global food businesses are driven by readily identified brand names. No matter whether a brand is expensive and available worldwide or modestly priced and on sale only locally, it will embody a guarantee of authenticity. That is, it will be what it appears to be and its origins are known, at least as regards the identity of the company producing it. Associated with a brand's authenticity is its consistency, the fact that it can be depended on to deliver a certain quality each time it is bought. A global brand such as McDonald's can be relied upon to provide a particular range and quality of fast food around the world. The element of trust, born of experience that consumers feel toward a certain brand simplifies the making of future choices for them from among the plethora on offer. Thus it makes possible a saving of time and effort through a reduction of perceived risk. In this respect, the appeal of a brand to a consumer can be said to be rational or functional. But it is also emotional or experiential. As with anything that communicates, there is a connotative or cultural dimension to consider, in other words, those less easily defined associations that are triggered in people's values. Some of these effects will be culturally determined, while others will be the result of individual personal experience.

But just as there are important rational and emotional drivers behind the development of global food brands, increasing resistance to multinational conglomerates and global brands—most famously perhaps by Naomi Klein and the No Logo lobby—has led to the development of food campaigns at a national or regional level. Rejecting many tenets of global food production—pressures to adopt ever intensive farming methods or genetically modified varieties—as well as expressing increased disquiet about the effects of "fast-food culture" on national diets and lifestyles, food experts have turned to examining the relationship between the nation-state, identity, and food culture.

As with many facets of globalization, cultural homogeneity on the surface—a McWorld—quickly gives way to local differences, and this is especially so when it comes to how local and national food cultures adopt but also adapt key Italian dishes. Take this quotation from the anonymously written StakeVentures blog from 2008, for example:

> http://www.flickr.com/photos/pelle/221531820/Argentina had nearly as many Italian immigrants as the US. What did they make of the Pizza? On the one hand you've got a Buenos Aires Deep Pan Pizza, but they also do thin crust, white

pizzas, and they are all very different to US or Italian pizzas. While the first pizza restaurants in Denmark were run by Italian immigrants, nearly all of them today are run by Middle Eastern immigrants, which have created strange little micro-fusions of Italian, Middle Eastern and Danish food. One of the most popular pizza toppings is shawarma meat and another called the pizza sandwich has evolved, which is basically a pita the size of a Calzone and freshly baked stuffed with fresh ingredients be it pepperoni or shawarma or ham. But hang on a minute. Aren't many Italian classics also products of early globalization? Pasta came from China, tomatoes from the Americas. Are the Italians eating Chinese food when they cook up spaghetti bolognese?[12]

At the same time it is important to point out that global food companies often change their products slightly to cater to regional or national markets. The concept of "glocalization" is very common. Swiss chocolate manufacturers will sometimes vary the amount of sugar they add to their produce depending on the final destination of the product. For France, for example, they have been known to add less sugar.[13] And the taste of Coca-Cola can vary slightly from country to country, again depending on the amount of sugar added.[14]

Where history demonstrates the extent to which a nation-state has been affected by the onset of globalization, it shows that its status has grown in importance not diminished. The fall of the Soviet bloc and Yugoslavia has shown that the tide of history has turned toward a period of renewed nation-state building, but one where the "slow sedimentation of multiculturalism," common in more organic developments of nationhood, has been replaced by a quicker recipe in order to guarantee cultural homogeneity and political compliancy: ethnic cleansing. So although the nation-state has been affected by globalizing tendencies and (on-going) regional conflicts or devolutionary debates, it still constitutes the basic social and political unit that promotes and nurtures citizenship. The durability of the modern nation-state can be accounted for by the fact that it is a social and cultural entity as well as a political construction. Anthony D. Smith identifies the "benefits of membership" a nation brings that help explain why it has remained so pervasive in the era of (high) modernity and globalizing pressures. These include an answer to the problem of personal oblivion and the promise of a glorious future; the provision of personal regeneration and dignity as part of a superfamily; and, most importantly, the prominence it gives to realizing the ideal of fraternity through culture, rituals, and symbols—for example, in the preparation and consumption of special culinary dishes on special occasions, such as Christian festivals or national holidays.[15]

The nation-state is therefore both a product of, and a reaction against, modernity. The chronic features of national identities include the following attributes: the construction of a reflexive-self by communities using signs provided by their culture, which operate by the call to traditional values and the remembrance of the glorious past (popular memory) and generate a sense of nostalgia and moral well-being. Such traditions are not god-given, but are manufactured, and involve the "selective interpretation of history" and some conception of Them and Us. Interpretations of traditions are invented largely within ideological frameworks. Finally, for nations, there is some conception of a territorial boundary.[16] National cuisines highlight a rather ambiguous relationship with the modern and postmodern, since they have developed as a result of the grand processes of capitalism, democracy, industrialization, nationalism, and urbanism. But national cuisines also play a fundamental part in the development of global food cultures, which are heavily dependent on hybridized forms of national cuisine.

According to Massimo Montanari, this association of nation with the global food-and-beverage industry highlights another key paradox of this debate. Whereas ancient civilizations or older forms of globalization, such as the Roman Empire, celebrated food of universal origin and made little attempt to associate food with territory—food was de-territorialized—twenty-first-century globalization emphasizes just that by linking global gastronomic tastes to specific localities.[17] So food, arguably, plays an important part in the reinforcement of national identity and stereotypes. Many of the signature dishes that we today recognize as Italian national cuisine actually gained popularity well after the unification of the country in 1861. And what we see as traditional Italian dishes today were in fact nineteenth-century inventions drawing on older regional or local foods.

The Unification of Italy and Emergence of Situated Food Cultures

The concept of a united Italy is more ancient than that of England, Scotland, or France.[18] In the third century BC, the Italian peninsula up to the Arno River was unified by the Romans into a political confederation.[19] The idea of a united Italy as a political concept (roughly encompassing its current geographical borders) and as a unitary linguistic culture was understood by Dante. Dante was a key figure in shaping the idea of Italy as a nation based on a homogeneous language and culture (both heavily Florentine in influence). If the age of Dante and the subsequent period of the Renaissance did not lead to the direct Italianization of Europe, it left a considerable cultural and artistic legacy and certainly contributed to the Italianization of the towns and villages within Italy itself and also resulted in the emerging link between Italian cities and food culture, as outlined at the start of this essay.[20]

The European nationalist movement of the eighteenth and nineteenth century was a reaction against much of Enlightenment thinking that espoused the rise of "a scientific and philosophical movement espousing universal, immutable truths and ideals."[21] While the Enlightenment emphasized the limitless potential of humankind through scientific observation and experiment, the nationalist movement retreated into local and subjective cultures—the feeling of instinctively belonging to a group, community, or nation.[22] The movement owes much of its strength to the writings of Rousseau, but he also included elements of Enlightenment thinking in his philosophy, including the belief in human goodness and in a social contract. In Germany, the nationalist movement was associated with promoting a language, rural-based *Volk* culture inspired through the writings of Herder. It is true to say that Herder was the most influential exponent of Romanticism; this was certainly the case in Italy, where Mazzini was later heavily influenced by his writings. These ideals, which embodied the concepts of linguistic and cultural diversity, influenced the development of regional food cultures.[23]

Italian writers of the period were less concerned with thoughts of nationalism or political independence. So when a nascent Italian nationalist movement did develop, it is not surprising that it was very different from its German equivalent. The main difference was that the construction of Italianism as a cultural identity was based on the social customs of a small minority of people. For one thing, Italian was only spoken by educated elites. Most Italian people spoke in the vernacular, lived in rural and remote areas, were tied to a feudal farming agreement of tenant and landlord, and enjoyed different social customs.[24] Therefore, the Italian movement was not born out of the vestiges of feudalism, as in Germany. In many ways, the problem of Italian-ness or *Italianità*, what it constitutes and who actually possesses it, has remained a salient one throughout the period of Italian unity. When Italy did achieve unification in 1861, Massimo d'Azeglio, the Piedmontese statesman, declared in the aftermath of the unification that "the Risorgimento has made Italy; the task now is to make Italians."[25] It was a sentiment echoed half a century later by Antonio Gramsci in his famous prison notebooks. For Gramsci, the Risorgimento was a revolution *passiva* and *mancata*; it was not a truly nationalist revolution since large swathes of the agricultural masses had been bypassed completely in the process of unification. Essentially, the

Risorgimento had produced a political union, a state, before it had created a nation.[26]

Food culture, for example, is a good case in point. Italy was not particularly admired for its cuisine abroad in the pre- or immediate postunification period. There was little or no common identification with national dishes, as regional and local preferences dominated, reflecting social realities across the peninsula. The key nationalist figure Giuseppe Mazzini, for example, placed no emphasis whatsoever on any national culinary tradition in his political philosophy or push towards Italian independence.[27] And disparities in cultural competence extended to food-related matters. Italians were very happy to criticize food in other regions. Food divided opinion as much as it united Italians. Little, if any, consensus existed as to what defined national cuisine. As John Dickie has recently argued,

"When it comes to food, Italians are as sedulous in their disgust as they are discerning about good eating. Taste and distaste, gusto and disgusto, are inseparable partners in the Italian civilization of the table."[28] Such disgust extended to attempts to popularize regional dishes through national symbols. The emergence of the Queen Margherita pizza, from 1889 onward, saw one of Naples' best-loved dishes popularized by Italy's well-liked queen. But the result wasn't the adoption of pizza as a staple national food. As Dickie again argues, "Italians had to learn to like pizza. Not only that: they had to learn not to loathe it."[29] In fact, notable Italians lined up to criticize Naples, Neapolitans, and their food culture. Carlo Collodi, author of *Pinocchio*, described the pizza as "a focaccia made from leavened bread dough which is toasted in the oven. On top they put a sauce with a little bit of everything. When its colors are combined—the black of the toasted bread, the sickly white of the garlic and anchovy, the greeny-yellow of the oil and fried greens, the bits of red here and there from the tomato—they make pizza look like a patchwork of greasy filth that harmonizes perfectly with the appearance of the person selling it."[30]

In the last decade of the nineteenth century, however, signs of an ever-increasing national identity embodied through a nascent Italian food culture did emerge. The publication, in 1891, of Pellegrino Artusi's *La scienza in cucina e l'arte di mangier bene* (Science in the Kitchen and the Art of Eating Well), brought together and codified many dishes from the Italian peninsula, turning those dishes into "a template of Italian national identity."[31] Even if Artusi could never realize at the time the impact of his book on successive generations of Italian society, he brought together different regional dishes and specialties and presented them under generic chapter headings (such as "Soups" or "Pastas"), providing 731 recipes in total, listed in alphabetical order by title of recipe, thereby emphasizing elements of similarity among culinary traditions and ingredients across the peninsula. For example, *ravioli alla genovese* is presented directly before *spaghetti alle acciughe*, although they come from different regions.[32] Artusi also prefaced each chapter with a short essay providing examples of best culinary practice from across Italy to Italian audiences. What Artusi did so well was to appropriate regional dishes and weave them into a national historical narrative. But, despite this, Artusi still used vernacular names for dishes, so differences remained in terminology brought about by dialects. And by no means were all contemporary Italian dishes recognizable from Artusi's recipes. Take the ingredients he provides for *pizza alla napoletana*, for example:

50 grams of ricotta cheese
70 grams of almonds
50 grams of sugar
20 grams of flour
One egg
Essence of lemon and vanilla
Half a glass of milk[33]

Far from providing ingredients for what today we associate as a pizza base with tomatoes, Artusi provides a recipe for a popular sweet dish of the period.

The Fascist Dictatorship

The rapid rise of an ex-socialist newspaper editor, Benito Mussolini, was abetted by the widespread discontent felt by many Italians in the postwar years and also by the ideological battles taking
place throughout Europe after the 1917 Russian Revolution. While
essential political rights were abolished under the Fascists after
1925, one feature of Mussolini's political policy was his promise to
modernize and renovate Italy in the style of the Roman Empire.
It was this sense of *sacro egoismo* that pushed Fascist nationalism. Plans to expand along the North African coast were a direct
appeal to the greatness of the Roman past and the promise of a
great Roman future. Yet, beyond the nationalist rhetoric of mod-
ernization and expansion, what Mussolini understood by the
term *modernity* remains somewhat ambiguous. He was somewhat suspicious of committing the regime to the urbanization or
industrialization of society. Under the Fascists, the structure of
industrial output never altered significantly. One reason for the
hostility toward pushing industrial production at the expense of
agricultural production was the threat of Communism. Yet, at
the same time, the industrial north and the business community
were important constituents for the Fascists. So the government
was not totally against industrial growth partly for fear of losing
powerful supporters; but there was little productive social legislation, and in many ways Italy remained a backward country.[34]

While Mussolini wanted to construct a "national culture" based
on Fascist doctrine and values, most cultural consumption in Italy
under Fascism was of foreign products such as films, novels, and
comic books. People enjoyed and demanded these products, and
the cultural industries were happy to supply them, ensuring a rapid
turnover of movies, books, and so on. Insufficient Italian cultural
goods were produced.[35] Fascists also had a rather ambiguous relationship with food. The development of Fascist autarky—self-
sufficiency—was extended to food policy, most notably through

the famous Battle for Grain campaign. Italians were regularly urged to consume Italian home-produced goods only. And there was little doubt who would be in charge in the kitchen. Women were either idealized in Fascist propaganda as "middle-class, urban homemakers inspired by American conceptions of home economics or as rural housewives, providing domestic stability as part of the national self-sufficiency effort."[36] Books, too, were encouraged by Fascist authorities to help housewives learn about cooking and housekeeping, including Fernanda Momigliano's 1933 *Vivere bene in tempi difficili: Come le donne affrontano le crisi economiche* (How to Live Well during Tough Times). The book, produced at a time when Italy and the Western world were still suffering economic crisis following the 1929 crash, produced advice on how to cook and prepare inexpensive Italian dishes. The success of Momigliano's book was due in part to its adherence to broader Fascist campaigns. In this sense, Momigliano's book put women at the forefront of a Fascist "kitchen autarky" policy.[37] In a rather sad footnote, and despite her status as an Italian patriot, Momigliano was forced to go into hiding in 1943 due to her Jewish ancestry.[38]

A more radical departure was Filippo Marinetti's *La cucina futurista* (Futurist Cuisine), first published in the early 1930s.[39] Marinetti, founder of Italy's futurist movement, advocated key contemporary concepts relating to industrial change, art and design, and modern forms of culture and entertainment. Marinetti saw Italian cuisine as being hindered by traditional dishes such as pasta. According to Marinetti, Italian cuisine retarded national development by advocating a rich and heavy diet, producing a workforce unsuited to modern demands. Marinetti instead advocated the use of alternative ingredients including fruits, proteins, and exotic flavors to provide a lighter, healthier diet to suit, as he saw it, the needs of a modern workforce. One can certainly see Marinetti's influence in Italian vegetarian and macrobiotic food culture, which has enjoyed renewed support in recent years.

It is interesting to compare and contrast briefly, as Carol Helstosky (2003) has done, the very different ways in which Pellegrino Artusi and Filippo Marinetti conceptualized food culture and nationhood. Artusi advocated a national adoption of existing city and regional food habits, promoted through the new urbanized middle classes, while Marinetti proposed breaking with traditional, regional food culture and introducing radical new national cuisine based on different ingredients in line with modern industrial requirements. But, as Helstosky argues, while Artusi and Marinetti might have disagreed on many aspects "they did share a common concern with what was possible for future generations of Italians and a realization that food served a material, aesthetic, and political purpose in Italian history."[40] Some of Marinetti's ideas actually gained favor among Fascist political elites due to his support of local food produce as opposed to imported foods such as grain for pasta.

And yet Mussolini was not a great food connoisseur. Fascism did not celebrate food in its propaganda or advertising. Nutrition, as defined by average daily calorie intake for workers in cities, actually declined from 2,954 calories in 1926 to 2,476 in 1936.[41] Fascist propaganda stressed self-sufficiency, hardly the solid basis for a food renaissance. Although groups like the Touring Club of Italy promoted Italian food through the publication of its *Gastronomic Guide to Italy*, in 1931, and through the efforts of the aforementioned Momigliano and Marinetti, it would require the ravages of war and substantive economic change in the 1950s and 1960s to popularize Italian food cuisine.

Italy in the Age of Democracy, 1945–2010

In 1945, the Italian nation was in ruins.[42] The very concept of nationhood entailed explicit overtones associated with the regime of the 1920s and 1930s. Yet, at the same time, the reconstruction of Italy (along with the rest of Europe) would require strong social cohesion and a sense of collective identity. Ties of allegiance extending beyond familial bonds to wider cultural symbols were required for renascent political and social bridge building. The destruction wrought on France, Italy, Germany, and the other nations of Europe did not entail the dissolution of the nation as a political, economic, and social reference point. Instead, their revival was deemed essential to the Allies in order to combat the new declared enemy, Communism. Identity and allegiance in Rome, Paris, and Bonn, therefore, became synonymous with differentiating against the Communist enemy in the Cold War era.

The postwar years saw the anti-Fascist alliance tending to the more urgent needs while convening a constituent assembly to construct a new constitution. The restoration and reconstitution of basic political and civic rights denied by the previous regime constituted an improvement in itself. The provision of basic social and economic norms and responsibilities also represented a qualitative improvement in the formal rights of Italian citizens. Successive governments undertook substantive industrial and, important for this essay, agricultural reforms, which resulted in Italy becoming an industrialized country and greatly increasing its food production.

State industries often took the economic initiatives that led to increasing growth, such as the expansion of the motorway network. It was state intervention in the south that secured more jobs and investment for the people of those lands. Finally, the Italian government was at the forefront of negotiations between European partners that culminated in the formation of the European Economic Community in 1957. Economic expansion had immediate and positive spin-offs for social provision. Growth in educational expenditure, cultural programs, health spending, social housing, and so on, ensured that there would be major improvement in the living standards and the quality of life in Italy, crucial to the development of a flourishing national food culture.

Between 1959 and 1962, the years that marked the high point of the economic expansion in Italy, gross national product (GNP) grew by at least 6 percent annually. In the longer term the GNP grew by an average of 5.3 percent in the 1950s and by 5.7 percent in the 1960s. Average incomes grew more in two decades than they had in the previous seven decades put together. Italians had more disposable income to spend on food, cooking equipment, cookbooks, travel, and dining out. The political and social consequences of this rapid rate of growth were explosive. Mass migration from southern to northern Italy and from the countryside to the city produced overwhelming social demands on housing, health, and education. But it also brought changes in food culture. Migration led to the development of new restaurants that catered for southern workers and that were run by migrants themselves, therefore bringing new dishes to many northern Italians who, due to the economic growth, could also afford to eat out more often. The massive expansion of the pizzeria in many northern Italian towns and cities dates from the 1950s onward, for example.[43]

The role of television in postwar Italy took on a strong social dimension. The public service broadcaster RAI, which enjoyed a monopoly until 1976, was a crucial reference point for many citizens during this period.[44] The upward social mobility of many Italians, matched also by the numbers migrating, created a society in rapid transition. RAI had to shape its program output according to the perceived needs of a country changing rapidly.[45] And with this expansion came television programs dealing with culinary issues (although fewer than one might expect for a key food nation) and, importantly, national advertising of food and drink products, which provided Italians with a wide choice of generic, standardized food and drink goods, devoid of any substantive regional affiliation, for mass consumption on a national scale. For example, Italy has long enjoyed a tradition of local cheese-making and regional cheese types—Umbrian Pecorino, Fontina from the Valle d'Aosta, Caciocavallo from the south, and so on—but modern production techniques and mass marketing saw the development and success of the nation's first genuinely commercialized and mass-produced cheese, Bel Paese. First created in Lombardy in 1906, this mild and accessible cheese is now made in both Italy and the United States. It invokes a sense of nation, as opposed to region, both through its wrapping, which, in Italy at least, shows a map of the entire Italian peninsula, and its name, from the book by Antonio Stoppani, meaning "beautiful country."[46]

The development of television and its impact on Italian food culture has always divided opinion among Italian culinary and media experts. On the one hand, programs like the 1957 documentary *Il viaggio cultural: Viaggio lungo la valle del Po*, were both critically acclaimed and provided urban and rural Italians with information about culinary and cultural traditions in one area of Italy. Subsequent programs, including *Occhio alla Spesa*, arguably provided Italians with knowledge of their culinary history and culture without denying the regional, city, and local roots of those traditions. On the other hand, the commercialization of Italian television, especially the dominant role of advertising as the primary source of funding, coupled with developments in the international television market, which has seen the expansion of cookery-related format programs, has led some, like Carlo Petrini, president of Italy's Slow Food organization, to condemn television's negative impact on Italian food culture and standards. Entertainment is seen by many to have all but eliminated the serious discussion of culinary matters, which befits a leading food nation. Television, through format programming and advertising, is seen to promote international food producers and a fast-food culture identified with globalization, which is leaving many Italians ignorant about their rich culinary traditions and methods for the preparation and consumption of food and drink.

But if modern mass media are seen to dumb down debates surrounding Italian cuisine, political developments in Italy since the early 1990s have led many Italian politicians to use regional and local food culture as part of a highly contested political space in the push toward greater devolution across the Italian peninsula. Autonomist parties, led by the current government coalition party, the Northern League, have used food culture as part of their political armory fighting against the powers of central government in Rome. The emphasis placed on supporting local or regional cultures is seen as vital in the broader struggle to gain greater economic, fiscal, and political autonomy for northern Italians. Another aspect of this debate is the reaction among some Italian politicians to the influx of ethnic minorities to Italy from Africa and Eastern Europe, which has led to a significant growth in new "ethnic" food shops and restaurants in the past decade. An article from the (London) *Times* in January 2009 helps illustrate this point:

> Luca Zaia, the Minister of Agriculture and a member of the Northern League from the Veneto region, applauded the authorities in Lucca and Milan for cracking down on non-Italian food. "We stand for tradition and the safeguarding of our culture," he said. . . . Asked if he had ever eaten a kebab, Mr. Zaia said: "No—and I defy anyone to prove the contrary. I prefer the dishes of my native Veneto. I even refuse to eat pineapple . . ." Davide Boni, a councilor in Milan for the Northern League, which also opposes the building of mosques in Italian cities, said that kebab-shop owners were prepared to work long hours, which was unfair competition. "This is a new Lombard Crusade against the Saracens," *La Stampa*, the daily newspaper, said. The centre-left opposition in Lucca said that the campaign was discrimination and amounted to "culinary ethnic cleansing."[47]

Italy is today recognized as one of the world's great food nations. I have argued in this essay that national cuisine has not always held such importance to Italians. It is only in the past century or so that such traditions have become firmly established. That said, it should still be recognized that Italian food continues to have strong regional flavors and, if anything, trends in recent years have been to rediscover and celebrate local and regional culinary traditions.

This is linked by many to the emergence of strong regional parties and political and cultural identities, as well as to a backlash against the dominant media discourses that advertise and promote large national or international industrial food interests and global food cultures. Hence food in Italy is likely to remain a highly sensitive issue in political and aesthetic debates. I finish with a brief quotation from novelist Michael Dibdin who, via his police hero, Aurelio Zen, best sums up the complex relationship between food, city, regional, national, and global cultures and the nation-state in Italy:

As so often since his transfer to Cosenza, Zen felt seriously foreign. He knew that if he had eaten even the smallest fragment of one of those peppers, he would have suffered not merely scorched taste buds but also sweaty palpitations like those preceding a cardiac arrest, leaving him unable to eat, drink, talk or even think for fifteen minutes. His neighbor, on the other hand, chomped them down without the slightest change of expression. That grim countenance would never betray any emotion, but he appeared content with his lunch. Zen toyed with his own food a bit longer, then pushed the plate away. Knobs of mutton knuckle protruded from the globby local pasta smothered in tomato sauce. Not for the first time, he asked himself how this bland yet cloying fruit had come to stand as the symbol of Italian cuisine worldwide, despite the fact that until a century ago very few Italians had even seen a tomato, never mind regarded them as a staple ingredient in every meal. As recently as his own childhood in Venice, they remained a rarity. His mother had never cooked them in her life. "Roba del sud," she would have said dismissively, "southern stuff."[48]

Notes

1. Sophie Braimbridge and Jo Glynn, *The Food of Italy* (Sydney, Australia: Murdoch Books, 2003), 10–15.

2. Massimo Montanari, *Il cibo come cultura* (Bari, Italy: Laterza, 2008), 110.

3. Montanari, *Il cibo*, 110.

4. Montanari, *Il cibo*, 112.

5. Jean-Louis Flandrin, *Arranging the Meal: A History of Table Service in France*, California Studies in Food and Culture (Berkeley: University of California Press, 2007). See also Stephen Mennell, *All Manners of Food: Eating and Taste in England and France from the Middle Ages to the Present*, 2nd ed. (Champaign: University of Illinois Press, 1996).

6. Marc Bloch, "Les aliments de l'ancienne France," in *Pour une Histoire de l'Alimentation*, ed. J. Hemardinquer (Paris: Colin, 1970), 232.

7. Quoted in P. Camporesi, "Introduzione," in *La scienza in cucina e l'arte di mangier bene*, ed. P. Artusi (Turin: Einaudi, 2007), ix.

8. Anthony Giddens, *Modernity and Self-Identity: Self and Society in the Late Modern Age* (Stanford CA: Stanford University Press, 1991), 50–58.

9. Giddens, *Modernity*, 3.

10. Alberto Melucci, quoted in Philip Schlesinger, "Europeanness: A New Cultural Battlefield?" *Innovation* 5, no. 1 (1992): 13.

11. M. Santos, "'Leave the Gun, Take the Cannoli': Food and Family in the Modern American Mafia Film," in *Reel Food: Essays on Food and Film*, ed. A. Bower (London: Routledge, 2004), 204.

12. "Bootstrapping tales: Why globalization won't make everything the same," http://stakeventures.com/articles/2007/09/18/why -globalization-wont-make-everything-the-same (last accessed January 18, 2009).

13. Montanari, *Il cibo*, 122.

14. Montanari, *Il cibo*, 122.

15. A. D. Smith, *National Identity* (Harmondsworth: Penguin, 1991), 162.

16. Philip Schlesinger, *Media, State, and Nation: Political Violence and Collective Identities* (London: Sage, 1991), 168–71. See also E. Gellner, *Nationalism* (London: Weidenfeld and Nicolson, 1997).

17. Montanari, *Il cibo*, 117–23.

18. Harry Hearder, *Italy in the Age of Risorgimento* (London: Longman, 1983), 156.

19. Hearder, *Italy in the Age*, 156.

20. Peter Burke, introduction to *The Civilization of the Renaissance in Italy*, by J. Burckhardt (Harmondsworth: Penguin, 1990), 14.

21. I. Berlin, *The Age of Enlightenment: The Eighteenth-Century Philosophers* (Oxford: Oxford University Press, 1956), 17.

22. Hearder, *Italy in the Age*, 157.

23. J. Gray, *Isaiah Berlin* (London: Harper Collins, 1995), 130–33.

24. See C. Seton-Watson, *Italy from Liberalism to Fascism* (London: Methuen, 1968).

25. M. Clark, *Modern Italy: 1871–1982* (London: Longman, 1984), 2.

26. Clark, *Modern Italy*, 2.

27. J. Dickie, *Delizia! The Epic History of the Italians and Their Food* (London: Hodder and Stoughton, 2007).

28. Dickie, *Delizia*, 199.

29. Dickie, *Delizia*, 201–2.

30. Quoted in Dickie, *Delizia*, 202.

31. Dickie, *Delizia*, 212.

32. Pellegrino Artusi, *La scienza in cucina e l'arte di mangier bene* (Turin: Einaudi, 2007), 133–34. Date of original publication is 1891.

33. Artusi, *La scienza*, 528.

34. Clark, *Modern Italy*, 263–66.

35. David Forgacs, *Italian Culture in the Industrial Era 1880–1980: Cultural Industries, Politics, and the Public* (Manchester: Manchester University Press, 1990), 72–82.

36. L. Tasca and S. Hilwig, "The 'Average Housewife' in Post–World War II Italy," *Journal of Women's History* 16, no. 2 (Summer 2004): 92–115.

37. Maria Giuseppina Muzzarelli and Fiorenza Tarozzi, *Donne e cibo: Una relazione nella storia* (Milan: Mondadori, 2003), 133.

38. Lepre Aurelio, "Fornelli d'Italia: I menu dei papi e la cucina dei poveri," *Corriere della Sera* 27 (November 2007): 46.

39. Filippo Marinetti, *La cucina futurista* (Milano: Sonzogno, 1932).

40. Carol Helstosky, "Recipe For The Nation: Reading Italian History Through *La Scienza In Cucina and La Cucina Futurista*," *Food and Foodways* 11, nos. 2–3 (2003): 113–40, http://www.informaworld

.com/smpp/title~content=t713642611~db=all~tab=issueslist
~branches=11-viiii.

41. Dickie, *Delizia*, 267.

42. See D. Hine, *Governing Italy: The Politics of Bargained Pluralism* (Oxford: Oxford University Press, 1993); and also T. Judt, *A Grand Illusion? An Essay on Europe* (Harmondsworth: Penguin, 1997).

43. This section draws on a number of interviews undertaken by the author in March 2010. My grateful thanks also goes to Professor Michele Sorice, LUISS, Rome, for extra information supplied in this section.

44. Matthew Hibberd, *The Media in Italy: Press, Cinema, and Broadcasting from Unification to Digital* (Milton Keynes: McGraw Hill/Open University Press, 2009).

45. See F. Monteleone, *Storia della radio e della televisione in Italia: Società, politica, strategie, programmi 1922–1992* (Venezia: Marsilio, 1992).

46. U.S. wrapping shows a map of the Americas.

47. R. Owen, "Italy bans kebabs and foreign food from cities," (London) *Times*, January 31, 2009.

48. M. Dibdin, *End Game: An Aurelio Zen Mystery* (London: Faber and Faber, 2007), 5–6.

Chapter Five

....

Teaching Wine Tasting

JOHN DUCKER

Much of my professional time these days is spent teaching others about wine and its pleasures. I am careful always to put this civilizing drink in the context of food, where I believe it belongs. I was first introduced to the pleasures of wine drinking in the 1960s, when no one in Britain could have anticipated the welter of bright New World flavors now crowding our supermarket shelves. Today at least 50 percent of the UK off-license wine market is from the "New World," which is providing an ongoing wake-up call in various "Old World" wine areas, particularly France. The 1960s and '70s were the heady days of "Cape Brandy," "British Wine," sweet Cyprus "Sherry," and the more affordable so-called London-bottled clarets, which although accurately bearing the name of their Bordeaux provenance were shipped to Britain in cask and bottled in unromantic-sounding places west of London like Basingstoke. My own earliest wine memories, apart from the surreptitious sips of El Rei Madeira I stole as a child from my father's wine cabinet— and which I found quite shockingly strong—were of the semisweet Liebfraumilch variety. One could safely pour out a glass of this silvery, totally anonymous "off-dry" libation when taking one's girlfriend out to dinner—and the chances were that neither she nor I would be offended. One could certainly hope for no more.

Dryer tastes in cheap white wine in my early tasting days led almost inevitably to Lutomer Riesling or to another underpowered, neutrally flavored shelf-filler from the former Yugoslavia. I knew people at the time who swore by liter bottles (or larger) of a barely alcoholic sweetish stuff from the prolific German vineyards of the Rheinhessen, labeled simply as "Hock," which they consumed uncomplainingly if unsuitably alongside their steak and fries. Among the long-lost red wines of the day were the dumpy straw-covered flasks of simple, cherry-flavored Chianti, the clustered "empties" of which tended to adorn the walls of Italian *trattorie* in London's Soho and in provincial towns. If stronger meat was required, a generic-branded red wine like Bull's Blood, from Hungary, generally filled the bill.

My own enthusiasm to learn more about wine was fueled in part by a visit to Paris shortly after my wife and I were married and where torrential rain forced us both to take immediate shelter. We found ourselves in the portico of a restaurant not far from the Gare de l'Est. To our amazement the ambience was unfamiliar, surprisingly un-French. Had we had stepped quite by chance into an upmarket, Ruritanian beer cellar? No Paris bistro here. Given the establishment's setting within a stone's throw of the Seine, rather than the Rhine, we little guessed how authentically *alsacien* the food would prove to be. Not only did we find ourselves introduced to the menu's curious offerings of dishes, including *surla-werla*, *flammekuche*, and *baeckeoffe*, but also to one of the most distinctive of the region's wines, Gewürtztraminer, which had been suggested by our waiter as a suitable partner for our main dish, a civet of wild boar. The advice he gave was inspirational, and we both felt that we had mined gold in a bottle. Our waiter would never have realized that his recommendation would prove such a catalyst to my later wine career. Every mouthful of food was aromatized and seasoned by this amazing spicy liquor.

We thought to ourselves that if this gestalt was just one of the authentic gastronomic manifestations of Alsace, then what else could the region offer? A visit to this magical eastern *département* of France was arranged as soon as time and our joint budgets permitted. I recall a visit to a village shop in northern Alsace in order to buy quiches or patés for a picnic lunch. My entrance had interrupted the shopkeeper's conversation with another customer (in a completely impenetrable local *patois*). Concluding my own shopping deal in my schoolboy French, the change was carefully counted back to me in German. The quiches were delicious, and *zewelwäia*—Alsace onion tart—is probably the most long-standing dish of my own domestic *repertoire de cuisine*.

Today I am still cooking, and I am keenly aware of how the British culinary landscape has changed across the years, as witnessed by some of the more dog-eared cookery books on my kitchen bookshelf, which I haven't the heart to throw out. For in addition to my food-writing heroines such as Elizabeth David, there were other pioneers of taste I followed slavishly in the '70s and '80s: Robert Carrier, Graham Kerr, even spy-thriller writer Len Deighton who was no slouch over a low gas and who, in the film *The Ipcress File*, gifted his fictional creation Harry Palmer with chat-up lines like "I'm going to cook you the best meal you have ever had."

Apart from working when I could as a "proper" actor, in the early 1970s I freelanced for a while as an out-of-vision announcer for BBC television. In my tiny studio I had opportunities to switch the monitor screens at the touch of a button to view the rehearsal outputs from the main studios elsewhere in the BBC Television Center. I remember that in one studio the best-known TV cook of the day, Fanny Craddock, was going through her paces in rehearsal, dripping cigarette ash over everything she prepared. I learned later that none of the studio crew—usually the first to rush to consume free food after a show—would touch a morsel once the show had finished. In retrospect I realize now that the essential concern of this doyenne of the pastry-board was not essentially with *food* at all, or balance, or taste, but with training her audience—as potential hosts at the dinner table—to avoid making what she considered unacceptable social gaffes.

Latterly, I have enjoyed a professional occupation in the world of wine. I am an accredited tutor for the Wine & Spirit Education Trust (WSET) and teach regularly for the Wine Education Service Limited, the most extensive independent nonacademic wine education service in Britain. This rather begs the initial and important question of how one can actually teach wine tasting in the first place as it is hardly a didactic or textbook exercise. The BBC's *Food and Drink* program used an imaginative technique some years ago when viewers were told which wines would be the subject of discussion the following week and were given the opportunity to buy them in advance of the program so they could taste and assess them at the same time as the presenter. A good idea in theory, it was limited in practice not only by the variability of supply of the featured wine throughout Britain in the appropriate vintage, but also by the inevitable variations of bottle condition, given the amount of time it might have been sitting on the retailer's shelves.

In considering the nonacademic recreational wine courses I have delivered for more than a dozen years of teaching, a clear picture emerges of participants who are generally "upwardly mobile," with disposable incomes, mostly from a professional or junior managerial background, around 75 percent female, and with an average age of less than thirty. Some students turn out to be professional personal assistants or company representatives tasked occasionally with taking clients out to restaurant meals, who attend the course principally as a means of enhancing their knowledge of what's what on the wine list. Others may be planning to join the wine trade themselves and want, through tasting experience, to get a foot on the first rung of the wine ladder. Even experienced professionals, candidates for the prestigious Master of Wine examination, may attend sessions on an ad hoc basis simply in order to supplement their necessary tasting practice. It has to be borne in mind that learning about wine has a wider dimension of conviviality, too, and it is unsurprising that a class of around twenty like-minded young people serves as a forum for social contact.

It goes without saying that, unlike spirits, wine is an enabling substance that tends to bring people together, ideally around food. Ever the hedonist, Ernest Hemingway was certainly aware of the wider dimension afforded by the fruit of the vine, as captured in this reflection from his novel *Death in the Afternoon*: "Wine is one of the most civilized things in the world and one of the natural things in the world that has been brought to the greatest perfection, and it offers a greater range for enjoyment and appreciation than, possibly, any other purely sensory thing."

It is easy to sound pretentious and high-flown about wine, but a proper study of the subject requires having one's feet firmly on the ground, hence my attraction to a pithy observation once made by the distinguished wine writer Hugh Johnson: "No matter whether it becomes a simple Vin de Pays or a great Cru Classé, all wine starts its life as sap inside a stick." These days wine studies have to be taught in the context of increasingly rapid change within the wine world itself. Viticulturalists and winemakers are living in potentially stressful times, and not simply as a result of global warming. Competition is fierce, particularly in the more commercial echelons of wine where promotional budgets may run into millions. At the other end of the scale, artisanal or "lifestyle" producers frequently suffer the economic squeeze between the need to keep their vine yields down in order to produce high quality against the requirement to produce and sell enough of their precious product to make the exercise financially viable. Variable vintages only add to their headache. Even the "rave review" syndrome can have a downside. The glossy magazines or popular wine pundits may heap accolades on a wine of this kind, then consumer demand grows so rapidly and to such an extent that either new vineyards have to be planted or further grapes have to be outsourced in an effort to meet supply, resulting in a likely compromise of the essential quality that put the wine on its pedestal in the first place. It takes at least five years for a vineyard to come fully on stream.

There are some glaring imbalances in the way wine is produced. Huge and subsidized overproduction of wine in some parts of the world is now leading progressively to compulsory retrenchment. Formerly an area of overproduction, Southern Australia has been a victim of serious drought for at least seven successive years, where in the wine-producing areas around Adelaide and eastward in Victoria's Murray River area the demand for irrigation water for the vineyards has outstripped supply. In contrast, many European wine producers—particularly in Languedoc-Roussillon, or in the Veneto in northern Italy and the Mezzogiorno in the south, in central Spain, and elsewhere—have been churning out an intolerable quantity of substandard "industrial" wine from high-yielding vines that simply goes down the drain, washed down with the added blessing of an annual European Union subsidy of around 1.3 billion euros. Compulsory cutbacks of around 15 percent of production are now to be put in place in the first instance, and, notwithstanding the pain caused to the growers, they will be paid subsidies for grubbing up their overproducing vines and planting more viable cash crops in their place.

Equally, a radical reform of the current French *appellation* system has long been overdue, urged progressively as a needful exercise in the face of growing competition within their own export markets from New World producers. To British and American consumers now fully accustomed to these vibrant fruit-driven styles of wine, the advantage is not simply one of taste but of a market presentation that is both easily understandable and user friendly. Front labels give helpful indications of both grape variety and vintage, and, if you are lucky, back labels give plenty of information on provenance and winemaking techniques involved. Arguably, the lack of finesse in wines with high alcohol levels, resulting from recent "hot" vintages in Australia and elsewhere, is causing the wine-wise to reassess their preferred sources of drinking, but "bright" New World flavors remain a strong market in Britain and elsewhere. Perversely, the *appellation contrôlée* (AC) regulations of France, and those of the *denominazione di origine controllata* (DOC) of Italy and the *denominación de origen* (DO) of Spain, have more often than not shrouded wine—or at least grape identities—in unhelpful obscurity and, as a wine educator, I find I have to guide my students around the additional pitfalls and confusions of "Old World" wine nomenclature. Faced with a restaurant wine list featuring French classic names, many beginners find themselves quite understandably at sea. What should they expect from wines that are simply labeled with village appellations? Unless having taken the plunge to taste them, how do the uninitiated guess at the inherent general characteristics of, say, Savennières, or Chinon, or of Chiroubles? Newcomers could more than easily assume that the wines of AC Pouilly-Fumé and AC Pouilly-Fuissé were born under a single star, although one is 100 percent Sauvignon Blanc, grown in the eastern reaches of the Loire Valley, and the other is 100 percent Chardonnay, produced miles away in southern Burgundy. Likewise, Tuscan Vino Nobile di Montepulciano, based on Sangiovese grapes, has nothing whatever to do with the eponymous Montepulciano grapevines that festoon the hillsides of Italy's Abruzzo region. As matters currently stand, it is a jungle that only systematic study can unravel.

So, can *taste* be taught? I think my starting point must be that if taste can be "acquired," then there is every reason to suppose that it can be formally nurtured. It is self-evident that experiences and memories of smells and tastes require *words* to give them shape, precision, and context—descriptors that afford a common ground for discussion and comparison. But it is, above all, what one *makes* of those remembered sensations that counts.

To stand at the beginning of learning about wine is to stand at the threshold of a bewilderingly complex world, with a landscape often further confused by a largely irrelevant overlay of wine "hype." In the early stages of a course, some less-practiced members of the group will not dare express an opinion lest it be found "wrong" or laughable by their tutor or their peers. My own approach is to create the most user-friendly forum for discussion that is possible in the circumstances. Classroom "received opinions" on tastes are important, and frequently supportive, if ultimately valuable only to a degree. My aim as a tutor must therefore be to build up students' personal confidence in wine appreciation, to get them to take ownership of their own judgments, their own values, their own convictions. Otherwise they will never fully grasp the subject for themselves. Tasting practice is essential, as is objective note taking.

With which mental and physiological faculties are we dealing in the endeavor to educate tastes in the context of food and wine? In no particular order, one could enumerate perception, memory, physical taste, imagination, and judgment. The very word *taste* may refer in simple empirical/evidential terms to the broad brush-strokes of "sweet," "salty," "acidic," or "bitter," and so on, or to the wider aesthetic of what is perceived to be of value, fine or less fine, when selectivity, consideration, and judgment have to be called into play. I hope, therefore, as a wine educator I can encourage in my sessions a *rapprochement* between the two senses of the word. My audience is already well disposed to learning about wine—which is an essential first step—but it may be undisciplined in its approach to making sense of it, therefore the need to help students make considerations of their own is paramount. My function is to raise not only the "how" but the "why" about the wines we are assessing together, and also to assist students in making their own personal evaluations on a comparative basis. The learning framework aims to support and enthuse the relatively uninitiated as they begin to quantify and qualify experience. Trust in their own palates is nurtured, and their experience broadened sufficiently to wean them away from an adherence merely to their immediate personal likes and dislikes.

Although wine is properly pleasurable in its social context, effective taste learning requires rigorous objectivity if progress is to be made. As a teacher I have to keep in mind how unfamiliar tastes may raise subjective likes and dislikes among the group. These are all very well and have their place, but unless the class is kept on track, these side issues can cloud proper analysis of the wine or the food match in question. If, then, objectivity is the prime requirement, the next important requisite is structure: a planned framework devised to explore the broader generic styles of wine.

Using six well-differentiated wines as examples, the first of the student sessions concentrates almost exclusively on the mechanisms of *how* we taste, and how tastes—or at least our perceptions of them—can change radically relative to the juxtaposition of other tastes. It is often mistakenly assumed that the tongue delivers subtleties of flavor, but the surface of the top of the tongue yields only broad indications of sweetness, sourness, saltiness, and acidity, together with the ability to discern textures. Science has even supplied a further possible gustatory indicator on the tongue's taste receptors: *umami* ("deliciousness," in Japanese), which is said to reflect the taste of glutamates. According to the Chinese, there is even a sixth category, specifying pungency as a separate taste. Where possible I will provide the class with taste comparators, for example, slivers of lemon or lime to lick once they have sampled a relatively low-acidic white wine. The result comes as rather a shock: having sampled the fruit, a further taste of the same wine will now reveal its initial flavor as greatly muted—whatever acidity the wine might have possessed now being overtaken by the much sharper citric attack of the lemon. The broader lesson, of course, is that it is fairly pointless to serve a very low-acid wine alongside a dish dressed with lemon juice or a vinaigrette. One might just as well serve bottled water. Likewise, students' perceptions are challenged once an astringent, tannic, red wine has been sampled, when I invite them to nibble a piece of cheese alongside. Returning to the wine, they now begin to perceive something different in their glass, with more apparent fruit and "user friendliness."

The polyphenol tannin, a perfectly natural constituent of plant matter found to a greater or lesser degree in red wines, particularly those made from grapes with thicker skins and/or matured in new oak barrels, has the effect of binding proteins. Reacting to the free proteins we already carry on our tongues, it can cause a dry or "furred" taste sensation. Tasting protein-based foods—such as cheeses, meats, or cream—alongside the wine sets up a barrier of further protein, diverting the tannic attack solely onto our tongues. In consequence, we perceive less harshness in the wine. There is an old saying in the wine trade: "Buy on an apple, sell on a cheese." In other words, an apple's acidity will tend to reveal potential faults, particularly in white wines, and a little cheese will soften the taste of tough young red wines if offered alongside at the point of sale!

It soon becomes evident to students that we taste with our *noses*, and I encourage them to become much more aware of the crucial part our sense of smell, acting upon the all-important olfactory bulb behind our nasal cavities, plays in the tasting process. Noses, especially trained, practiced noses, can reveal literally hundreds of subtleties of scent and hints of flavor but tend to tire easily. It may seem surprising, but relatively few wines actually smell of grapes, the very substance from which they are made, so my very first step in the education process is to try to raise students' general awareness of what *anything* smells like. It may sound ridiculous, but anything from old leather armchairs to new-mown hay to dry sidewalks newly washed by rain—let alone the varied palette of the dried herbs and spices in their kitchens, store cupboards, or the fruit and vegetables on market stalls—may serve as a means of tuning their olfactory machinery and establishing a vocabulary of descriptive adjectives to help in writing up their notes. It is very rewarding in consequence to see how confidence grows across the weeks of a course alongside the variety of wines chosen for tasting and discussion, aided and abetted no doubt by the private wine discoveries they make individually, at home or elsewhere.

Taking the word *taste* in its purely aesthetic sense, deconstructed across the spectrum, say, of the classical era, one can accept that the aim of the artists or craftsmen of the day was to create a purity of balance between potentially disparate elements. This is not quite as neutral as it may sound—such creations pointed up the inherent tensions within them that, uncontrolled, may have led otherwise to disharmony. It is this tension that provides both the aesthetic and the excitement. Equally, the form of a classical building, the sweep of a symphony or the harmony of shape and color in a painting contains the energy of its complementary forces—and I am prepared to stretch this somewhat abstract concept to apply to the creation of fine wine. Put at its simplest, the aim of any fine winemaker is to provide a *balance* within his or her wine between fruit, sweetness, alcohol, and acidity, and of tannin, too, should the basic material tend in that direction. Even assuming all these factors are suitably controlled, one then has to add the "wild card"—somewhat beyond anyone's direct control—of vintage variance year after year. Notwithstanding the application of state-of-the-art technology, the exercise of viticulture and vinification is often conducted "against the odds" and at the mercy of whatever nature throws at the vineyards. I once stayed at a small Bordeaux château at harvest time where, on a particularly drizzly day, the anxious proprietor kept rushing out into the vineyards with his saccharometer to test the sugar levels in his grapes, lest they fall too far and compromise the price he would be able to achieve for his vintage.

There is no question that wine "hits" us on many levels. I shared a lecturing assignment on a luxury cruise once with a fellow wine tutor who began by telling her audience that the enjoyment of wine touches all five of our senses: *hearing*, as when a cork is pulled and wine pops and fizzes or glugs its way into a glass, with all the expectations that may follow; *sight*, as when we enjoy the subtleties of color it displays, possibly giving indications of age; *scent*, as in the aromas that fill the bowl of the glass; *taste*, as in the gustatory pleasure it offers; and *touch* as in its apparent body and texture on the surface of our tongues.

For all its undeniable potential for complexity, wine can be understood at its simplest across three very basic taste categories: (1) simple primary flavors; (2) primary plus secondary flavors, that is, oak maturation, yeast, oxidation and so on, and (3) tertiary flavors that, taken together with the above, demonstrate reductive qualities, in other words, the taste of maturity.

The classes I teach are invited to make systematic notes on each wine across the elements of appearance, nose, and taste and, following open discussion, to write down what conclusions may be drawn regarding the individual characteristics and quality of each example. Detailed note taking is very important, where objective evidence of sight, smell, and flavor can be written down and referred to as an aide-mémoire. I am quick to warn students that unsupported comments like "gorgeous" or even "fruity" are completely meaningless indicators and are of no help whatsoever when referring back to their notes. One needs to encourage specificity in writing wine notes: to write down that a wine's flavor is of "apples" must surely then open the further question of what kind of apples—tartly acidic ones like English Granny Smiths, for example, or sweetly fragrant ones like Gala or Cox's Orange Pippin. Equally, is the flavor of the apples fresh or cooked?

The follow-up session, based on viticulture and vinification, explores the different ways in which vines are grown and trained across the world and the general effect of varied environments on production styles: the saying that "All wine is made in the vineyard" is well founded. Basic information on standard winemaking techniques is also offered, including procedures for fortified wines like Sherry, Port, and Madeira, and the *méthode Champenoise*. The remaining sessions look specifically at different parts of the winemaking world, with selected generic examples of local wines to match. My own role in these particular sessions is to put the wines in the context of their regions of origin, having due regard for considerations of climate and weather patterns, soils, grape varieties, and the general production methods used. I suggest possible food matches, open to discussion by the class; and within the ambit of an enjoyable tasting exercise, I try to encourage an appropriate degree of personal tasting rigor from each participant.

The nurture and development of a sense of comparative *value* in the wines tasted in the course is important too. Alongside the study of wine purely for its inherent elements, perceptions of quality can be contrasted with price. In point of fact, most of the wines chosen for the course fall into a midrange price bracket, where the "variables" are not so glaring. It is generally at the top end of the price spectrum that difficulties arise, when the "value-for-money" factor is compromised by considerations of scarcity or fashion. In this giddy stratosphere one is arguably leaving the world of wine behind and venturing into the world of investment, buying into "big names" and big reputations with an eye to the future, and it is salutary to discover that at this level the quality-to-price ratio is often staggeringly uneven. The most extreme example I have ever heard of is of a single *bottle* of 1845 Château d'Yquem on a wine list in an exclusive London restaurant offered at £30,000 (or approximately $48,000 in U.S. dollars).

From time to time, my teaching colleagues and I are called upon to engage in some challenging tasting assessments ourselves. I have been an occasional judge at the annual International Wine Challenge run by *Wine International* magazine, where literally hundreds of different wines, grouped into broad categories, are tasted "blind" and annotated for typicity, quality, style, and cellarage potential. Elsewhere I have joined "triage" panels for importers or generic trade bodies testing new wines coming on to their market. Whereas many of my students assume that my day spent tasting around a hundred wines is simply an imbiber's heaven, I assure them that, an experienced palate aside, a disciplined tasting across a range of young and possibly unready wines requires not only superlative concentration and clear note taking but also considerable stamina! The use of spittoons is essential on such occasions to prevent one's judgment becoming clouded by alcohol. I refer my students to the annual burden of the tasting panels at the top Bordeaux châteaux to forecast quality, style, and cellarage potential for future development and, in direct consequence, the prices asked for the wine *en primeur*. These dense, inky cask samples from new vintages will frequently taste impossibly hard and unyielding. The Champagne blenders, too, have the unenviable task of assessing maybe fifty or more *cuvées* from disparate vineyards in order to blend a consistent nonvintage house style from year to year. So valued are their tasting skills and their precious noses that, like royalty, some top Champagne houses will not allow two of their blenders to fly in the same plane together lest misfortune befall them. It is indeed the journey from sap to wine that is the eternal variable and the endless fascination. And no matter what—with sufficient practice—the taste of wine will always tell the truth about itself and that journey: its fruit, its age, its origins, and the way it has been made.

Part Two

....

Theorizing and
Contextualizing Taste

Chapter Six

....

The (Extensive) Pleasures of Eating;

Or, Why Did This Meal Suddenly Become Less Delicious When I Found Out My Server Has No Health Insurance, the Cook Worked Ninety Hours Last Week, and the Recipes Were Published in a Cookbook Whose Author Collected Them from the Women of South India, Whom She Fails to Credit, Even in Her Acknowledgements?

LISA HELDKE

In a review of vegetarian cookbooks for his magazine *Cook's Illustrated*, in 2000, editor Christopher Kimball writes:

Vegetarianism as a lifestyle ain't what it used to be. Deborah Madison, the reigning queen of this culinary niche and author of *Vegetarian Cooking for Everyone* (Broadway Books, 1997), admits to a taste for red meat and has, on occasion, been seen consuming a sizzling steak in public. Mollie Katzen, author of *The Moosewood Cookbook* (Ten Speed Press, 1977), espouses wholesome cooking, "whether that contains meat or not." And Madhur Jaffrey has now turned her considerable talents to the subject of vegetarian cooking, but from an international perspective, bringing numerous ethnic specialties together in one giant tome. Vegetarian cooking is growing up, shedding tie-dye for L.L. Bean and taking on a more sophisticated, less politically sensitive palate. At last, it seems, vegetarian cooking can be welcomed into the fold of legitimate culinary pursuits now that it is first and foremost about taste and technique rather than health and politics.[1]

This passage made me frantic the first time I read it. After thinking about it for a while, I came up with the following set of interconnected reasons why. I begin with the most trivial (and most tangential), and tack my way into the more important, which will be the topic of this chapter.

First, Kimball writes that Jaffrey has "now turned her considerable talents" to vegetarianism—as if her most recent work were the first book of vegetarian cookery she had written. But in fact, Jaffrey wrote another cookbook, entitled *Worlds of the East Vegetarian Cooking,* a dozen years ago; she has been *writing* about vegetarian cuisine for at least that long.

Secondly, this error, while trivial in one sense, strikes me as quite revealing and disturbing in another. As Kimball well knows, Jaffrey comes from—and regularly writes about—India, a country of vast, varied, and *sophisticated* vegetarian culinary practices, growing out of several different religious traditions—a country in which vegetarian cooking is not only deeply established, but regarded as perhaps *the* "legitimate culinary pursuit" (to use Kimball's phrase). It is particularly galling to find him dismissing vegetarian cuisines "of the past" and praising those of "the present" by praising an author who *comes from* one of the world's oldest and richest vegetarian cultures.

Thirdly, this oversight makes Kimball's claim that "we" are "now" making vegetarian cuisine culinarily sophisticated both ahistorical and acontextual. Never mind centuries of Indian cookery that arise out of the practices of Hinduism and other religious traditions; never mind centuries of Buddhist cookery in such culinary centers as Japan and China; to Kimball, vegetarianism is *only now* becoming culinarily sophisticated, because only now is it being developed by people who supposedly put taste before politics. (People who shop at L.L. Bean know to keep their politics out of the kitchen, apparently.[2])

My fourth point has to do with Kimball's evidence for the claim that vegetarians (in the United States) are actually putting taste before politics. It seems to consist of his observation that several well-respected authors of vegetarian cookbooks are known to eat meat, at least on occasion. The reasoning seems to go like this: Anyone who eats meat can't be one of those strident vegetarians who only care about animals, and if the best and the brightest of our vegetarian authors are among those who sometimes eat meat, well, then vegetarianism has hung up its manifestos and is ready for the big time. Correlatively, if a meat eater is actually interested in vegetarian cooking, it must be because there is something genuinely (read "aesthetically") interesting about vegetarian cuisine. Meat eating, apparently, is apolitical, and can have the effect of neutralizing the moral and political crankiness of vegetarianism.

With my fifth reason for dismay, things start to get interesting, as I read between the lines, tunneling underneath Kimball's review to address the kinds of cultural presuppositions about vegetarians on which I think his review relies. Kimball's review implies that vegetarian cooking has actually been thwarted aesthetically by its practitioners' emphasis on political concerns, such as the welfare of animals, and health concerns, such as an interest in reducing fat consumption. (Given his silence on the great vegetarian cuisines of Asia, we might also surmise that a commitment to a religious tradition thwarts the development of a cuisine.) Such concerns, extraneous to the *proper* aesthetic appreciation of food, have made vegetarian cuisine unsophisticated and, well, just plain bad tasting. Vegetarianism was immature (aesthetically immature) precisely *because* it was politically sensitive.

This view of vegetarian food probably sounds quite familiar. Since at least the sixties, vegetarian food has had a reputation in the United States as the food of health faddists, antiwar hippies, humorless feminists, and cloth-shoe-wearing tree-huggers; so-called vegetarian staples like tofu and brown rice have been the butt of innumerable jokes.[3] "Everybody knows" that vegetarians don't care if food tastes good, so long as it saves the earth. "Everyone knows" that, at the very least, political commitments leave vegetarians unconcerned about whether the foods they create and eat are aesthetically pleasing; at most, those commitments actually prevent the vegetarian from producing aesthetically desirable foods.

But now vegetarian food has an opportunity to become "a legitimate culinary pursuit," as it loses, or at least loosens, its political commitments.

Finally, in making his pronouncement about the bright future of vegetarian cuisine, Kimball presumes a dichotomy between "culinary sophistication" and "political sensitivity"—between "taste and technique" on the one hand and "health and politics" on the other. Such a presumption is hardly unique to Kimball, of course; it is a standard feature of many mainstream views of vegetarianism. Vegetarian cooking, by choosing to emphasize politics, health, or religion, places itself on the wrong side of the divide. It isn't just that aesthetic and political/moral concerns are completely different concerns; it is that the pursuit of the one (at least when that one is "ethical concerns") spells the ruination of the other. You cannot both produce sophisticated cuisine and pursue an ethical, social, or political agenda.

This is just the point I want to challenge. This chapter is my attempt to develop the claim that there are some experiences that are aesthetically rich in part precisely *because* they are morally rich.[4]

Vegetarianism probably represents the most familiar case of alleged politics-over-aesthetics on the contemporary culinary scene in the United States, but it is certainly not the only culinary practice that chooses the wrong side of the divide. Other contenders might include organic farming, buying locally grown food, and choosing to buy from worker-owned cooperatives (unless, of course, one can prove that one does these things to procure aesthetically superior food).[5] The proper relationship between aesthetics and ethics/politics is clear; place "taste and technique" at the forefront of culinary art, and minimize, ignore or deny, concerns of an ethical or political nature, unless they can actually be shown to have a direct bearing on taste. An illustration: in a program I once saw about the raising of veal calves, Julia Child was interviewed about the relative merits and demerits of veal calves that were allowed to run around during their attenuated lives. Child asserted—no doubt accurately—that the taste of this free-range veal was utterly different from that of pen-raised veal—and went on to argue that it was utterly inferior to the latter. She expressed genuine outrage at the suggestion that someone might choose to eat a product she regarded as culinarily inadequate, for a reason as flimsy as the relative happiness of an animal. For Child, it seemed clear that ethical concerns constituted an actual obstacle to aesthetic commitments—an obstacle to be resisted at all costs.

How well does this dictum—If it is about aesthetic taste, it can't be about ethical concerns, and if it's about ethical concerns it can't be about taste—serve or account for our actual aesthetic appreciation of food? How well does it describe or account for the kinds of aesthetic decisions that a cook makes? If adhered to, would it improve cuisine—and enlighten our experiences of it? My answers are, "poorly," "poorly," and "not likely." Why?

Adopting a sharp dichotomy between aesthetic and ethical considerations would impoverish our aesthetic experiences of food by drawing our attention away from many of the very things that give food its significance. An aesthetic of food ought to be able to help us reflect on aspects of Thanksgiving dinner or a Passover Seder or a meal at the local organic vegan restaurant other than the fluffiness and savoriness of the respective mashed potatoes, matzo balls, and kelp puffs. It ought to give us tools for reflecting on the ways history, heritage, religious conviction—and, yes, environment and ecology—enter into our experience of the meal. After all, most of us are mostly today not ashamed to admit that such "extra-aesthetic" elements enhance our *aesthetic* appreciation of paintings, poems, musical compositions, even constitute an essential element of them.[6] So why retain it for food?

Can the Aesthetic Appreciation of Food be Multidimensional?

More pointedly, why denigrate the role of political, social, and ethical commitments in cuisine? Why are these seen as a contaminating influence? In the case of someone like Kimball, I believe he criticizes what might be called "political vegetarianism" out of a sincere desire to shore up the aesthetic legitimacy of food. Kimball, like many food writers, obviously believes wholeheartedly that food can be an object of aesthetic appreciation; indeed, many believe the stronger claim that food is an actual art. But of course not everyone agrees—food is on decidedly shaky ground in most aesthetic theories. If you're trying to make it clear even to the dubious that food is art, then vegetarian cuisine—with its commitment to things other than "taste and technique," with its reputation for tasting bad—needs to be hidden in the closet, whipped into shape, or publicly ridiculed and drummed out of the category of "cuisine." Otherwise, cuisine in general will never be able to take its rightful place in the art pantheon.

Those who advocate such a route to legitimize the aesthetic value of food put me in mind of a practitioner of the social sciences who attempts to prove that anthropology and psychology are "real" (read "hard") sciences. This social scientist polices the ranks of the various disciplines, criticizing anyone who, for example, tries to use autobiography in their work and call it social science. The self-appointed police officer knows that the social sciences have a much lower chance of being accepted as hard sciences if practitioners use such unorthodox methods. Autobiographical anthropologists threaten the scientific legitimacy of the social sciences *in general* in the same way that vegetarian chefs who "put politics before taste" threaten the aesthetic legitimacy of cuisine in general. If you're worried about your own claims to membership in some category, you're going to be doubly vigilant in your efforts to root out anything that might be taken as a counterexample. You are *not*, for example, going to be interested in making room for renegades who are trying to expand the methodologies of science to include autobiography. You are going to interpret science as narrowly as possible—and make sure that all practitioners of the social sciences adhere to this narrow interpretation.

Food loyalists, eager to prove to the dubious that food is an art form, frequently engage in just such self-policing, by severely restricting the scope of aesthetically relevant features of food. Carolyn Korsmeyer, in her book *Making Sense of Taste*, discusses several theorists who attempt to negotiate food into the category of fine art.[7] Such arguments tend to be characterized by very narrow readings of *both* aesthetic criteria *and* the activity of eating.

For example, Korsmeyer notes that most defendants of food as art focus their attention very narrowly on the sensory qualities of food—primarily its taste, but also its smell and appearance. And they end up resting their defenses on such extraordinary instances of "eating" as wine tasting, in which the potation is literally spat out after it has been tasted. But even with this stringent (and bizarre) conception of food, those who defend the "art-ness" of food describe it as a minor art form, since (among other things) taste is a lower sense than hearing and seeing and since food doesn't seem to refer—doesn't seem to "mean" anything outside of itself—an accusation that leaves taste stranded in the realm of the utterly subjective.[8]

Such a position is characteristic of those who reduce the aesthetic appreciation of food to its sensuous qualities alone. But why take this approach? As Korsmeyer says, "It would be a sacrifice of richness and breadth for the significance of foods if this were the only grounds on which it could be aesthetically justified."[9] To restrict our aesthetic appreciation of food to "the savor of the tastes themselves" means that we lose access to "the terrain of deeper aesthetic significance that foods display in their practical contexts, including ritual, ceremony, and commemoration."[10] Thanksgiving, Passover, and vegan restaurant meals are significant for reasons beyond fluffiness and savoriness—or even fluffiness, savoriness, and a pleasing golden-brown color. There is more to the aesthetics of food than meets the tongue—or even the tongue and the nose together. Critics miss the point of 1960s-style vegetarian food, if they write it off as aesthetically unsophisticated because its practitioners were motivated by deep political commitments. For Korsmeyer, choosing to weigh the aesthetic value of a cuisine on the basis of taste and technique alone means impoverishing oneself with no good reason.

The Aesthetic Significance of Food

Korsmeyer herself is actually deliciously uninterested in arguing food into the category of art, per se. Among her reasons: "The concept of art, dominated as it is today by the idea of *fine* art, is a poor category to capture the nature of foods and their consumption"—poor precisely because fine art exists in a climate deeply influenced by the idea that "aesthetic qualities of works of art . . . inhere in the works themselves, free of surrounding context."[11] In other words, Korsmeyer doesn't want to argue that food is art, because making such an argument seems to require her to adopt just the impoverished set of aesthetically relevant criteria that many advocates of the food-is-art view adopt. It is too big a sacrifice, for too little gain. (Big deal if we get to treat food as art, only to have to ignore all the aspects of it that give it significance.)

On the other hand, Korsmeyer *is* interested in making a case for the *aesthetic significance* of food; she develops a notion of the aesthetic that is rich, complex, and contextual. It is a notion of the aesthetic in which the ethical, political, social, and religious aspects of cooking and eating are anything but irrelevant to aesthetic appreciation. And while she doesn't say so in so many words, I think she would like the aesthetic appreciation of food to become more of a paradigm for the aesthetic appreciation of art.

I am interested in Korsmeyer's theory because I think it presents an important challenge to the way of thinking on which Kimball's view relies. I think it more fully represents the kinds of aesthetic experiences of food I actually have, *when I experience food aesthetically*. (Our fullest, most aesthetically rich experiences of food are, I believe, just those in which we attend to many aspects of its context.) Korsmeyer's theory pushes me to expand the scope of the aesthetically relevant. I look to her theory to give me a way to understand how the aesthetic value of food can actually depend upon such ethical considerations as the working conditions of the people who prepared the food, the environmental impact of growing the food, and other ostensibly unaesthetic qualities. I want to consider the possibility that at least sometimes the presence of moral commitments is actually a necessary condition for certain kinds of aesthetic value. What would it be like for my aesthetic experience of food to be deeply imbued by the ethical context of its creation? How would my various food practices—growing, cooking, eating, eliminating—be transformed were I to seek to create such multilayered aesthetic experiences? What I seek is a way to make aesthetic sense/aesthetic relevance of the matter of who grew my tomatoes and how they live—or even who is the source of my recipes, and how were her or his contributions compensated or acknowledged?[12]

To lay the groundwork for this argument, I begin by explicating key aspects of Korsmeyer's theory.

Cognitivist Theory and the Meaning of Food

The single most important feature of Korsmeyer's theory (for her, as well as for my, argument) is its cognitivist approach. Most theorists writing about food have argued that taste "tells us something only about the subject doing the tasting. It yields no information about objects in the world."[13] Food, these theorists further explain, doesn't "mean" anything beyond itself—it does not refer, represent, denote. Korsmeyer disagrees. Food *does* have meanings; it connects to objects in the world in all sorts of ways. If this seems implausible, consider, for a moment, just two of her minor examples. Croissants were invented to *represent* the Austrians' defeat of the Ottoman Turks in 1683, and chicken soup *expresses* comfort to someone suffering from a head cold. (I understand that many consider the story of croissants' origin to be discredited. The legitimacy or illegitimacy of the story, while certainly relevant for some purposes, is not particularly relevant to Korsmeyer's point; another, more credible, origins story would do just as well.) Borrowing from Nelson Goodman's cognitivist theory, she invites her readers to consider food as one of Goodman's symbol systems. She argues that food is *pervasively* symbolic. Croissants and chicken soup only begin to tell the story, a story that also includes everything from candy corn to the bread and wine of communion to the bear meat eaten by a character in the novel *Cold Mountain*.

She uses this starting point to show *how* food means something beyond itself—and how understanding the multiple layers of food's meaning can enable us to plumb its full aesthetic depths. Rather than "zeroing out" the political commitments of vegetarians, the environmental commitments of organic vegetable farmers, the religious commitments of cooks in a *glatt* kosher restaurant, or the family history of the diner eating kimchee, this method invites us to take them into account as sources of meaning—meaning that can deepen and enrich the literal savor of the food in our mouths.

How does the theory accomplish this? Symbol systems function as "systems of meaning that have obvious cognitive functions."[14] By "cognitive" or "symbolic functions," Korsmeyer and Goodman mean the various ways that symbols symbolize—the ways they point to something outside themselves. As Korsmeyer notes, Goodman's theory does not sharply separate the aesthetic from the nonaesthetic; the same kinds of symbolic functions can be found in artworks and in objects with no particular aesthetic significance. Not all instances of representation, for example, are aesthetically significant. Furthermore, in different contexts, the same symbol may be interpreted in ways that highlight or minimize its aesthetic significance. Korsmeyer writes that "rather than presenting necessary and sufficient conditions to define the aesthetic, Goodman identifies five 'symptoms' of the aesthetic"— five different cognitive functions that aesthetic objects tend to manifest.[15] Three of them are particularly significant for aesthetic experiences involving food; they include representation, exemplification, and expression (which Korsmeyer, following Goodman, terms "metaphorical exemplification"). I will sketch out her descriptions of each, as a way to show how an aesthetic experience is constituted out of layers of meaning.

Representation

First, representation. A candy skull *represents* the real thing to a Day of the Dead celebrant. Korsmeyer lists dozens of such foods that represent something outside themselves, generally by simply looking like something else. (Other examples I thought of include ginger pigs, Hanukah geld, and a cake made in the shape of Mount Rainier.) Such resemblances generally do not amount to much aesthetically (we might be amazed by the inclusion of astonishingly realistic glaciers in the appropriate places on the faces of the carrot cake Mount Rainier, but they won't bring us to rank the cake with the *Mona Lisa*); nevertheless, the sheer number of representations points to "the pervasiveness of meaning in food."[16] Those who argue that food doesn't refer beyond itself will have to somehow account for the fact that "an enormous amount of what we put in our mouths represents (in one sense or another) something else."[17] And they will have to come up with a different ground for denying the aesthetic relevance of food, since many foods meet this criterion, although meeting it alone is not a sufficient condition for making a food aesthetically significant or valuable.

So if the actual fact of visual representation is of no particular aesthetic consequence, then of what aesthetic interest is representation in food? Korsmeyer's answer points to context. She suggests that reflecting on a familiar reference, or coming to understand an unfamiliar one, can, and often does, add a layer of *aesthetic* meaning to a food. For example, in coming to learn that a pretzel was originally shaped to look like the arms of a monk in prayer, "the experience of eating a pretzel is transformed very slightly and perhaps achieves the aesthetic predicate 'witty.'"[18] And for a patriotic Austrian, learning that the shape of the croissant was inspired by the crescent moon on the Turkish flag (so that they are symbolically eating Turkey, relishing its defeat each time they eat one) adds a layer of meaning to the food that makes the experience of eating a croissant considerably different from (and arguably more aesthetically significant than), say, eating a bagel. (For me, the aesthetically pleasurable experience of biting through buttery, papery layers of a well-made croissant and finding its soft, yeasty interior has been altered somewhat bitterly, by learning that even this wonderful delicacy is seen by some as a kind of war memorial. Does it still *taste* the same to me? Part of what I want to argue, ultimately, is that it doesn't. Or, more accurately, that the complex aesthetic experience of eating a croissant—and of which literal tasting is only a part—has been altered with the introduction of this new information. Of course it's been altered yet again by learning that this is inaccurate history—now I'm led to wonder about the appeal of such an apparently false anecdote.) On the more elaborate end of the spectrum of representation, the fantastical cakes of the nineteenth-century chef Antoine Carême, fashioned to look like everything from Greek and Roman ruins to Chinese pavilions, reveal such skill and beauty that we can understand why Carême described pastry making as the chief form of architecture. While we might not agree with Carême's grandiose assessment, we would nonetheless be moved to agree that his creations merit aesthetic approbation for the cleverness and subtlety of their replication.

As Korsmeyer points out, representations of these sorts generally depend upon vision for their effect—not taste. (However, she does note that a Thanksgiving meal might be said to represent the first Thanksgiving—a kind of representation that is not visual.) But whereas others might see this dependence on vision as a reason to discount the aesthetic significance *for food* of such representations (since food is supposedly all about taste), Korsmeyer argues that it instead "illustrates the unremarkable fact that the experience of eating involves more than one sense."[19] Eating also engages our senses of smell, sight, touch, even sound. (Listen the next time you bite into a croissant.)

Korsmeyer acknowledges that representation constitutes a fairly limited aesthetic element of food—even the elaborate stunt cookery of a Carême serves a chiefly decorative function. Nevertheless, it is worth noting that attention to food's representative properties already moves us beyond the sphere in which Kimball's review makes aesthetic judgments about cuisine. While someone like Kimball would likely agree that *appearance* is important—foods must *look* beautiful, and must visually display the cook's knowledge of proper technique—such a person would not, in general, regard *resemblance* as contributing any aesthetic value to a dish qua cuisine. If such representation gave the food item any aesthetic value at all, it would be as a sculpture or painting, or as a piece of some decorative visual art like embroidery. Such an understanding of food pares away aspects of our experience of food, to get at an aesthetic core of "taste and technique"; Korsmeyer builds up the aesthetic significance of food out of just such rejected aspects. One considerable source of fun in vegetarian food derives from the whimsy that inspired vegetarian cooks to create "turkeys" out of everything in sight—nut loaf, tofu, mashed potatoes. (Surely everyone eating such a turkey simulacrum had to remove their tongues from their cheeks to do so.)

Exemplification

The next cognitive function Korsmeyer discusses is *exemplification*, which comes in two forms. An apple may exemplify redness, crispness, tartness. Chicken soup exemplifies saltiness, blandness. A bowl of cereal *exemplifies* breakfast to an American eater. Stated most plainly, exemplification attends to the fact that foods possess particular qualities—taste qualities, as with the apple, but also qualities like belonging to a particular meal, as with cereal. Exemplification describes the fact that the eater's attention is drawn to these qualities.

As Korsmeyer notes, most aesthetic writing about food focuses on taste exemplification—on the ways food manifests the qualities it is expected to have.[20] Indeed, the countless parodies of vegetarian cooking one finds in popular culture tend to rely on the stereotype of humorless vegetarians who use ingredients in ways that fail to allow their exemplary qualities to speak, or who select ingredients that exemplify unappealing qualities (like blandness), simply because they meet some set of political criteria. Insert tofu, brown rice, and bean jokes here.

While most aestheticians focus on taste exemplification, Korsmeyer's reading of exemplification goes deeper than this, as her inclusion of the cereal example illustrates. Here we can see why Korsmeyer understands exemplification as a cognitive function; foods come to "'mean' the meal that they provide."[21] Cereal exemplifies breakfast for an American because it possesses "implicit properties" as a result of its location within a particular social context—a context that may be as small as a particular family, or as large as an entire nation.[22] It may include elements of religious practice, food availability, ethnic heritage, constraints of work life, ethical commitments, or any number of other aspects of one's surroundings, all of which combine to make certain foods embody— *mean*—particular times and/or places. While a caramel roll *meant* breakfast to me, to my Swedish college roommate, it threatened violent illness—to her, fluorescent pink, salty, fishy caviar in a tube spelled 7:00 a.m. Foods possess properties as a result of occupying "a particular place in the rhythm of nourishment that is represented by mealtimes."[23]

While such exemplified properties regularly go unnoticed (who recognizes the ubiquitous?), a change in the context brings them into sharp focus. Being in the presence of my roommate made it very clear to me that the connection between caramel rolls and 7:00 a.m. was all about context. Ditto when I visited her in Sweden, and was confronted with what looked, in the morning hours, like a tube of toothpaste on the breakfast table. Tastes, Korsmeyer concludes, are always *embedded* in meaning—foods exemplify different properties as a result of the different contexts they come to inhabit.

(While it is somewhat beside my present point, I am interested in expanding this notion of exemplified properties beyond the "rhythm of nourishment" that Korsmeyer describes, to include what we might call the "agricultural rhythm" and the "rhythm of preparation." For just as foods occupy particular times in the day, they also occupy particular times of the year, and particular places on the globe, among other things. And just as Korsmeyer suggests we can come to render explicit the implicit meanings lodged in the structure of our meals, so too, I think, can we make explicit the implicit meanings buried in our agricultural and cooking practices. Will we be able to taste them, the way we can taste the "wrongness" of caviar for breakfast? I don't know; but fortunately, on Korsmeyer's account, tasting is not the end of the story. But am I extending the notion of exemplification too far here, by extending it to qualities of a food that may not be literally perceptible by the tongue? I don't think so—but I may be wrong, in which case I need another place to put them. And I'm not comfortable putting them into the other possible category, the one I'll describe in a moment: metaphorical expression.)

To take Kimball as an example again, he is sometimes comfortable acknowledging the aesthetic importance of this aspect of cuisine. In editorials in his magazine, he often waxes rhapsodic about the relationship between times of the year and the foods he is eating on his farm in Vermont. It is clear that at least some elements of context are aesthetically important to him—seasonality and location, for example. It might not be a tremendous stretch for him to include in that category such things as the working conditions of those who grow his food or the lives of those animals that become his food.

Metaphorical Expression

Apples may exemplify crispness and tartness, but in other contexts, they may *express*—or *metaphorically* exemplify—anything from temptation to poison to motherhood to appreciation for a teacher, depending, of course, upon the contexts in which they are embedded. Metaphorical exemplification is the third "symptom," or cognitive function, of the aesthetic particularly important for food. Sometimes we identify an expressive function in foods because of a natural property they possess—bitterness and sweetness are two common examples of flavors that come to express experiences that we describe with the same adjectives. A tongue-in-cheek organization does "research" on the meaning of bitter melons, the bitterest food humans normally consume. "Do bitter personalities grow bitterer bitter melons?" is one of the questions they currently are "researching."[24] Any number of common metaphorical expressions attests to this cognitive feature of food—eating crow, sour grapes, the sweet taste of victory, and so on. But Korsmeyer takes us into, and beyond, the everyday level of food's expressiveness to reveal the aesthetic potential of this cognitive property. She illustrates the depth of "complex propositional understanding" that even a simple flavor like salt can possess, by retelling an old English fairytale in which the relationship between salt and meat comes to stand for a daughter's love for her father. In the story, the father comes to understand the depth of his daughter's love (which she describes as "the way fresh meat loves salt") when he is served a meal without any salt. The father comes to understand his daughter's love with his very body, as he takes the savorless meat into his mouth. Korsmeyer concludes, "This is the force of 'aesthetic' apprehension: that some truth or realization of discovery is delivered in a way that touches one intimately, that focuses and concentrates insight with the poignant immediacy of the blind father's taste of saltless meat."[25]

It is not difficult to multiply examples of food's expressiveness—and it is also not hard to notice how deeply contextual such examples are. For example, while chicken soup might express thoughtfulness and comfort to someone whose mother made it for them as a child when they had a cold, to a vegetarian that same soup might express violence and wanton cruelty—the taste of the soup becoming inseparable from the life of the chicken that flavors it. Similarly, the smell of bacon might, for some, evoke the love of the grandmother who made BLT sandwiches, during summer vacations, while to someone who keeps kosher, the smell of such *trayf* meat might make them literally ill. And while a meal in an Ethiopian restaurant might spell comfort to both my New York–raised Jewish friend Naomi and my Somali acquaintance Jamila, their experiences of comfort will probably bear little resemblance to each other, rooted as they are in such dramatically different contexts.

As Korsmeyer, interpreting Goodman, shows, aesthetic experiences happen where the project of drawing out symbolic connections is the most nuanced and layered—their multilayered character explains "the insight and emotional depth for which art is valued."[26] Simply put, there is a lot to draw upon in an experience that has depth and complexity. Recognizing the similarity between a triangular orange-and-white piece of candy and a kernel of corn is unlikely to be an aesthetically rich experience—not much room for subtlety and not many layers of meaning here. (As Korsmeyer observes, not all experiences of food are aesthetically significant—but this is hardly to its detriment. Neither, it can be argued, are doodles on the phone pad, or the music they play while you are trapped in an elevator.) We must look to much more complex and nuanced food experiences than this to see the aesthetic depths of which food is capable. The fairytale points us in such a direction. Ceremonial meals present us with still more examples—examples in which the various symbolic uses of foods combine in multiple ways to create events of considerable aesthetic weight. Korsmeyer points to Thanksgiving, the Passover Seder, and Holy Communion as three meals that manifest, often in deep and profound ways, all of the kinds of symbolic connections I've discussed—representation (wafer and wine denote body and blood—even become them in some denominations of Christianity); exemplification (warmth, savoriness, and heaviness of Thanksgiving foods); and expression (salt water expresses the tears shed by the Israelites in captivity). The fact that these symbolic connections are, in each case, multiple and are encased in ceremonies that emerge out of, and take place in, multilayered cultural contexts, all contribute to the aesthetic potential of such ceremonial meals.

(I must note a consequence of Korsmeyer's theory that may strike readers as ironic. If we adopt her position, we are forced to acknowledge that food may taste bad and yet be aesthetically very significant. On Kimball's account, this of course would make no sense, because the aesthetic value of food is so completely tied to its taste/smell. For Korsmeyer, however, while it is certainly extremely lovely if, at a Seder, the harosset is made with crispy, flavorful apples and the matzo comes fresh from a bakery rather than a box, much of the aesthetic significance of the meal will remain, even if the quality of the flavors is poor. So long as the foods are recognizable, they get to count, as it were. To require food to be always delicious in order to be aesthetically significant would be the equivalent of requiring that paintings always be beautiful.)

The Communality of Food

My comment about contexts hints at a second central feature of Korsmeyer's aesthetic theory—her conviction that food is communal, and that to understand it as aesthetically significant requires attention to its communality. For Korsmeyer, it is communal in at least two senses.

The Intimacy in Giving and Receiving Food

First, literal, sensory taste is a sense that is both inward- and outward directed; in her words, it is an "intimate" sense. (Korsmeyer develops her conception of taste by carefully and exhaustively discussing theories of taste—both physiological and aesthetic—to show that those conceptions that understand taste as a purely subjective, inward-looking sensation are inadequate. I will not rehearse her very compelling arguments here.) The operation of eating results in external objects literally becoming part of oneself; given that the objects in question are so often *presented* to us by someone else (and, in our culture, given that that someone else is often a total stranger serving you in a restaurant or fast-food place), the activity of eating involves risk and trust (I have to believe that you won't poison me or make me sick, intentionally or accidentally). As such, it is no surprise that many cultural bonds focus on eating; when you depend upon another for your safe sustenance, the potential exists for a deep connection to that other. (In commodity culture, rather than developing a deep connection, we tend to develop legislation to protect ourselves from dangerous food. While this might appear to minimize the need to trust others, it more accurately just shifts the focus of our trust to government inspectors.) Little wonder, then, that so many rituals of eating have grown up around this feature of it. Korsmeyer notes that Bedouin tradition dictates that once you share salt and bread with someone, you are responsible for that person's protection.[27] And Aristotle cites the parable describing friends as people who have eaten salt together.[28] Any aesthetic understanding of food must always come back to, or remember its roots in, this fundamental fact about eating—that it places us in intimate contact with any number of others. (We can perhaps best see these intimate connections when something goes wrong with the connection—when, for example, a mass-produced food is found to have been contaminated. I had a small experience of the degree to which I trust unknown others—and am thus "intimate" with them in Korsmeyer's sense—when I opened a foil packet of soup and out dropped a large metal nut. Suddenly I was acutely aware of how dependent I was upon others for ensuring that the things I put in my mouth would not poison me.) In the United States, and in fact in industrialized nations all over the world, that ever-expanding group of others is, by and large, anonymous, so we tend to erase them from the story. (We'd rather not be responsible to the folks who "share" the fruits of their labors with us, thank you very much.) But to ignore the intimacy of taste as if it were aesthetically irrelevant is, in effect, to make wine tasting—tasting without ingesting—the standard for eating.

Such intimacy is not only a burden, however. Participating in this activity makes us vulnerable in a way that experiencing arts based on the "distal senses" of hearing and seeing normally does not. You can literally die—or be horribly betrayed—by taking into yourself something that you ought not. But Korsmeyer also points out that the possibilities of horror are the flip side of the possibilities of community, friendship, and so on that food enables.[29] This is true of special as well as mundane instances of eating. The Passover Seder, and a meal of the year's last garden tomatoes shared with a neighbor, both represent instances of the community that can form around, or be strengthened by, an eating experience. Eating is rooted in this "profound foundation of trust." Surely that fact colors this experience in ways so profound that our aesthetic system needs to be able to address them.[30]

The Cultural Context of Food

Food preparation and eating are communal in a second way. Foods exist in cultural contexts, and the symbolic meanings they have are meanings they acquire in context. Aesthetic appreciation of any depth requires that we have at least some access to this cultural context—to the community out of which this food has developed its meanings. This might mean being a part of, or knowing something about, the religious practice, the historical significance, the social convention, or the family tradition of a dish or a meal. It might mean knowing something about, or possessing, the Scandinavian penchant for fish and caviar. Absent this understanding, the food becomes literally *unintelligible* (note the cognition word), even if it tastes good in some one- or two-dimensional way. I think, for instance, of how ill equipped I would be to participate in a tea ceremony, because I know so little about it. The tea I tasted would quite literally not be the same drink as the one consumed by a knowledgeable participant; I would swill down a beverage, while they would participate in a multilayered experience, one in which everything from the style of the cup to the art on the walls of the tea house, to the manner in which the tea was poured, could evoke a response from them.

A more everyday example of tea drinking will illustrate the importance of context more concretely. Recently, a student came to see me about a paper with which she was struggling. I knew she was from Japan, though I didn't know much beyond that. I offered her a cup of *genmaicha*, a green tea mixed with roasted brown rice that I knew to be Japanese in origin. She accepted—something of a surprise to me, since she wasn't really eager to prolong the visit to my office—and then this very shy, very quiet student proceeded to drink the tea with obvious and deep pleasure. I asked her if *genmaicha* was common in Japan. "Yes," she replied, "very common," but then said nothing more, as she closed her eyes and drank. I felt oddly like a voyeur, and also strangely left out, watching this woman go on a little trip home while drinking a cup of tea. I wanted to know about this tea—when would she typically drink it? how would it be prepared? among whom was it common?—and worried about whether I'd prepared it at all correctly. Was it too strong? Too weak? Was it okay to give it to her in a mug? Was the water the right temperature? Absent any knowledge of her context, and in the presence of someone to whom this drink was as familiar as home, my experience of this tea suddenly became both more frustrating and more full of potential—frustrating, because there was so much I didn't know, but full of potential, because I was coming to see that it was there to be known, and to see that knowing it would enhance my appreciation of this tea.

(Thinking about attention to context as an element of aesthetic appreciation, it strikes me that Kimball's emphasis on the importance of technique as an aesthetic criterion could be understood as attention to context. When you appreciate what you know to be the complex preparations that have gone into the making of a seemingly simple dish in a fine nouvelle cuisine restaurant, you are actually relying on your knowledge of context. You can only appreciate that dish fully because you know something about the culinary tradition in which it is situated. Without a very detailed understanding of that context, the food before you may seem to you to be ordinary, or even bad.)

It would be ridiculous to try to make any general statements about the ways food is rooted in social context. But any aesthetic that hopes to address the deep potential of food needs to pay attention to that rootedness. In paying attention to human connection, one is inevitably drawn into consideration of the ethical and political dimensions of our intertwining.

Yet another aspect of Korsmeyer's account, that I will not explore here, is her observation that food is *temporal*.[31] Foods are fresh, and then they rot. They are in season, and then they are out. Eating itself takes time; it cannot be accomplished in an instant.[32]

In contrast to views of food-as-art that reduce it to the experience of tongue and nose, I want a food aesthetic that draws upon all its potential layers of symbolic meaning—including layers that are ethical and political in nature. As someone with a variety of ethical commitments that I take very seriously, and upon which I nevertheless often have difficulty acting, I am interested in increasing their hold on me by situating them also within an aesthetic framework. As someone interested in encouraging others to see the ethical consequences of their food choices, someone who realizes that her entreaties often make her sound like a shrill harpy—everybody's least-favorite dinner guest—I am frankly interested in the strategic value of being able to plead my case on aesthetic, as well as ethical and political, grounds. Therefore, I want to explore the prescriptive power of Korsmeyer's theory.

It may seem odd to use her theory prescriptively. Korsmeyer, after all, observes that aesthetic worth or value can be present even in really painful experiences. But while Korsmeyer is suggesting that painful features of our eating *are* parts of our aesthetic experience, I wish to use her work to make a claim about the sorts of foods we ought to create in the future. I am suggesting that we ought to promote foods that enable a certain kind of aesthetic pleasure. There is a subcategory of experiences—pleasurable aesthetic experiences—in which moral concerns are a necessary contributor to aesthetic pleasure. We ought to try to create such experiences *and* we ought to cultivate the kind of aesthetic faculty that would enable us *to* appreciate them, aesthetically. We ought to make decisions using this faculty, to enable ourselves to have extensive pleasures.

In that spirit, in this last section of the chapter, I want to think about how to move from using her theory to *describe* aesthetic experiences, to using it as a way to *create, expand, and enrich* my aesthetic experiences of food.[33] I would like to increase my capacity for what Korsmeyer calls "aesthetic apprehension," for receiving those "truths or realizations" that are "delivered in a way that touches one intimately, that focuses and concentrates insight," as well as my capacity to create the sorts of eating experiences that have the multidimensionality that will enable them to serve in this capacity.[34] And I think Korsmeyer gives me the tools to do so—the means I can use to begin to pay different kinds of attention to my food experiences, and thereby begin to seek out particular kinds of food experiences and reject others.

A caveat: Korsmeyer notes that much of our experience of food has no particular aesthetic richness about it—eating, for example, is an everyday activity that we often do in everyday ways. While I understand and accept that pronouncement to some degree—surely we could not withstand three or more profound aesthetic experiences a day every day of our lives, could we?—I think there is substantial room to expand and deepen the quality of our aesthetic attention to food, even everyday food. While three profound experiences might exhaust us, surely we could substantially increase our daily aesthetic intake without doing grave harm to ourselves, couldn't we?

For the time being, I am going to limit myself to examining the possibility of developing the capacity for aesthetic *pleasure*, because this is the focus of Wendell Berry's essay "The Pleasures of Eating," upon which I will draw here.[35] I recognize that pleasure is only one among many forms of aesthetic apprehension—and in some ways the easiest one to deal with. In making this choice, I do not mean to deny the possibility that foods could be aesthetically challenging or disturbing—to suggest that they could not be the source of poignant, concentrated insight of the sort Korsmeyer is describing, and would not be valuable because of that. (And, in fact, I think it is a problem that Berry only talks about aesthetic pleasure.)

The Industrial Food System and Its Displeasures

According to Berry, eating ought to be an *extensive* pleasure. Berry is useful because, among other reasons, he can move the discussion from description to prescription. Berry wants to tell us what to do.

In the current food system, which Berry describes as an "industrial food system," eaters are defined as "consumers," and the pleasure (by which he means aesthetic pleasure) we are urged to take in our food is a very thin pleasure indeed. Berry writes, "'Life is not very interesting,' we seem to have decided. 'Let its satisfactions be minimal, perfunctory, and fast.' We hurry through our meals to go to work and hurry through our work in order to 'recreate' ourselves in the evenings and on weekends and vacations."[36]

In contrast, Berry urges us to see eating as a complex relationship with soil, plant, and animal—in short, an "agricultural act."[37] When we do so, we come to take great "*dis*pleasures in knowing about a food economy that degrades and abuses those arts and those plants and animals and the soil from which they come."[38] Seen from the perspective of an agricultural eater, industrial eating stops being very pleasurable at all. For the agricultural eater cannot utilize the thin conception of pleasure engendered by the industrial view—a conception on which food satisfies so long as it looks like the box, tastes salty enough, and doesn't take long to prepare. The agricultural eater understands that eating is—or should be able to be—an extensive pleasure. Here is Berry's first pass at an explanation of extensive pleasure:

> People who know the garden in which their vegetables have grown and know that the garden is healthy will remember the beauty of the growing plants, perhaps in the dewy first light of morning when gardens are at their best. Such a memory involves itself with the food and is one of the pleasures of eating. The knowledge of the good health of the garden relieves and frees and comforts the eater. . . . A significant part of the pleasure of eating is in one's accurate consciousness of the lives and the world from which food comes.[39]

This is a wonderfully evocative passage; its imagery has inspired me considerably over the years. Understood from the perspective of a fully fleshed-out aesthetic theory like Korsmeyer's, however, Berry's notion of an extensive pleasure is pretty bare bones. It is not entirely clear how he is using the word "aesthetic," for example. And because we don't know what he means by the aesthetic, it is also not entirely clear (compelling illustrations notwithstanding) why anyone should be persuaded to call the pleasure of eating vegetables from his own garden an aesthetic pleasure rather than, say, a purely moral pleasure, an ecological pleasure, or even an economical pleasure. While Berry powerfully suggests (to me, the converted) that there exists a class of food experiences in which aesthetic pleasure cannot be divorced from ethical satisfaction, the prescriptive power of those suggestions needs some unpacking. Korsmeyer's aesthetic account is ideal for this task.

Reclaiming the Extensive Pleasure of Eating

So where to begin to fill out Berry's account? I start by observing that Berry implicitly understands what Korsmeyer makes explicit: eating is a communal, an intimate act. I see the negative side of its communality in his observation that "we cannot be free if our food and its sources are controlled by someone else"—which is how he would describe the current industrial food system, in which a very few corporations hold enormous control over the foods that eventually make their way into our supermarkets.[40] Berry understands communality to include not just other persons, but also the very animals and plants that we eat. He wants to know that the "animal has [not] been made miserable in order to feed me" and that the fruits and vegetables he eats "have lived happily and healthily in good soil."[41] "A significant part of the pleasure of eating," he writes, "is in one's accurate consciousness of the lives and the world from which food comes."[42] As Korsmeyer might say it, that pleasure comes from reflecting—with gratitude, perhaps—upon those animals and plants that literally become one, which is perhaps the most intimate connection of all. I would add that such pleasure would be enhanced by knowing that those who prepared one's food did so uncoerced and safely, and were adequately compensated for their work.

A second important feature of Berry's account that Korsmeyer can explain is this: the aesthetic pleasure I take in a particular food can be diminished or increased as a result of my coming to know more about it—specifically, more about its representational, exemplificatory, and expressive qualities. Berry invites this approach, I think, by his use of words like "knowledge" and "ignorance"; he suggests that an extensive pleasure requires us *not* to be ignorant in certain ways. And if we require ignorance of certain sorts in order to experience pleasure, then that counts as evidence that our pleasure is of a considerably thinner sort. Developing the capacity to experience extensive pleasure does likely mean reducing the number of aesthetically pleasurable experiences that one will have involving food (which gives rise to the inevitable question of why anyone would be willing to do so—why give up blissful ignorance?). But it may also have the longer-term effect of bringing me to seek out, make possible, foster, and demand that the foods I eat be prepared—from ground to table—in ways that can give me extensive pleasure. Done in concert with many others, this could have a profound positive effect on the food system, and all those who work within it.

Conscious Cultivation of Extensive Pleasure in Eating

So what do we do? We cultivate our capacity for experiencing extensive pleasure. One way to do so is obviously to increase our attention to, and understanding of, the number and variety of symbolic layers on which we experience any given food. In his own list of suggestions, Wendell Berry urges us to *learn* a great variety of things: the origins of our food, the economy of industrial food production, the best farming practices, the life histories of food—and to make food choices on the basis of that knowledge.[43] In Korsmeyer's language, we might rewrite Berry's urgings as suggestions to attend to the exemplificatory and expressive qualities of foods—to render explicit the implicit meanings of our foods by situating them in the contexts (both environmental and social) in which they were grown, the ways in which they were grown, and the contexts (environmental and social) in which they were prepared, and then making food choices on the basis of those meanings.

Through coming to learn about best farming practices, for example, we might learn to see particular foods as *exemplifying* not only particular times of the day (cereal in the morning), but also specific times of the year, and specific regions of the globe. If I, a Minnesotan, start to understand strawberries as exemplifying late June (as they would, for any Minnesotan rooted in an agricultural, rather than an industrial, understanding of eating), I experience considerably less aesthetic pleasure from those big, bright red strawberries I find in the produce sections of my markets in January. Rather than exemplifying a particular time (of the day or the year), these industrial strawberries seem to exemplify a desire to get outside of time, to make time irrelevant, to trick it. Once I start paying attention to their *apparent* timelessness, I might be led to inquire into the farming practices that are used to create that appearance. Will the berries also come to *express* unjust working conditions for farm workers, petrochemical intensive agricultural techniques, and the exhaust fumes of thousands of highway miles?

Furthermore, the failure of these berries to exemplify many of the sensory qualities I think of as characteristic of a strawberry— juiciness, for example—also might lead me to explore the reasons that supermarket strawberries have become woody, flavorless lumps. Contemplating my bowl of berries as having been bred to travel, ripen at a time convenient for mass picking, and look uniform thus further diminishes my aesthetic pleasure in them. The superficial pleasure I feel upon seeing something fresh and red in my January grocery stores might turn to deep displeasure, even revulsion, as I attend to the layers of exemplification and expression in which they are embedded.

In making these suggestions, I hope I am operating in the spirit of Korsmeyer's project. At the same time, I know that I am pushing her theory in at least two ways. First, by suggesting that foods have implicit meanings because of their situation in agricultural cycles, I push beyond her claim that foods exemplify because of their place in the framework of meals. I think there is justification for this, but at the same time, I am aware that I may have pushed the notion further than she would countenance. After all, in all her examples of exemplification—from the crispiness of apples to the "breakfastiness" of oatmeal—there is the definite sense that one can literally *taste* the property of the food in question. (Yes, we quite literally *taste* how wrong caviar is in the morning, if we are raised in cereal land.) In the case of strawberries in January, we might be able to cultivate that same feeling of inaptness of taste. But I'm not sure that I could guarantee that, in all cases of inaptness, one would be drawn to attend to the exemplified property by taste—or by any sensory experience at all, for that matter. And if it becomes a *purely* cognitive matter—purely a case of something I know to be the case about a given food—then have I stretched the notion of exemplification to its breaking point? For example, if it is true that milk from cows treated with recombinant bovine growth hormone (rBGH) tastes exactly like milk produced by cows not taking the hormone, can we still make an aesthetic argument about the experience of drinking that milk? I think it is exactly this sort of appeal that opponents of rBGH often use to urge people not to buy it. "Imagine the cow as you drink the milk." But doesn't there need to be some (sensible) quality manifested in the milk in order to say that this milk expresses certain properties?

To make this matter more three dimensional, consider this story, which I was told some time ago by the German filmmaker Helma Sanders Brahms, when she visited my college. It is a familiar enough kind of story; you no doubt have a version of your own. Brahms told me that, when she gave birth to her daughter twenty-three years ago, Werner Herzog came to visit her and brought her, among other things, a sausage, which he claimed came from very special animals raised naturally and freely in the pure mountain countryside of Moldavia. Brahms ate the first half of the sausage with relish, marveling at the deliciousness of the meat, the delicacy of the flavors, and so on. Then, when she got to the center, she removed the band around the sausage, and underneath it, she found the words "made in Munich for" and the name of a cheap German market chain. The second half of the sausage, she reported, had no savor.

The second way in which I am extending Korsmeyer is by suggesting that we ought to cultivate a particular kind of context—an agricultural context—and reject another kind—an industrial one. While Korsmeyer of course insists that the meaning of food is embedded in context, she does not anywhere suggest that one ought to change the context in which one understands food to be embedded. This is a level of prescriptiveness with which she might indeed be uncomfortable. For in suggesting that one change the context, I am of course suggesting that one try to replace one set of meanings with another.

Consider this example. Unlike "jet lagged" strawberries, a raspberry pie from the berries in my parents' yard vibrantly exemplifies the qualities of raspberries—their jewel-like color and tangy flavor. It also expresses—or metaphorically exemplifies—the love of my mother and my father, because eating that pie conjures up images of them tending the raspberry canes in their yard every spring, summer, and fall, picking the ripe berries, freezing them in their coffin-sized freezer, and then bringing them to me when they come to visit. (Raspberry pie, not chicken soup, spells parental love in our family.)[44]

Both kinds of experiences—the unseasonable strawberries from the supermarket and the homegrown raspberries of my family garden—can come to have a multilayered character that, at least in principle, enables some degree of the "insight and emotional depth" that give aesthetic experiences their weight and value.[45]

But in the case of the strawberries, an exploration of the layers leads me to an aesthetic experience that I would describe as deeply poignant, bordering on tragic—in marked contrast to its pleasant surface appearance. In the case of the raspberries, my exploration of the layers has (so far) only served to enhance and heighten that pleasure (which is not to say that it would necessarily remain so, no matter what I learned).

As I noted earlier, Korsmeyer suggests that not all eating has much cognitive—or, therefore much aesthetic—significance. However, I think that is to some extent a contingent, rather than a necessary, fact. While I don't mean to suggest that every meal can have the rich significance of a Seder, Christian communion, or a Hmong New Year meal, I do believe that many of our ordinary eating experiences are rich in implicit meanings that could be made explicit, thereby enriching the aesthetic significance of those experiences. Why do we tend not to do so? No doubt for many reasons—but surely one of them is that, in the industrial food system so many of us inhabit, making those meanings explicit will almost guarantee that our eating experience is less pleasant, not more so.

So why *wouldn't* we continue to be satisfied with thin pleasure, if the alternative, at least in the short term, is extensive *dis*pleasure? One reason surely is that even that thin pleasure is a very fragile thing, susceptible to being upset if our consciousness is permeated by an unpleasant or inconvenient feature of the food we eat. Such unpleasantnesses might include seeing a chicken truck drive by, getting lost in southern Wisconsin and coming upon a migrant worker camp, reading a statistic about the average distance traveled by one's food. It takes some work to ignore these facts—and over time, it may become more work than paying attention to them. Eventually, it may even require more work than does doing something to change one's participation in this industrial system.

Another reason is simply that thin pleasure is just that—thin. And if we have the capacity for aesthetic depth, and if aesthetically rich experiences do, as Korsmeyer suggests, "deliver" a "truth or realization or discovery . . . in a way that touches one intimately, that focuses and concentrates insight with poignant immediacy," then it might well behoove us to take advantage of the opportunities for aesthetically rich experiences where we find them.[46] In other words, multilayered aesthetic *dis*pleasure (to use a flat, inadequate word) might actually be far preferable to thin *pleasure*. (Note that, on Korsmeyer and Berry's accounts, even the gourmet may have only a relatively thin aesthetic experience of a food, if all they concentrate on are its sensuous properties. Perhaps Kimball, with his emphasis on "taste and technique," would be similarly impoverished.)

In her discussion of why food is not an art form, even though it is aesthetically rich, Korsmeyer notes that the history of food and the history of art are fundamentally different. "On its own, food is assessed only for a relatively narrow band of exemplified properties; art is assessed for all symbolic function."[47] In effect, what I am calling for is for food to be accorded the same treatment—not so that it can become an art form, but so that our aesthetic appreciation of it can attain whatever depth of which it is capable.

The summer I wrote this chapter, I was living in a boathouse on the Maine coast that has become my summer home. In my search for recreational reading that might speak to the place I was living, I came upon a memoir by Alix Kates Shulman describing several summers she spent alone on an island in Penobscot Bay, Maine.[48] Imagine my surprise when, instead of finding myself escaping from my work, I found a vivid example of someone cultivating the kind of capacity for aesthetic apprehension of food I've been advocating.

After her first (long, tedious, and ultimately disappointing) trip to the island grocery store, Shulman decides to make use of the copy of Euell Gibbons that she finds on her cabin shelf and teach herself how to eat of the things living around her. What began as a means of saving time and avoiding expensive, limp produce eventually becomes a passionate commitment to eating with the intimate understanding that her life and health are directly intertwined with the life and health of every living thing she encounters. The list of foods she eventually harvests (all in a ten-minute walk from her door) spans a full page. And she doesn't stop at Maine; she learns to eat what's growing in the mountains of Colorado, between the cracks of a Cleveland sidewalk, and in the backyards of Santa Fe.

Her descriptions of eating captivate me because, although she is deeply motivated by a set of ethical, environmental, and political concerns, hers are so clearly not the descriptions of food eaten by someone operating out of some Kantian moral imperative—eating devoid of pleasure, so one can be sure one is *really* motivated by duty. Quite the reverse; her meals are luscious, extravagant feasts, filled with unbelievable delicacies, cooked into dishes she creates through a wonderful process that employs equal parts daring, experimentation, and creativity. Her city friends, meanwhile, worry about her; isn't she starving to death? How can she possibly be getting by without anything to eat? A French friend writes to ask if she isn't "longing by now for a *boeuf en daube* or a *galantine de volaille*?" (She and her visiting friend laugh, she writes, "as we stuff ourselves with bouillabaisse."[49]) Hers is not the subsistence of an environmental martyr; it is the repast of a gourmet, an *extensive* gourmet.

I close with a passage from Shulman's work, a description of a meal she and her friend create and enjoy together one late summer day.

We browse through my cookbooks, perusing recipes, not as formulas or prescriptions but as hints and inspirations for impromptu inventions. Then we assemble our ingredients, take up our instruments—our knives, mixing bowls, measures—and begin. We slice green apples from my tree, scrub mussels and crabs, extract periwinkles from their shells. Margaret mixes dough and rolls out the pie shell; I measure the rice and season the mussel broth with juniper, bayberry, Irish moss, and a dash of wine. Then we build our salad, sampling each wild thing as we add it to the big wooden bowl. On top of the greens I sprinkle some of the goosefoot "strawberries" and a fistful of yellow charlock blossoms, bright and mustardy. Presentation counts. . . .

We set the table on the front deck facing the empty beach. Margaret pours the wine, I bring out the steaming paella, dense with mussels and periwinkles, dotted with red crabs and tiny peas. On the floor I place a pot for the empty shells, which we'll return to the sea. Our gorgeous salad shines in the wooden bowl, with its array of red, yellow and varicolored greens. . . . From our steaming plates rise invisible vapors, wafting delicious aromas to our nostrils, and I feel like a birthday child wishing on candles. We wish. Then we click our glasses, pick up our forks, and fall to.[50]

Notes

1. "Vegetarian Cooking for Carnivores," *Cook's Illustrated*, May/June, 2000, 31. The title evokes the image of recipes for use by lions and bears (animals that *really* consume only flesh) rather than by omnivorous humans like Kimball, Katzen, and Madison. While the matter of vegetarianism is of only tangential relevance to this paper, I would note that this title is a good example of a not-uncommon occurrence—the nonvegetarian who comes to vegetarianism with a chip already on his shoulder. Vegetarians often notice that the very food on our plate may get interpreted by others as a silent reproach, a tacit moral attack on them for their choice to eat meat. Some nonvegetarians sometimes choose to respond to vegetarians' perceived attack by drawing special attention to their meat eating, giving it more prominence than perhaps it does in their actual diet. Thus the name "carnivores" for people who in fact eat far more than just meat.

2. Peg O'Connor notes that there is something disturbing about Kimball's reference to L.L. Bean—the quintessential emblem of one kind of American middle-class correctness—when one considers that vegetarianism was often associated with hippies, and hippies were often dropouts from the middle class. Kimball seems, then, indirectly to rejoice in bringing these dropouts back into the middle-class fold, and watching as they trade their VW microbuses for Subaru Outback station wagons.

3. For a fascinating history of vegetarian food in the United States from 1966 to 1988, see Warren Belasco, *Appetite for Change: How the Counterculture Took on the Food Industry*, 2nd ed. (Ithaca: Cornell University Press, 2006).

4. While I rarely find it helpful to reduce natural language expressions to formal logical ones, in this case I think it might be useful. While Kimball argues that $(x)(Ax \rightarrow -Mx)$ or even, more strongly, (x) $(Ax \equiv -Mx)$, I am arguing that $(x)(Ax \rightarrow Mx)$. (A and M here stand for something like "is aesthetically valuable" and "is morally praiseworthy.") I'm not arguing for a biconditional, because I don't want to say that all morally relevant experiences are automatically aesthetically relevant. In the end, logic can't quite capture the connection I'm talking about, because it cannot show the causal connection that I am most interested in positing—the causal relationship between aesthetic and moral significance.

5. In the time since I originally wrote this paper, there has been a remarkable sea change in the United States regarding local food. Now the prejudice sometimes seems to be that "local food equals delicious food," while "imported food equals aesthetically inferior food." Regardless of the shift in elite consumer preferences, my point remains—aesthetic commitments are regarded as standing across a deep divide from ethical or political ones. Indeed, the defensive retorts made by aesthetes worried that their choice of locally grown produce might be mistaken for a political act ("The local ones just *taste* so much better"), illustrate that point.

6. Carolyn Korsmeyer notes that what she calls the "strict view" of aesthetic attention is fading from fashion. See *Making Sense of Taste* (Ithaca: Cornell University Press, 2000), 106.

7. See, especially, chapter 4, in Korsmeyer's *Making Sense*.

8. Korsmeyer, *Making Sense*, 104–14.

9. Korsmeyer, *Making Sense*, 142.

10. Korsmeyer, *Making Sense*, 143.

11. Korsmeyer, *Making Sense*, 141, 143.

12. Appealing again to logic, I want to argue that $(x)(Ax \rightarrow Mx)$, where there is understood to be a *causal* connection between M and A. I'm not saying $(x)(Ax \cdot Mx)$, or $(x)(Ax \equiv Mx)$. But I am saying that there is a relationship of necessity here—that moral considerations sometimes figure necessarily into the depth and significance of an aesthetic experience.

13. Korsmeyer, *Making Sense*, 99.

14. Korsmeyer, *Making Sense*, 115.

15. Korsmeyer, *Making Sense*, 118.

16. Korsmeyer, *Making Sense*, 118.

17. Korsmeyer, *Making Sense*, 119.

18. Korsmeyer, *Making Sense*, 119.

19. Korsmeyer, *Making Sense*, 127.

20. Indeed, as she notes, one needn't employ a cognitivist analysis of food to understand the flavor properties of food as aesthetically significant.

21. Korsmeyer, *Making Sense*, 129.

22. A notion she borrows from anthropologist Mary Douglas. See Korsmeyer, *Making Sense*, 129–31.

23. Korsmeyer, *Making Sense*, 131–32.

24. See www.bittermelon.org.

25. Korsmeyer, *Making Sense*, 134.

26. Korsmeyer, *Making Sense*, 117.

27. Korsmeyer, *Making Sense*, 132.

28. *Nichomachean Ethics*, chapter 3, http://www.sacred-texts.com/cla/ari/nico/nico084.htm.

29. Korsmeyer, *Making Sense*, 193.

30. Korsmeyer, *Making Sense*, 101.

31. Korsmeyer, *Making Sense*, 145.

32. Korsmeyer, *Making Sense*, 216.

33. I should note here that Korsmeyer herself expresses skepticism at the thought that a philosophical theory can make something come to

be the case—that a philosophical argument that food is art, for example, will actually make food be art—but I presume she won't object if I pronounce myself persuaded by her theory and choose to alter my own behavior on the basis of it.

34. Korsmeyer, *Making Sense*, 134.

35. Wendell Berry, "The Pleasures of Eating," in *What Are People For?* (San Francisco: North Point Press, 1990).

36. Berry, "Pleasures," 375.

37. Berry, "Pleasures," 377.

38. Berry, "Pleasures," 378.

39. Berry, "Pleasures," 378.

40. Berry, "Pleasures," 375.

41. Berry, "Pleasures," 378.

42. Berry, "Pleasures," 378.

43. Berry, "Pleasures," 377.

44. Indeed, as I offer the final edits to this chapter, the story has acquired additional resonance, since my father died this fall, and I have eaten the last of his raspberries.

45. Korsmeyer, *Making Sense*, 117.

46. Korsmeyer, *Making Sense*, 134.

47. Korsmeyer, *Making Sense*, 143.

48. Alix Kates Shulman, *Drinking the Rain* (New York: Penguin Books, 1996).

49. Shulman, *Drinking the Rain*, 145.

50. Shulman, *Drinking the Rain*, 133–36.

Chapter Seven

A Short Poetics of Cruel Food

JEREMY STRONG

Beneath the candelabra, beneath the five-tiers bearing towards the distant ceiling pyramids of home-made cakes that were never touched, spread the monotonous opulence of buffets at big balls: coraline lobsters boiled alive, waxy chaud-froids of veal, steely-tinted fish immersed in sauce, turkeys gilded by the ovens' heat, rosy foie-gras under gelatine armour, boned woodcocks reclining on amber toast decorated with their own chopped guts, and a dozen other cruel, colored delights.

Giuseppe di Lampedusa

What might "cruel food" signify? What dishes, products, and practices might be assembled under such a title? It is uncontroversial to state that for both animals and people there exist countless examples of suffering and injustice in relation to the production and availability of food. The conditions of their existence, their abbreviated lives, and often-protracted deaths are the subjects of many other works and impassioned media interventions, though human and nonhuman travails are rarely considered jointly other than through the well-worn rhetorical figure of describing especially abject circumstances as "unfit for animals." Focusing on human experience, a global economic system in which oversupply and obesity coexist with famine and starvation might justifiably merit the polemical conjunction of "cruel" and "food." A concern for animals would likely register the short, cramped, sunlight-free lives of battery hens—obliged to stand upon wire floors, spattered in the excrement of their neighbors, and nourished with antibiotics to prevent their succumbing prematurely to the infections such circumstances encourage—as a self-evident food cruelty. The same could easily be argued for the conditions of cattle raised on concrete feedlots. Fattened on a cheap and easily transported cereal diet rather than upon the grass, for which their complex digestive system actually evolved, their topsy-turvy predicament also routinely requires chemical intervention to avoid their unscheduled demise.

However, this study has a still more distinct focus. For the examples given above do not meet a criterion for what I here term cruel food; they lack a *necessary* and *manifest* connection between foodstuff and cruelty. Not *necessary*, in that eggs, chicken, and beef do not have to be produced by such means. Not *manifest* in that industrial producers do not like to reveal, and the consumers of industrially produced foodstuffs do not like to think about, the unpleasant aspects of food production. To make this distinction is not to assert that such modes of production are not cruel. They are. Rather, it is to acknowledge that the cruelty arises, at least in the main, as a consequence of industrial methods conceived to produce food cheaply for consumers who do not know, or do not wish to know, of the cruelties practiced on their behalf. There exists, I contend, another species of cruel food: culinary experiences and food items in which the element of cruelty figures not as a by-product but as a vital ingredient.

In the introduction to his excellent book *In The Devil's Garden: A Sinful History of Forbidden Food*, Stewart Lee Allen observes an important aspect of how we regard food and the pleasures of eating: "We now judge a dish largely by how guilty we feel about eating it—at least judging from today's advertising—and if it is not considered 'sinful' we find it less pleasant."[1] It is necessary to add a critical caveat; the "sin" Allen describes is largely represented and understood as a sin against oneself rather than, as is the case for the food experiences described in this chapter, a pleasure bought at the price of suffering by other sentient beings. In particular, his observation chimes precisely with that genre of food advertising in which a host of products are figured as decadent and happiness-inducing because of their propensity to make consumers fat. The appurtenances of this genre are wholly familiar, especially its use of sexualized images to amplify the theme of guilty, secret, bodily pleasures. Fresh cream cakes are "naughty but nice," for example.[2] Chocolate and ice creams are consumed (and presumably expelled between takes) by slim models for whom this surfeit of ingestion provokes sexual rapture as the longed-for object threatens to, and frequently does, spill from their mouths. Lascivious voice-overs mount adjectives upon images of foodstuffs being carved and greedily deconstructed, even bursting open in their enthusiasm to surrender the glistening delights of their insides. The figuration of these calorific pleasures as "sinful" is related to the transformation of Lent into a springtime slimming exercise or health kick, an act of denial (of alcohol, chocolate, cigarettes), with oneself as the sole beneficiary. With the attainment of the lean and youthful form enshrined as the proper object of watchful dedication, foodstuffs that militate against this resolution have become the moral tempters of our age. The triumph of their advertising is in acknowledging, even celebrating, the succulent devilry of these foods while simultaneously defusing their threat by representing their consumers as slender angels. Real consumers are presented, not with a consequential equation of *either* this (food) *or* that (body), but a fabulous yoking of *both/ and*.

The topic of this chapter intersects with aspects of the above, especially the themes of decadence and surfeit. However, whereas the notion of overindulgence as sin turns the matter and its repercussions narcissistically inward, cruel food is notable rather for the foregrounding of extrinsic pain (pain not directed toward the self) as the price of delight. There is rarely a masochistic dimension to cruel food, while elements of sadism may regularly be discerned. A key question of this chapter is, in fact, whether cruel foods represent a particularly heightened version of the exchange in which some suffering, or at the very least the loss of life, is simply the acknowledged cost of many edible outcomes, or whether cruelty is reveled in as a structuring element of our relish. In this latter formulation, knowledge of (or even participation in) the cruel quality of a particular dish would constitute a defining strand of the taste experience as, for example, the fair-trade guarantee channels and allows the gratification of the ethically purchasing coffee drinker. Hence, Brillat-Savarin's assertion that "a true gourmand is as insensible to suffering as is a conqueror" may constitute an especially direct proposition of a necessary correlative between fine food and pain, but his invocation of insensibility stops short of dissipated viciousness.[3] Sensual pleasure is still wholly vested in the materiality of the food experience, not in the knowledge that it has caused suffering. To participate in a culinary economy of life and death, in which the breeding, keeping, transporting, slaughtering, and eating of animals is conducted for human satisfaction, is necessarily to occupy a place on a spectrum of ethical positions. The confines of the present volume preclude all but the briefest engagement with those aspects of moral philosophy that pertain to killing and human-animal relationships. Yet in a chapter that many readers may, quite properly, approach in terms of right and wrong, it is necessary to address some salient perspectives.

A Foray into Ethics

The so-called Golden Rule of Christianity, to do unto others as one would have them do unto oneself, does not stymie the use and consumption of animals (or even the enjoyment of cruel foods) provided the "others" of the axiom is understood to signify only other humans. Common to philosophical traditions from classical antiquity until comparatively recently is the absence of accounts that afford what we might nowadays term *rights* (or even significant capacity for sensation) to animals. Descartes regarded them as machinelike, incapable of feeling, a perspective that facilitated his prompting that we should regard their screams of pain as nothing more than the sounds emitted by a clock. Kant took the view that it was indeed wrong to be cruel to animals but purely because the practice might incline us to be cruel to people, too; he did not allow them any intrinsic status. Spinoza counseled against feeling pity for animals, arguing that the natural difference between their emotions and ours made it wholly justifiable that we should use them as we please. For Wittgenstein, the key issue was "consciousness," in particular the higher levels of self-awareness enjoyed uniquely by humans because of our capacity for language. The lack of such a capacity in animals made it impossible to regard them as endowed with consciousness. Utilitarian philosophy, as developed in the writing of Jeremy Bentham and John Stuart Mill, had the great advantage of developing an emphasis upon the consequences of actions, in particular the consideration of outcomes in terms of pleasure and pain, two categories of especial relevance to this chapter. Utilitarianism assumes happiness to be the goal of human life and encourages calculations that consider the probable consequences of actions in terms of the balance of happiness and unhappiness, a method that may factor sentient nonhuman life into its workings. Notably, Bentham acknowledged animals' capacity for mental activity and suffering, key considerations that continue to shape discourses addressing animal rights and our responsibilities: "A full-grown horse or dog is beyond comparison a more rational, as well as a more conversable animal, than an infant of a day or a week or even a month, old. But suppose they were otherwise, what would it avail? The question is not, Can they reason? nor Can they talk? but, Can they suffer?"[4]

The last quarter of the twentieth century saw the publication of an increasing number of philosophical and scientific texts that challenged the "speciesism" inherent in most Western thought.

Work such as Peter Singer's *Animal Liberation* and Mary Midgley's *Animals and Why They Matter* helped shape the agenda of the animal rights movement by refuting those arguments that sought to postulate animal pain as different in kind from that experienced by humans and, in particular, by problemizing the issue of what affords people a superior claim to suffering-free lives over that of animals.[5] For many, though nonetheless a minority, a vegetarian (even pet-free) life that eschews the exploitation of animals for human nourishment, health, and vanity is the obvious solution to the ethical issues raised by meat eating and parallel practices such as animal testing. Overwhelmingly however, it is the utilitarian approach that continues to govern human-animal interactions, though few would recognize that their "commonsense" position was thus limned. It would now be rare to encounter the view that animals, especially the complex mammals and vertebrates we tend to eat, are incapable of feeling pain and discomfort in a largely identical fashion to humans. Nonetheless—such a "commonsense" submission might proceed—it is still acceptable to keep, kill, and eat them provided they are raised in a manner that acknowledges and accommodates their capacity to feel and are slaughtered in as instantaneous a fashion as possible. Such measures being in place, the gain to humans outweighs the loss to animals, not least because (their capacity for pain notwithstanding) the value of their lives does not approximate to the value of ours. To be sure, the adopting of such a position is significantly abetted by a supermarket culture that largely omits the facts of food production from the images and narratives of taste, mealtimes, and gustatory pleasure that it peddles to consumers.

In *The Ethical Gourmet*, a volume that combines recipes and food-sourcing advice, Jay Weinstein espouses an approach to eating that is precisely utilitarian. A theme consistently returned to is that consumers should not only purchase meat that has been reared according to superior welfare and environmental standards, but also that they should eat *less* of that meat in order to strike the proper balance between their pleasure and its many-sided cost:

> The better part of our nature laments the suffering of any creature, even if that suffering is at our hands. To reconcile our two desires—both to eat meat and to minimize the suffering and environmental impact of doing so—we need to reassess the place meat holds in our diet. The goal here isn't to eat no meat—it's to eat less meat. If, instead of putting a one-pound lamb shank in front of every guest, you divide one shank among four people as part of a rustic pasta dish, you've reduced the animal suffering and environmental damage linked to that meal by 75 percent. If one steak, instead of being one serving, is sliced into four gorgeous, satisfying portions, that meal generates only a quarter of the suffering and pollution that would otherwise be generated.[6]

A difficulty with Weinstein's formula is, obviously, the easy arbitrariness with which his "correct" balance has been struck.[7] What makes quartering, as opposed to halving or division into tenths, the appropriate scale of reduction? Does the hypothetical steak weigh a pound too? Is a whole lamb shank or steak per diner plain wrong, or could a sufficient interval between meat-based meals render it acceptable? What are the relative weightings one should afford to animal suffering and environmental damage? These questions are, of course, far easier to pose than to answer, and Weinstein is to be applauded for producing a volume that so directly foregrounds the consequences of consumption as well as indicating practical alternatives to or mitigation of the most problematic modes and products. Such publications and related television programs both reflect and create an increasingly informed segment of the Western public for whom the variously constituted credentials of their food are a prime concern. Ethical and other discourses including environmentalism, animal welfare, authenticity, health, and fair trade coalesce and occasionally compete for the attentions of consumers driven by considerations other than price. It is rare, however, that purchasers expect, or are expected, to sacrifice taste and quality in an exchange in which they are already paying a premium.

Generally, the food media conveys an impression of improved welfare standards, artisan and local production, equitable treatment of workers, organic farming, and so on, all serving to effect not simply an improvement—however defined—in the process but also in the material properties of the eventual product. One of the features of late capitalism, among its many and contradictory lineaments, has been a resentment in some quarters of the ever-more-powerful multinationals and a suspicion of the science, technology, and politics that serves them. Consumer considerations such as those listed above and the popular reception of texts such as *Supersize Me* are evidence of this positioning, which includes a desire to recuperate less industrial, less globalized means that ostensibly eschew the imperatives and teleology of capitalist production. Yet the currents of the free-market mindset run deep and, although we may accept paying a premium as a consequence of the diseconomies of scale and other financial disadvantages that attend nonmainstream methods, we still expect a better product when we pay a higher price.

Cruel foods occupy a conflicted position in relation to the various altruistic or "issue-conscious" modes and products that have increased in significance and market share over the last decade. On the one hand, there is an obvious dissonance between the moral or quasi-moral standing of the latter and the foregrounding of, or at least acquiescing to, cruelty that defines the former. Equally, as dishes and practices that sit outside the mainstream, cruel foods adjoin other types that are defined by consumers' particularity and their increased interest in and knowledge of foods. As I have argued elsewhere, food choices, and in particular the selection of esoteric foodstuffs, may be interpreted as the signs of a "distinction-seeking culture" in which culinary choices, attitudes, and aptitudes carry key social meanings.[8] This is not to argue that cruel foods are a new creation of trendsetting foodies. Rather, it is to acknowledge that they coexist more easily than might be imagined with a contemporary "consequentialist" food culture concerned with *inter alia* food miles, local markets, rare breeds and dwindling species, vernacular dishes and distant rainforests, workers' cooperatives, and genetic modification. Time for some specifics.

The Seven Cruelties
Death Agonies

The theme of an agonizing death is shared by several cruel foods and is here addressed as a matter distinct from the pain and discomfort experienced by animals throughout their lives. It may be linked to the issue of freshness, but more so to the erasure of that complacent void that now generally separates animal and completed dish. M.F.K Fisher described in 1936 a meal in Burgundy in which the enthusiastic servant brings for inspection her trout, alive in a bucket: "'Here is the trout, Madame. You are to eat it au bleu, and you should never do so if you had not seen it alive. For if the trout were dead when it was plunged into the court bouillon it would not turn blue. So, naturally, it must be living.... Any trout is glad, truly glad, to be prepared by Monsieur Paul. His little gills are pinched, with one flash of the knife he is empty, and then he curls in agony in the bouillon and all is over. And it is the curl you must judge, Madame. A false truite au bleu cannot curl.'"[9]

The defining features of the dish, the color and curl, certify for the diner its living evisceration and the manner of its death. This transcends any simple warranty of freshness; the fact of its prior presentation confirms the diner's dominion over those creatures that supply the table. Like a Roman emperor presiding at the amphitheater, this is the power of life and death, hinged on the whimsical desire of a moment. Other foods implicate their consumers no less completely in fatal transactions but this dish emphasizes how the diner occasions the proxy hand of death. If blue trout abbreviates the life-death-preparation-consumption sequence, live sashimi completely overturns it. *Ikizukuri* involves the cutting of fillets from a living fish, which are then served immediately. Frequently, the fish is reconstructed for serving, its organs and spine still intact, in order that it may remain visibly alive while its flesh is eaten. More familiarly, seafood restaurants with tanks of crustaceans offer a version of this mortal choosing and, just as there are those who delight in selecting their supper from the fated prisoners who bump and huddle together, so others cannot bear this responsibility and make their choice from the list of the already dead.

The spectacle of death, and the taking of pleasure in it, is central to the practice described by Seneca of bringing live mullet to the table in glass jars. Deprived of oxygen, they change color in their death throes. As with blue trout, color signifies the authenticity of the end-of-life moment and is sought by the diner not merely as the guarantee of "real" death but as a "sado-aesthetic" experience in its own right in which beauty and agony are inextricably bound:

> "There is nothing," You say, "more beautiful than a dying mullet. Let me hold in my hands the glass jar where the fish may leap and quiver in the struggle for life. See how the red becomes inflamed, more brilliant than any vermilion! Look at the veins which pulse along its sides! Look! You would think its belly were actual blood! What a bright kind of blue gleamed right under its brow! Now, between life and death, it is stretching out and going pale into a gradation of color of infinitely subtle shades."[10]

A repeated motif of many cruel foods is the prominence afforded to information about the lives and deaths of their associated animals. Campaigners seeking to ban certain foods and practices use information, and particularly images, to prevail upon consumers to amend their purchasing habits. Naturally this assumes that consumers do not fully grasp the facts behind purchases they regard as essentially benign, but can be made to realize the wrongness their buying engenders when presented with a transparent account of what is involved. This polemics of exposure has been employed to influence consumer behavior by drawing attention to human and animal welfare standards, economic relationships, and political conditions with products and issues as diverse as fur, chocolate, eggs, vivisection, and apartheid. Although it can be effective for a majority of consumers and mainstream products, it clearly fails as a mode of persuasion and engine of change in instances where cruelty is acknowledged or even celebrated. The decadent diner of ancient Rome presented with an undercover PETA video of a protracted mullet asphyxiation would have his appetite whetted, not subdued, by such a piece of gastro-snuff-porn.

Whether or not their deaths are actually worse than those routinely experienced by countless millions of other animals in both industrial and faith-specific circumstances, it is notable that certain foods foreground aspects of difference and particularity that apply to their killings. The fact that a particular dish involves or necessitates an unusual end affords it a property of exclusivity, just as celebrated brands, notions of *terroir*, the cru system, and protected denominations afford distinction to consumers by demarcating their purchases from others. At La Tour d'Argent Restaurant in Paris the signature dish is *canard pressé*, for which the duck is smothered so that the blood, which forms a critical component of the sauce, is not lost but remains in the flesh. Ortolan, to be discussed at length later, die by drowning in Armagnac. Plutarch describes particularly barbaric methods of slaughter in his *Moralia*: "In slaughtering swine, for example, they thrust red-hot irons into their living bodies, so that, by sucking up or diffusing the blood, they may render the flesh soft and tender. Some butchers jump upon or kick the udders of pregnant sows, that by mingling the blood and milk and matter of the embryos that have been murdered together in the very pangs of parturition, they may enjoy the pleasures of feeding upon unnaturally and highly inflamed flesh."[11]

An echo of this blood-milk admixture may be found in *Moby Dick*, where the narrator, Ishmael, describes one of the consequences of a whale hunt: "When by chance these precious parts in a nursing whale are cut by the hunter's lance, the mother's pouring milk and blood rivalingly discolor the sea for rods. The milk is very sweet and rich; it has been tasted by man; it might do well with strawberries."[12]

As Anca Vlasopolos observes, this troubling taste recommendation is omitted from several editions of *Moby Dick*, perhaps because it is so perverse.[13] The notion that the treatment described by Plutarch would enhance the quality of the resulting tissue has been discredited by modern research in meat science, which identifies increased levels of preslaughter stress as causative of quite the opposite effect. Yet the fallacy continues to persist, as for example in this report from *The Independent on Sunday* (London) on a restaurant in Canton specializing in rat. The proprietor, Mr. Zhang, opines that the mode of killing is critically important: "'Put the rat in hot water. The temperature must be just right, about 65 degrees. Wait until it stops squirming, fish it out before it dies and pluck its hair, cut open its belly and chop off its tail and head.'"[14]

Certainly a species of culinary Orientalism, in which the exotic and the pitiless are linked in the occidental imagination, underpins the Western fascination and revulsion with such stories. Weird meals and grisly food practices are merely the side dishes to an overarching fantasy of cruel and corrupt despots, harems overflowing with odalisques and concubines, and the perils—and allure—of such places for Westerners. This reaches its apotheosis in the myth of the live monkey brain dinner, here described by Paul Levy:

Naturally, there are a lot of famous Chinese gastronomic atrocity stories. The most famous one features live monkey brains, and I have been told it fifty times—but always at second hand, by someone whose friend, husband, or mother has absolutely, definitely witnessed it. It is claimed that decadent Chinese gourmands give banquets at which little boys are employed to shove shaven-headed monkeys up through a table with a hole in the center, following which the host slices off the top of the animal's head with a machete, and the diners eat the still warm brains with long silver spoons.[15]

Levy recounts how the tale arose in 1952 as a hoax perpetrated on campaigning journalist Arthur Halliwell by other British journalists based in Singapore. Halliwell reported the story in *The People*, linking it to a Chinese millionaire who then sued for defamation. The tables with a central hole do exist, but are merely for holding the chafing dishes used in traditional "steamboat dinners."[16] Although this origin does not preclude the subsequent possibility of life imitating art, the dish appears to exist only as a travelers' myth and in a variety of screen manifestations. Of these the 1978 pseudo-documentary *Faces of Death* and the second installment of the Indiana Jones franchise, *Indiana Jones and the Temple of Doom* (1984), where they are served chilled as dessert, are the most notable. In a stroke of breathtaking chutzpah, Spielberg relocated the monkey brain feast to India where, taken alongside the film's overarching imperialist tone, the motif proved highly offensive to a largely Hindu, mostly vegetarian citizenry for whom the monkey-god Hanuman is a key figure in the sacred Ramayana. The film was promptly banned in India, a fate more usually reserved for the excessively graphic *Faces of Death*.

Verbs and adjectives of violence predominate in menus and cookbooks more generally, often eclipsing the central nouns in a welter of searing, skewering, beating, and mincing. While it is the joints, cuts, and fillets of once-living foodstuffs that are the primary focus of such treatment, the orgy of bellicose procedures extends to the inanimate so that, as is frequently observed, even the cream does not escape whipping. By displacing brutality toward creatures into brutal treatment of their meat, this aestheticized language restores to consumers some connection to the active bloody business of hunting, butchering, and preparing food. "Restaurantese" is often derided for its flowery descriptions—for "foreign" words, provenance-obsession, and general prolixity—but the centrality of violent terms suggests a quite different need, however mutated, to retain and convey something of the life-and-death story that precedes the arrival of the plate. Our psychological relationship with animal-derived foodstuffs is further complicated by the counterdiscourse of soft sensuality operating within this idiom, of foods that are nestled, enrobed, bathed, and rested. Perhaps, like tyrants, our determining power is demonstrated not only through acts of force but also through arbitrary mercy and our oscillation between those poles.

Confinement

To a certain extent the issue of confinement may be said to apply to most of the animals we eat, certainly to virtually all the mammals and birds. Domestication and centuries of selective breeding have resulted in docile creatures that grow faster and bigger than their wild forbears and which, by means of enclosure, may be managed more economically than otherwise. The rearing of fish, from medieval carp keeping through to modern salmon farming, similarly indicates the increased rewards and predictability of supply that come with confinement. Cruelty arises, of course—the example of salmon is especially redolent of the mismatch between the great traveling lives for which they evolved and the cramped pens they must endure—but is not specifically sought either as a means or end. Other products and dishes however have specified confinement, often of the most unimaginable nature, as a prerequisite of achieving the desired taste experience.

Veal, the flesh of calves, has long provoked discussion and concern in terms of the practice of keeping the animals in confined spaces and deprived of sunlight, the opportunity to exercise, and iron in order that their meat be white and tender. Mrs. Beeton lamented another aspect of veal-related cruelty as early as 1861, stating that "there was no species of slaughtering practiced in this country so inhuman and disgraceful as that, till very lately, employed in killing this poor animal; when, under the plea of making the flesh white, the calf was bled day by day, till, when the final hour came, the animal was unable to stand. This inhumanity is, we believe, now everywhere abolished."[17]

The practice of bleeding has ceased but the Dutch "veal crate" system maintains the endeavor for whiteness on an industrial scale. Banned in certain countries, crates permit calves only sufficient space to stand up or lie down. Their diet is based on powdered milk and specifically excludes the grass and other feed that calves not destined for veal would ordinarily encounter. Jay Weinstein, describing the situation in the United States, maintains that "with the exception of the small amount of humanely raised meat, sold mostly by mail order, veal is produced in reprehensible conditions."[18] And Hugh Fearnley-Whittingstall observes that veal has been "widely rejected by the British consumer for the much-publicized cruelty of the crate production system."[19] Fearnley-Whittingstall also draws attention to a significant ethical complication in the veal debate; namely, that a thriving dairy industry routinely and inescapably produces an oversupply of dairy calves that are unsuitable for beef production and which, with a dwindling demand for veal, will be shot shortly after birth.[20] In short, yoghurt-eating vegetarians and meat eaters who reject veal have simply traded the cruelty of confinement for bovine infanticide. He does, however, offer an ethical alternative to this impasse, namely rosé veal, which eschews the crate and restricted diet but results in a meat that is darker than that produced by the Dutch system. As is often the case with volumes and articles that address ethical food issues, Fearnley-Whittingstall argues for a satisfying coincidence between the morally preferable method and the resulting taste experience. He describes rosé veal from a British organic producer as "robust and tasty," "far more interesting to eat than any white veal I have ever tried."[21] "Rosé veal" is also, of course, an interesting linguistic and marketing maneuver in that it decenters a traditional criterion of "vealness" or veal quality, namely whiteness. It establishes instead an alternative product category, which not only accommodates but actively foregrounds the property of darkness which, according to the traditional formulation, is a key marker of nonveal. The mitigating adjective may also work to denature the negative connotations that have accreted around the unadorned noun.

The cruelty of veal production seems primarily constituted in the restriction of movement. Practiced to impede the development of mature muscle, the reduction of living space also accrues additional financial advantages for practitioners in terms of other overhead costs. This denial of locomotion, itself a compounding of the denial of liberty upon which most animal keeping is predicated, is profoundly redolent of human-on-human punishment and torture. It is notable that, even for regimes that subcontract, locate offshore, or otherwise disclaim their torturing, a strict control of space, light, and movement is still admitted to be the foundation for "approved" psychological strategies to demoralize and break detainees. A sense of the unnatural pervades consideration of crated veal; notwithstanding that, again, one might contend that all human-animal interactions have been unnatural since earliest domestication, and increasingly so with the industrialization of agriculture. There is the unnaturalness of limbs that will never begin to test their physical possibilities—as opposed, for example, to the spectacle of exuberant lambs running and leaping in a field, and the unnaturalness of an artificial and prolonged infancy that deliberately results in a creature less developed than its age should suggest.[22] In this respect, veal production runs contrary to the current norms of meat production in which an *accelerated* development is sought, with the animal acquiring the optimum slaughter weight in the minimum time as well as achieving the best ratio of feed consumed to meat produced.

In many instances it is less than straightforward to assign a particular culinary practice to one of the seven cruelties. Several dishes and processes combine elements of more than one cruelty, and—as will be seen later—the preparation of ortolan merits consideration as a separate and extraordinary cruelty of its own. The matter of confinement forms a bridge to the topic of the next section, concerning fat and fattening, in that the former has frequently been practiced to achieve the latter. The Romans kept edible dormice in small clay vessels, called *dolia*, where their enforced immobility and force-feeding resulted in plump and tender creatures.[23] These were often conserved in honey and served sprinkled with poppy seeds. Plutarch also recorded that "it is a common practice to stitch up the eyes of cranes and swans, and shut them up in dark places to fatten."[24]

Fat and Fattening

This section might also be termed "force-feeding" since that practice, especially in relation to foie gras production, figures heavily in what follows. Yet since the yielding of unnatural proportions of fat is the outcome, and since other fat-related cruelties will be considered, too, the matter will be bracketed under a rubric of ends rather than means. The fattened liver of ducks or geese, foie gras is a product that may simultaneously connote both the apotheosis of fine dining and the worst of animal welfare. A sense of decadence links both meanings: the former in terms of the physical richness of its taste and texture combined with the high value the product commands, the latter in terms of a moral degeneracy that knowingly accedes to cruelty in exchange for such a pleasure. Foie gras aficionado Michael Ginor rhapsodizes about the "magical taste experience" of his first bite, a sensation that set in train a lifelong enthusiasm and his establishing of the Hudson Valley Foie Gras label.[25] His comprehensive, if monomaniacal, volume *Foie Gras: A Passion* includes images from Egyptian tombs as early as the third century BC that depict force-feeding—also termed "cramming" and *gavage*—of geese and other birds.[26] He cites the earliest recorded instance of ethical issues being raised in relation to force-feeding in a third-century Babylonian parable by Rabbah bar-bar Hannah that speaks of fattened geese and concludes: "The Israelites will eventually have to account for their conduct before Justice."[27] Much debated since by Jewish scholars, for eleventh-century Ashkenazi scholar Rashi of Troyes, the meaning of this final line was clear; the Jews, who in some accounts had learned the practice of cramming during their Egyptian bondage and had found goose fat to be an invaluable—and permitted—cooking medium, as they journeyed north and west across Europe, would account before Justice "for having made the beasts [geese] suffer while fattening them."[28]

Ginor's account of the evolution of modern foie gras production methods is essentially a story of improvements in science, breeding, and technique that have simultaneously led to the creation of ever-larger livers and a decrease in bird mortality during their rearing. He seeks to address many of the criticisms leveled at foie gras, its makers, and consumers: the blinding of birds and the nailing of their feet to planks to prevent their movement and facilitate cramming does not continue, if indeed the former ever took place. Ducks and geese have a natural propensity to develop enlarged fatty livers to store energy for their migrations, hence force-feeding merely capitalizes upon their existing physiology and cannot be compared to doing the same to people. The esophagus of a duck or goose is also flexible and keratinized, allowing large objects—like feeding funnels—to be inserted with "no discomfort." French scientists have demonstrated that although stress-related corticosterone levels are high in ducks during the first feeding, they are at normal levels for subsequent feedings.

Other accounts of the foie gras business take a different view of the cruelty issue. In his 1953 book *Blue Trout and Black Truffles*, Joseph Wechsberg describes a visit to Périgueux to meet Charles Barbier, foie gras connoisseur and general manager of a canning factory that processed the livers of geese reared by small-scale peasant farmers.[29] Barbier describes the cramming process for his visitor: "'When the geese are six months old, they are put into wooden cages and the farmers begin to feed them forcibly, stuffing the maize down their throats. Not very pleasant for the poor animals, but then, monsieur, some of the nicest things in life don't start out in a pleasant way. Rough diamonds are not a pretty sight. And Madame Dubarry came out of the slums, didn't she?'" He raised his hands after this aside, and continued, matter-of-factly: 'After six weeks the geese get so fat they can't move any more. You have to kill them or they might suffocate.'"[30]

In this account a degree of suffering is simply the necessary price. The visit concludes in Barbier's office with a block of chilled foie gras truffé and a bottle of Château Margaux. Whether the acknowledgment of cruelty impaired or inflected Wechsberg's enjoyment of the experience, he did not record. An often-cited passage from *Larousse Gastronomique* exemplifies the perspective that the force-fed bird is inconsequential, merely the vessel and means of production for its extraordinary liver: "The goose is nothing, but man has made of it an instrument for the output of a marvelous product, a kind of living hothouse in which there grows the supreme fruit of gastronomy."[31] It is interesting to note that whilst some defenders of foie gras emphasize the natural capacity of migratory waterfowl to enlarge their livers, this justification of force-feeding stresses and celebrates the determining agency of man. As early as Pliny's *Natural History*, which describes the process of cramming and asks, "Who was the discoverer of so great a boon?" the product and process were emblematic of man's (and, of course, Romans') special capacity to dominate and shape the rest of creation.[32]

For ethical gourmet Jay Weinstein the true cost of foie gras is such that he can no longer continue to enjoy it. He concedes that developments in production have mitigated many of the cruelest aspects but is still left with the problem of force-feeding: "The debate about whether foie gras production is inhumane has gone on long enough. It is. No, they don't use nails to keep the ducks and geese in place during force-feeding any more. But it's widely acknowledged in the scientific community that these animals live the final weeks of their lives in great discomfort, permanently gorged. . . . I love foie gras. Its buttery texture is one of the most pleasant culinary experiences I know. But I can no longer abide the cruelty that creates it."[33]

His weighing of the pleasure and pain involved has concluded in the assessment that he should desist. The foregrounding of *his* feelings—of the sensual pleasures of foie gras, of what *he* can no longer abide—indicate that the factoring in of pain and the desire to avoid it applies not merely to the birds but also to himself. Knowledge of the conditions of production impinges on the eating to the extent that pleasure is marred and/or that an element of consumer pain—of conscience, guilt, doubt—is introduced. Weinstein is hopeful that "enlightened agriculturalists" will find a way to make foie gras ethically defensible by encouraging over-eating and thereby obviating the need to cram.[34] Yet presumably, this artificially induced gorging would raise ethical issues of its own, particularly if it still resulted in discomfort for the birds as a consequence of their unnatural development.

Foie gras continues to be a hotly disputed topic, with changes in legislation and significant individuals' personal stances presenting consumers, campaigners, and waverers with a shifting landscape of messages. Production of foie gras will be illegal in California from 2012, and several high-profile restaurateurs have discontinued its use. Evidence of this fast-moving environment may be adduced from two of the volumes considered in the present study; Ginor's 1999 book includes foie gras recipes by, and a short biography of, celebrity chef Charlie Trotter, while Weinstein's later volume describes Trotter's "outing" in 2005 by the *Chicago Tribune* for his deliberately low-key but ethically prompted elimination of foie gras from his menu.[35]

A particularly eccentric-seeming example of human endeavors to yield increased amounts of fat from animals involves the breeding of fat-tailed sheep. Roughly a quarter of the world's sheep are described as fat-tailed and, although rarely kept in Europe and the United States, they are common across North Africa, Arabia, and as far east as Western China. Mrs. Beeton was familiar with the term and associated the type with "Palestine and Syria."[36] The term "fat-tailed" actually encompasses a variety of tail shapes and dimensions—the common feature being that the appendage stores a fat that is especially prized for its delicate flavor and capacity to melt at low cooking temperatures. Tail fat may be used in dishes as diverse as lamb confit and baklava. Modern texts on sheep production and farming include many illustrations of fat-tailed breeds, the tails of which range from very broad, but comparatively short, through to longer tails that reach as far as the ground. However, it is the animals with tails so absurdly distended that they must be placed upon miniature carts that have compelled the fascination of writers for at least 2,500 years. Herodotus described these creatures and their manmade adaptations as early as the fifth century BC: "One kind has long tails no less than four and a half feet long which, if they were allowed to trail on the ground, would be bruised and develop sores. As it is, the shepherds have enough skill in carpentry to make little carts for their sheep's tail. The carts are placed under the tails, each sheep having one to himself, and the tails are then tied down upon them."[37]

In a letter to the journal *Greece and Rome*, Juliet Maguinness describes her first response to this account, one that will surely chime with most readers, namely, the impression that this is "merely one of Herodotus' tall stories."[38] However, she acknowledges that numerous commentators have offered parallel accounts, spanning antiquity to more recent volumes. Early Jewish sources—the Mishna and Gemara—refer to the carts and their purpose, and *The Oxford Companion to Food* and *In The Devil's Garden* have near-identical illustrations of a sheep with a very long, very fat tail resting upon a low two-wheeled cart harnessed to the animal at its forequarters. The latter identifies the image as a "seventeenth century engraving."[39] Interestingly, although volumes in animal science addressing sheep breeds and husbandry routinely consider fat-tailed types, they have no images of or references to the carts, even as a disappearing oddity.[40] Yet Jewish food scholar Gil Marks recalls seeing Arab sheep in Israel with their tails on a cart and identifies the practice as still current in Iran and parts of Central Asia.[41] In his introduction to the 1981 Picador edition of Robert Byron's *The Road to Oxiana*, Bruce Chatwin—admittedly a writer in the Herodotus tradition of telling "the truth and a half"—also recounts seeing in Afghanistan a ram with a tail so large it was tied to a cart.[42] The geographical and historical span of tail carts is further indicated in a 1959 letter to *Greece and Rome*, again motivated by discussion of Herodotus's original description, which describes the practice of cart-fitting taking place as far afield as South Africa. T. J. Haarhoff writes:

> One of the prominent S. African wool farmers, Dr. Eitel Hayward, tells me that his father-in-law used to tell of the little carts they built to place under the tails of the sheep that were bred in the north-west parts of the Union. The wheels resembled cotton-reels. A tail could weigh as much as 20–25 pounds. There are cases where a sheep with a tail of this weight, on being suddenly scared, broke the tail at the base. This might indicate the reason for the "cart." My friend says the length of the tails of these sheep in Namaqualand (north-west part of S. Africa) could be from 30 to 36 inches. . . . But farmers are doubtful whether this cart arrangement could ever be of practical use. Many think it was applied in a

sportive spirit. And a Cypriot, who is also a classical scholar, Dr. Nikolaides, says that these sheep, which he calls "Turkish," had wheels put under their ponderous tails by children "for fun."[43]

These accounts open several interesting avenues in relation to a poetics of cruel food. That selective breeding should result in animals so misshapen that their tails are an impediment to natural locomotion, prone to injury, and even liable to snapping off seems a self-evident example of a cruelty practiced for gustatory ends. Though it should be acknowledged that virtually all human-directed animal breeding produces creatures in which a loss of characteristics and proportions that have evolved naturally over countless millennia is the corollary of a gain in other qualities sought by the breeder (meat, fat, reproductive capacity, and so on). The development of numerous breeds of dog (generally for nonculinary ends) is a related example of how desired characteristics are acquired at the cost of breed-specific health problems. Equally, the cart may be regarded as a humane intervention applied to reduce discomfort and the risk of injury, though this in turn requires appreciation in an economic context; namely, that the desire for valuable fat generated the physical disproportion in the first instance, and that a desire to preserve it necessarily inflects any endeavor to safeguard the tail (and its sheep). All of which assumes that the carts actually work. If not, as the skeptical Dr. Nikolaides suspects, the adaptation simply becomes one of the many torments great and small inflicted upon animals for human entertainment.[44]

Just as the genetic capacity to store fat renders certain sheep and the fowl used for foie gras susceptible to human exploitation, so the already-discussed edible dormouse finds that this propensity is instrumental in securing its status as an object of human culinary interest. Its Latin name, *Myoxus glis*, identifies fatness as a core characteristic, and it is also frequently described as the fat dormouse. A hankering after fat is not restricted to our interactions with domesticated or otherwise confined animals, though it is invariably the case that the wild forebears of those creatures upon whom we have practiced generations of selective breeding are significantly leaner than their farmyard counterparts. Allen describes a Dutch fondness for "the marine flavored fat of young herons, which was obtained by shaking fledglings out of their nest." He notes that the visit of a foreign dignitary to Zevenjuizen Forest in the seventeenth century occasioned the shaking down of more than five hundred birds for lunch.[45] This last example introduces two further categories of cruelty: infanticide and profligacy.

Infanticide

An undeniable arbitrariness suffuses the consideration, in a meat-eating culture, of whether or not it is appropriate to slaughter animals at an especially early stage. Seen from a moral-vegetarian perspective, the Rubicon has already been crossed, while the career carnivore might cite the inevitability of the creatures' place and fate in the meat business as reasons why a relatively premature end is neither here nor there. Yet there is clearly a desire among many consumers to believe that the animals we eat have experienced, indeed even "enjoyed," decent lives prior to their consumption. Most animal-derived foodstuffs that are marketed as ethical emphasize the comparative freedoms they afforded their charges during their lifetime; for example, the freedom to range or move about, or the freedom to engage in natural behaviors. Louis Owens describes how free-range chickens raised by smallholders "roam and scratch in the dirt, flirt with one another, fight, worry about hawks and bobcats, make love, and live full chicken lives."[46] Likewise, a common defense of foods that are hunted or fished in the wild is precisely that they have lived unfettered natural lives up until they are shot or hooked, while closed seasons prevent the taking of young stock.[47] An anthropomorphic impulse contributes to this desire in that, although we may stop short of expecting "meaningful" lives for farm animals, and although the fact of slaughter looms heavy over the whole affair, improved welfare conditions consistently represent movement on a spectrum toward what people think they would prefer for themselves.

Other foods, however, emphasize the extreme youth and lack of development of the animals they feature, though a conscious cruelty does not connect all such instances. For example, the Mediterranean tradition of consuming baby lamb—that is animals of up to eight weeks in age and weighing around twenty pounds—was significantly determined by the economic imperative to use redundant male lambs prior to the journey to summer pastures.

In parts of Spain and Portugal, roast sucking pig is a celebrated dish involving piglets of two to six weeks old that have only ever fed on their mothers' milk and weigh up to seven pounds. Gastronomic lore and ceremony surrounding *cochinillo asado*, as it is described in Spain, lays particular emphasis on the size, tenderness, and generally frangible nature of the roasted animal. The brevity of its postpartum existence is manifested through a range of structuring differences, physical properties that distinguish the dish from adult roast pork: the browned skin or crackling has the texture and thinness of parchment; subcutaneous fat (which the piglet has had scant time to acquire) should have been entirely rendered away beneath; the flesh should not have the color or muscular development of an older animal. Nowhere is the culture of *cochinillo* more valorized than in the city of Segovia, and especially in the Meson de Candido. A statue of Señor Candido in the Plaza Mayor shows him about to carve a piglet not with a knife but using the edge of a plate, so yieldingly insubstantial is the roasted infant carcass.

If the consumption of very young creatures accentuates the bitter sense of animals reared only to die, this is further compounded by dishes and processes that involve the simultaneous slaughter of unborn animals and their mothers. If all meat-eating occasions death, such practices amount to a doubling of this fatal tariff as well as an all-too-obvious inversion of the norms of birth. Internet sources and blogs brim with accounts of such activity; these are mostly mythic, frequently bedeviled by poor spelling and grammar, and often marked by misunderstandings of other cultures. Sensationalist content and the promise of grisly images generate the possibility of curious surfers clicking onto the many advertising links that accrue upon and form a major raison d'être of such pages. The only large-scale and well-documented occasion for the practice relates not to the food industry but to the production of fetal lamb fur, known variously as broadtail, *karakulcha*, and *cha*.[48] Bukhara in Uzbekistan is the center of this trade, which also encompasses the fur of young newborn animals, though differences and gradations exist between the pelts of those animals slaughtered as young lambs and those killed with(in) their mothers while yet unborn; further differentiation exists in terms of pelts by fetal age. The karakul sheep used in the trade, which are commonly subjected to crude and inhumane slaughtering methods, belong to the fat-tailed family, though—in a cruel irony—the tiny skinned lambs' bodies are worthless as meat and are discarded.

Although most Western meat eaters would reject the concept of fetal flesh, it is striking that the motif should figuratively reappear across so many cultures in the form of ostentatious dishes, usually roasts, in which smaller animals are stuffed inside the larger. The turducken (a *tur*key, containing a *duck*, containing a chick*en*) is an increasingly popular U.S Thanksgiving dish that owes its ancestry to more elaborate multibird extravaganzas of the French and English court. Recipes also circulate for camels stuffed with sheep, chickens, and eggs, and for sheep stuffed with lamb, and for goat stuffed with kid. A connecting theme that links all these, from the bona fide and commercially available to the wildly impractical and macabre, is that the carving and serving process should be a public ceremony in which the layers of content are exposed before diners' eyes. The connotations of generosity and lavishness that such dishes convey are not merely a question of total meat volume; rather, it is the suggested *mise-en-abîme* of costing a life-within-life-within-life. As Claude Lévi-Strauss has theorized, roasted meat—as opposed to boiled—already entails prodigality as a consequence of the loss of juices versus the total conservation of the sealed boiling vessel, a symbolism that eventuates in his statement, "The boiled is life, the roast death."[49] The munificence of the multicreature roast is thus constituted in its many deaths, actual and symbolic.

Profligacy

This category verges close upon another entrant from a deadly list: gluttony. Yet gluttony is not necessarily cruel, save in the sense that its practitioners may be contrasted to the many who must endure deprivation and hunger, and that the overabundance supplying the former could be redirected to the latter. However, under the heading of profligacy, it will be dishes in which surfeit and wastefulness acquire a willfully malign aspect that form the central topic. In *The Twelve Caesars* Suetonius observed of the Emperor Vitellius that his "ruling vices were extravagance and cruelty."[50] This included inviting himself to meals that necessitated enormous expense, sometimes to several unfortunate hosts on the same day; but his greatest extravagance was a giant dish he dedicated to the Goddess Minerva: "The recipe called for pike-livers, pheasant brains, peacock brains, flamingo-tongues, and lamprey-milt; and all these ingredients, collected in every corner of the Empire from the Parthian frontier to the Spanish Strait, were brought to Rome by naval captains and triremes."[51]

Layers of profligacy accumulate in this description: the implication that the rare creatures are killed merely to acquire a tiny body part or organ, the concentration and number of animal deaths the dish requires by using only such parts, the vast amount of human labor and travel it occasions.[52] Only its preindustrial status saves the dish from the crowning shame of generating a truly whopping carbon footprint; a cost that one suspects would have troubled

Vitellius very little. The zero-carbon claim cannot be made for the following anecdote concerning French author and gastronome Raymond Roussel. The labors his epicurean tastes set in train were indulged in an age before such considerations existed, but for the modern reader it is difficult to ignore the environmental consequences:

> Raymond Roussel fancied raspberries. Every day during the height of the summer season, one of his Rolls-Royces descended toward his property in the Alpes-Maritimes, while another returned to Paris, bearing a small basket of the precious fruit. Like the emblem on his letterhead—the "RR" of his initials reversed and interlaced in specular echo—the "RR" on the radiator of the first Rolls would find its mirror image in the redoubled "RR" of the second one, as they crossed paths, in palindromic elegance, halfway between Roussel's properties in Neuilly and the South. These raspberries, his own, were consequently the most expensive imaginable.[53]

Admittedly, compared to the many animal-related foods and practices considered in this chapter, it seems counterintuitive to contemplate interactions with the plant kingdom in terms of cruelty. Yet even for those who might forgive Roussel's raspberries as mere extravagance, the example of "millionaire's cabbage" is surely freighted with sufficient *schadenfreude* and decadent prodigality to justify categorization as a vegetarian cruel food.

At the top of the stem of the coconut palm grows the small apical bud. As the only growing point, its removal condemns the tree to death. The finality of this fact, and the disproportion between the many productive outputs associated with a living tree as opposed to this tiny harvest, ensures both its status as a delicacy and the rarity value its popular title evokes. Millionaire's cabbage, like Vitellius's Shield of Minerva, is a distillation of death. It is a flagrant reverse economy that foregrounds the paucity of edible volume gained as an index of an enormous not-consumed, off-plate, but nonetheless expended cost. Without the consumer's knowledge of this cost, the dish is nothing. Environmental discourses frequently stress the unsustainability of Western modes of consumption that exceed our implicit "one planet" resource quota, and the disappearing rainforest is commonly cited as evidence of our shrinking supply and growing demand. The millionaire's cabbage is then the closest approximation to the literal consumption of trees; a genuine one dish/one tree (minimum!) equation and embodiment of the forest eating that connects cheap hamburgers, palm oil, and destructive logging.

Cruelty on the Side

Foods may also be garnished with cruelty. Settings, events, and entertainments have all evoked or featured cruelties for the benefit of, and sometimes at the expense of, diners. M.F.K Fisher's summary of the culinary signs of Rome's decay describes its nadir in "Heliogabalus' trick of fattening his prized conger eels on living slave-meat."[54] Accounts of the debauched emperor's excesses have doubtless been exaggerated by his successors and by writers and artists for whom the decadent and sexually ambiguous youth has proved a rich source of inspiration and invention. Alma-Tadema's 1888 painting *The Roses of Heliogabalus* is such an example; seated with a few favored friends upon a raised dais, the emperor watches as an unimaginable volume of rose petals fall from concealed ceiling panels to smother his other, evidently less-favored, guests.

The cruelty of Japanese *nyotaimori*, which translates as "female body presentation" and is also known as "body sushi," consists in its humiliating treatment of the model from whose naked body the food is taken. Its piece-by-piece removal by diners mirrors the objectifying mode of the striptease in that more of her body is revealed as more sushi is eaten. Unlike the stripper however, who might be said to control the revealing process, the model is entirely at the mercy of her consuming audience. At best, the practice reduces the model to the status of receptacle who must endure the discomforts of ogling, banter, and prodding with chopsticks. At worst, she assumes a status equivalent to the other commodified flesh with which her skin so closely merges. Unsurprisingly, nyotaimori restaurants are popular in organized-crime circles.

In fiction, few characters have enjoyed such a sustained relationship with cruel food as Hannibal Lecter. Across a series of Thomas Harris novels and their movie adaptations, the cannibal psychiatrist has combined his enthusiasm for acts of meaty horror with an appreciation of gastronomy, the arts, and luxury goods. Intentionally or otherwise, the books and films have assumed an increasingly comic aspect in tandem with the amplification of their gastro-pornography and product placement. Jonathan Demme's adaptation of *The Silence of the Lambs* (1990) established Anthony Hopkins as the definitive screen Lecter and retained many of the culinary motifs and references from the book. Census-taker's liver with fava beans and Chianti was endlessly quoted and parodied.[55] And Lecter's selection of rare lamb chops after hearing Agent Starling's story of childhood trauma encapsulated his capacity to aestheticize human fear and transmute it into culinary experience. Indeed, the lamb chops function as the appetizer for his subsequent murder and partial consumption of his guards prior to arranging their deconstructed corpses into a macabre *tableau décédé*. An increasingly baroque and polymorphous food cruelty develops across the texts, which includes: Lecter eating other characters; a character cutting off pieces of his own face to be eaten by dogs; carnivorous pigs trained to eat Lecter as part of an elaborate revenge plot; and Lecter cooking and feeding a lobotomized victim material from his own recently exposed brain. These imagination-straining themes form the grisly counterpoint to Lecter's appreciation of glass and chinaware, upscale delicatessens such as Dean & Deluca, and the artistic glories of Florence. While the absurdity of the specifics has swelled, the formula has remained constant: taboos, violence, and the bloodily raw meet fine discrimination, culinary etiquette, and the carefully cooked. Just as Lecter's food pleasures span bites from still-living victims through to a preference for Anatolian figs with his foie gras, so his relationships range from long-nurtured antipathies to a paternal and faintly erotic regard for Clarice Starling.

Ortolan

A small and endangered French songbird, known as the bunting in English, forms the culmination to this survey of gustatory cruelties. The unfortunate honor is achieved firstly because the dish combines many elements of those cruelties already discussed, and secondly by its achieving notoriety through featuring in the last meal of French President François Mitterand. Described by Michael Paterniti in a 1998 article for *Esquire* magazine and much referenced since, this occasion and its menu are redolent of the topics of this chapter: death and decadence, consumption and finality, suffering and pleasure. The quotation from *The Leopard* with which the chapter commenced describes the culinary excesses of a crumbling aristocracy in Risorgimento Italy. The dish with which it concludes is now indelibly associated with the demise of a powerful individual who, dying of cancer, invited his friends and family for a final extraordinary meal. Marennes oysters (of which Mitterand personally consumed upward of two dozen) were succeeded by foie gras, then capon. Illegal in certain countries, capon is a cockerel castrated in order that it develops a distinctive plumpness. Hence, even prior to the arrival of the ortolan, this is a supper in which cruel and luxurious foods loom large. Given Mitterand's other excesses that led to comparisons with Louis XV—the architectural follies of the Pyramide du Louvre and Opéra de la Bastille, the mistress and natural daughter, the regal hauteur—a decadent send-off was surely to be expected.

Allen describes the process by which ortolan are prepared, a scheme in which the cruelties of *confinement, fattening,* and *death agonies* may immediately be discerned, as well as a connection to those masters of cruel food, the Romans: "The birds must be taken alive; once captured they are either blinded or kept in a lightless box for a month to gorge on millet, grapes, and figs, a technique apparently taken from the decadent cooks of Imperial Rome who called the birds beccafico, or "fig-pecker." When they've reached four times their normal size, they're drowned alive in a snifter of Armagnac."[56]

The creature is quickly roasted in a hot oven then placed whole in the mouth. In some accounts a cloth is placed over the diner's head; perhaps to conceal oneself from the judgmental gaze of God, perhaps to concentrate the aromatic experience. Endeavoring to reconstruct Mitterand's last meal, Paterniti describes his own experience of eating ortolan:

> I sever the head and put it on the plate, where it lies in its own oil slick, then tentatively I try the body with bicuspids. The bird is surprisingly soft, gives completely, and then explodes with juices—liver, kidneys, lungs. Chestnut, corn, salt—all mix in an extraordinary current, the same warm, comforting flood as finely evolved consommé. . . . Here's what I taste; Yes, quidbits of meat and organs, the succulent, tiny strands of flesh between the ribs and tail. I put inside myself the last flowered bit of air and Armagnac in its lungs, the body of rainwater and berries. In there, too, is the ocean and Africa and the dip and plunge in a high wind. And the heart that bursts between my teeth.[57]

In this tasting of the end-of-life moment, "the last flowered bit of air," the drowning medium of the Armagnac, as well as the traces of its traveling existence, ortolan ingestion embodies the critical quality of cruel food eating: its rapacity. All consumption is predicated upon taking, and, with meat eating, that means the taking of life. Although contemporary Western food culture downplays this cost, cruel foods foreground, jubilate, and dramatize the deaths and other forms of expense they necessitate. Multiple deaths, peculiar deaths, infant deaths, deaths close-at-hand, and deaths for seemingly infinitesimal gustatory rewards are cruel food's mainstay. To taste, or to claim to taste, or to want to taste, the markers of the ortolan's migratory journey in its flesh and organs is a measure of this rapacity. It is an imperialism of taste, a desire to annex and conquer more than one's proper share. For Mitterand this aspect of the dish was symbolically apt, ortolan being not only perhaps the acme of classic French gastronomy but absorbing also nuances of Africa, the continent where he had resisted the waning of Gallic power and influence. In a last defiant gesture against the imminent closure of his own being, Mitterand ate two of these rare birds, savoring the rich embodiment of their lives. He refused all food thereafter.

Notes

Giuseppe di Lampedusa, *The Leopard*, trans. Archibald Colquhoun, 158 (London: Harvill Press, 1996).

1. Stewart Lee Allen, *In the Devil's Garden: A Sinful History of Forbidden Food* (New York: Ballantine Books, 2003), xviii.

2. A British advertising slogan penned by Salman Rushdie in the 1970s.

3. Quoted in Allen, *Devil's Garden*, 221.

4. Quoted in Peter Singer, *Writings on an Ethical Life* (London: Fourth Estate, 2002), 33.

5. Peter Singer, *Animal Liberation* (New York: Random House, 1975); Mary Midgley, *Animals and Why They Matter: A Journey Around the Species Barrier* (Harmondsworth: Penguin, 1983).

6. Jay Weinstein, *The Ethical Gourmet: How to Enjoy Great Food That Is Humanely Raised, Sustainable, Nonendangered, and That Replenishes the Earth* (New York: Broadway Books, 2006), 44.

7. In fairness, it should be admitted that a stock criticism of utilitarianism is the difficulty of its practical application.

8. Jeremy Strong, "The Modern Offal Eaters," *Gastronomica: The Journal of Food and Culture* 6, no. 2 (2006): 30–39.

9. M. F. K. Fisher, *The Art of Eating* (Hoboken: Wiley Publishing, 2004), 478–79.

10. Quoted in Allen, *Devil's Garden*, 222.

11. In Colin Spencer and Claire Clifton, eds., *The Faber Book of Food* (London: Faber and Faber, 1993), 343.

12. Herman Melville, *Moby Dick, or, the Whale*, ed. Tony Tanner (New York: Oxford University Press, 1998), 348.

13. Anca Vlasopolos, "Intercourse with Animals: Nature and Sadism during the Rise of the Industrial Revolution," *Interdisciplinary Studies in Literature and Environment* 16, no. 1 (Winter 2009): 29–30.

14. In Spencer and Clifton, eds., *Faber Book of Food*, 344.

15. In Spencer and Clifton, eds., *Faber Book of Food*, 515.

16. In Spencer and Clifton, eds., *Faber Book of Food*, 516.

17. Isabella Beeton, *Mrs. Beeton's Book of Household Management*, ed. Nicola Humble (Oxford: Oxford University Press, 2000), 201.

18. Weinstein, *Ethical Gourmet*, 154.

19. Hugh Fearnley-Whittingstall, *The River Cottage Meat Book* (London: Hodder and Stoughton, 2004), 84.

20. Fearnley-Whittingstall, *River Cottage Meat Book*, 85.

21. Fearnley-Whittingstall, *River Cottage Meat Book*, 86.

22. An all-too-brief phase before they acquire the true dullness of adult sheep.

23. Allen, *Devil's Garden*, 54.

24. In Spencer and Clifton, eds., *Faber Book of Food*, 343.

25. Michael A. Ginor, *Foie Gras: A Passion* (New York: John Wiley and Sons, 1999), xi.

26. Ginor, *Foie Gras*, 3.

27. Ginor, *Foie Gras*, 11.

28. Ginor, *Foie Gras*, 11.

29. Most foie gras production now employs not geese but Mullard ducks—the sterile offspring of female Pekin ducks artificially inseminated with the sperm of Muscovy males. With large throats that lessen incidences of funnel damage and strong disease resistance that allows industrial-scale housing, these produce optimum results. Only

the male hatchlings are destined for foie gras. The females produce a smaller liver and are reared for meat.

30. Joseph Wechsberg, *Blue Trout and Black Truffles: The Peregrinations of an Epicure* (Chicago: Academy Chicago Publishers, 2001), 152.

31. Quoted in Alan Davidson, *The Oxford Companion to Food* (Oxford: Oxford University Press, 1999), 312.

32. Michael A. Ginor, *Foie Gras: A Passion*, 5.

33. Jay Weinstein, *Ethical Gourmet*, 196.

34. Jay Weinstein, *Ethical Gourmet*, 197.

35. Jay Weinstein, *Ethical Gourmet*, 197.

36. Beeton, *Mrs. Beeton's Book of Household Management*, 176.

37. Quoted in Alan Davidson, *The Oxford Companion to Food*, 290.

38. Juliet Mcguinness, "Fat-tailed Sheep: Another Classical Echo," *Greece and Rome*, 2nd ser., 4, no. 2 (October 1957): 173.

39. Allen, *Devil's Garden*, 72.

40. The following volumes were reviewed and no reference to tail-carts found: C. V. Ross, *Sheep Production and Management* (New Jersey, Prentice Hall, 1989); John B. Owen, *Sheep Production* (London: Bailliere Tindall, 1976); R. G. Johnston, *Introduction to Sheep Farming* (St. Albans: Granada Publishing, 1983); G. J. Tomes, D. E. Robertson, and R. J. Lightfoot, *Sheep Breeding*, 2nd ed. (London: Butterworths, 1979); M. H. Fahmy, ed., *Prolific Sheep* (Oxford: CAB International, 1996).

41. Letter to the author, June 16, 2008.

42. Robert Byron, *The Road to Oxiana* (London: Picador, 1981).

43. T. J. Haarhoff, "Correspondence: Fat-Tailed Sheep," *Greece and Rome*, 2nd ser., 6, no. 1 (March 1959): 67.

44. I am conscious that Haarhoff's letter, with its serial displacement of sources, is suggestive of a fable by Eco or Borges, a process itself compounded by my own sourcing from a fifty-year-old journal. While I make no claim with regard to the accuracy of what Haarhoff reports, the correspondence is entirely genuine.

45. Allen, *Devil's Garden*, 71.

46. Louis Owens, "The Hunter's Dance," in *On Killing: Meditations on the Chase*, ed. Robert F. Jones, 183–94 (Guilford: The Lyons Press, 2001), 193.

47. Such measures exist mostly to secure future sport and supply. Creatures that are regarded as vermin as opposed to game species enjoy no such prohibition.

48. See "Karakul Sheep and Lamb Slaughter for the Fur Trade" by the Investigative Services Section of the Humane Society of the United States (2001), www.hsus.org.

49. Claude Lévi-Strauss, *L'origine des manières de table* (Paris: Plon, 1968), 401–3.

50. In Spencer and Clifton, eds., *Faber Book of Food*, 332.

51. In Spencer and Clifton, eds., *Faber Book of Food*, 332.

52. Hugh Fearnley-Whittingstall's meat creed—based on the modern Western preference for muscle-based meat over organ meat—is "Waste is not acceptable. It's all or nothing" (182). In contrast, Vitellius' infamous dish gives pride of place to the culinary oddments, rendering as by-product the overwhelming bulk of each creature slaughtered.

53. Allen S. Weiss, *Feast and Folly: Cuisine, Intoxication, and the Poetics of the Sublime* (New York: State University of New York Press, 2002), 115–16.

54. M. F. K. Fisher, *Art of Eating*, 31.

55. Changed from the comparatively obscure Amarone of the original, Harris's choice of the more robust wine is probably the better partner to an earthy offal dish.

56. Allen, *Devil's Garden*, 73.

57. See www.esquire.com/features/The-Last-Meal-0598.

Chapter Eight

"Los Pajaritos del Aire"

Disappearing Menus and After-Dinner Speaking in Don Quixote

ROBERT GOODWIN

Miguel de Cervantes Saavedra's *Don Quixote* was published in Madrid, in two parts—the first in 1605, the second in 1615. It recounts the midlife crisis of Alonso Quijano, a late sixteenth-century Spanish gentleman of limited means who reads too many romances of chivalry, which he apparently believes to be true accounts of history. Suffering from a limited diet and a lack of sleep, he takes it into his head to become a knight-errant, adopts the name Don Quixote, and sets out across Spain in search of chivalric services to be performed. He engages with the world on the basis of his chivalric romances, but travels with a down-to-earth and gluttonous squire, Sancho Panza, a peasant farmer who is happy to take a holiday from his wife, but who is sufficiently ignorant to half-believe Quixote's assurances that it is usual for chivalric servants to be ultimately rewarded with the governorship of some island. As they proceed, these two physiological stereotypes—the fat man and the lean man—learn to negotiate both with each other and with a usually benign world. This intensely ironic work contains philosophical, political, and moral discourse and plenty of commentary on literary theory as it holds up a superficially absurd mirror to early modern Spain. It became an immediate best-seller across Europe and is now considered one of the most influential literary works in the Western cultural canon.

The appearance of *Educated Tastes* falls neatly between the four hundredth anniversaries of the publication of the two parts of *Don Quixote*, which have recently encouraged a vast scholarly output. Yet despite the current interest in cultural objects among literary critics and the burgeoning importance of food to cultural studies in general, only a handful of scholars have addressed the representation of food in *Don Quixote*.[1] This is all the more surprising, given that Cervantes introduces his titular hero in terms of what he eats: "Not long ago, somewhere in la Mancha, the name of which I do not remember, there lived one of those gentleman with a lance in the rack, an old buckler, and a speedy greyhound. He had more beef than mutton in his pot, he had pickled meat most nights, *duelos y quebrantos* on Saturdays, lentils on Fridays, and a squab on Sundays, which used up three-quarters of his income" (1:1).[2]

B. W. Ife has made a summary analysis of this diet and concludes that Quixote would have suffered nutritional deficiencies: "The consequences of long-term malnourishment of this order would be wasting of the flesh and loss of muscle tone." Moreover, his diet provides about 10 percent of the recommended intake of vitamin E, which would have caused "weakened red blood cells and neurological dysfunction, causing loss of muscle coordination, and vision problems." While Ife emphasizes he is not suggesting that "biochemistry can be used for character analysis in literary texts," all of these symptoms are typical of Quixote, and he argues that Cervantes intended Quijano's diet to offer a credible background to his reinvention of himself as Don Quixote.[3]

In that context, it is noteworthy that Cervantes's father was a barber-surgeon, at the humblest level of the medical profession. Javier Puerto lists a number of medical works Cervantes may have known and notes that Quixote himself indicates knights errant need to be "doctors, and principally herbalists" (2:18).[4] Juan de Aviñón's fourteenth-century *Sevillana medicina*, published by a Sevillian doctor, in 1545, refers to lentils as "bad and melancholic." Miguel Sabuco's *Nueva filosofía* (1587), based on observation and folk remedies, explains that such melancholic foods cause fear, suspicion, unhappiness, and bad dreams, all characteristics of Quixote.[5] Likewise, Aviñón explains that "mutton" (*carnero*) is "the most noble of meats" and is good for the blood and strengthens the natural heat of the heart, while Quixote's "pot" had more "cow meat," which engendered bad humors and also caused melancholia.[6] Sabuco also notes that "insufficient food, drink, and sleep, or serious acts of thinking or studying after a meal, all do the same damage . . . and when hunger reaches its limits the desire to eat disappears," causing "anger" and "irritation." While most readers of chivalric novels presumably thought of them as relaxation, Alonso Quijano was very much a scholar of the genre, devoted to reading them after dinner; moreover, Don Quixote rarely eats and is frequently quick-tempered.

The connection between diet and mental state is explicit at the beginning of part 2 of *Don Quixote*, when his friends urge his housekeeper to give him "comforting foods, appropriate for the heart and the brain, which was the cause of all his misfortune, according to sensible theories" (2:1). Later, the housekeeper remarks that she had "used up more than six hundred eggs," in order to make Quixote better when he was brought home "on an ox-cart, imprisoned in a cage," apparently convinced "that he was bewitched, arriving in such a sad state so that even his mother would not recognize him: weak, jaundiced, his eyes sunk deep into the attics of his mind" (2:7). Aviñón notes that eggs generate good blood and quickly form good humors, while another important medical work recommends eggs.[7]

Further evidence of Cervantes's awareness of a connection between diet and madness comes in the first chapter of part 2, in an account of a graduate from Osuna, who, on the verge of being released from the Seville madhouse, goes to say goodbye to another inmate: "I'll take good care to send you presents of food and you should eat them; for I can let you know, as someone who has suffered because of it, that all of our madness comes from having our stomachs empty and our minds full of air" (2:1).

Quijano/Quixote's first serious encounter with the outside world is at an inn, which Quixote believes to be a castle, where the innkeeper is described as being "very pacific" of temperament "because he was fat" (1:2). Quixote then eats his first ever meal that we know of at this fat innkeeper's castle, on a Friday, a day of abstinence. Where Quixote's belief that the inn is a castle is apparently a hallucination, a trick of language is presented as initially deceiving him over his meal: the only thing on the menu is salt cod, known as *truchuela*, "little trout," and Quixote indeed mistakes the cod for trout (1:3). This may have been a mistake some readers had initially made themselves, but such readers, unlike Quixote, probably realized the truth on tasting it. However, a popular contemporary proverb tells us, in the words of Sancho's wife, that "the best sauce in the world is hunger" (2:5) and Quixote is indeed very hungry at this moment. Shortly before arriving at the inn, he and his horse are "tired and dead with hunger," and we learn he is looking for "some castle or a sheepfold where . . . he might satisfy his great hunger." The point is further emphasized soon afterward when Quixote has trouble dismounting, "like a man who had not eaten all day" (1:2). Quixote, then, has been traveling all day in the Spanish sunshine without food and without sleep the night before, thinking about the inevitable biography that some wise man will write about him and which he must act out. These are circumstances under which anyone might be prone to hallucinations, while the nature of those hallucinations is a consequence of his reading.

Quixote's first meal establishes that his character and his hallucination are carefully juxtaposed with a verisimilar account in which the castle is an inn and some courtly maidens at the door are prostitutes. Cervantes indicates that those hallucinations are a product of what he expects from his reading, telling us that Quixote pulled up short of the castle, waiting for a dwarf to trumpet his arrival, while explaining that in reality a passing pig-herd blew his horn, which "represented for Don Quixote what he desired at that moment." Quixote, as opposed to Quijano, is entirely dependent on chivalric novels for his knowledge of the world. Therefore, he sees inns as castles because castles were the usual kind of building in which knights errant spent the night in chivalric novels. Similarly, in such fictions, young women are usually beautiful maidens.

Even within the story itself, Quixote is presented as Quijano's quasi-literary invention, who functions in the real world, and at one level the work can be understood as a simultaneous critique of early modern Spain and the chivalric novel, as each is seen through the prism of the other. (Quixote's literary identity as supplied within the story by Quijano is at times indistinguishable from his literary identity as text, as created by Cervantes.) However, Cervantes usually maintains the distinction by underpinning this all-important intellectual conceit of a living quasi-text within a text by giving a sense of verisimilitude to the juxtaposition of Quixote and the world around him, anchoring the reader's perception in the realistic world. To do this he establishes a sense of realism both through the narrator's reference to inns or prostitutes and by offering a plausible explanation of the circumstances that give rise to Quixote's warped perception. One of Quixote's friends underscores the importance of verisimilitude in fiction when praising the successful chivalric romance *Tirant lo blanc* because it describes knights who eat, die in their beds, and make wills before their death (1:6). Alonso Quijano will make a will and from time to time does sleep, while only three or four chapters in *Don Quixote* contain no mention of food.[8] As Quixote says himself before tucking into his *truchuela*, "hard work and the weight of arms and armor cannot be born without good government of one's stomach" (1:3), although this is advice he frequently ignores.

For Cervantes, feeding his characters is a question of verisimilitude. As Arthur Terry has explained, the many references to food in the work, when taken together, "provide a ground base of realism in a novel where many fantastic things happen."[9]

Cervantes presents the superficially ridiculous Quixote against a background of contexts that make him, his madness, and Sancho's decision to join him, plausible. He uses hunger, the dark (1:20), a lack of sleep, and the reader's expectations derived from mental schemas to create a sense of familiarity about the world Quixote moves through. However, that sense of realism goes beyond the mundane and the practical, and as the book develops, the moral and intellectual prerogatives and "realities" of Counter-Reformation Spain and its literature are brought into play.

Early-modern Spanish intellectual theorizers, and the wider community more generally, were obsessed with the idea of a deceptive relationship between appearance and underlying reality. When that underlying reality was revealed, the individual experienced a kind of epiphany in which the essential moral truth was exposed, a process referred to as *desengaño*, which approximately translates as "disillusionment." Cervantes sought to represent that process by drawing attention to the superficial artifice of his creation and then contrasting it with a strong sense of verisimilitude. *Don Quixote* is characterized by slippery dialectic illusion, which constantly shifts between the appearance of reality and the over-riding dialogic struggle between fantasy and pragmatism, which has been described as "the Sanchification of Quixote and the Quixotification of Sancho."[10] I suspect that as he wrote part 1, even Cervantes at first struggled to control every head of this unruly hydra he had created, but as he settled into constructing part 2, with the benefit of hindsight, he harnessed his beast through the wholly unexpected expedient of exploiting Quixote and Sancho's real (as opposed to verisimilar) celebrity, a celebrity Cervantes himself had experienced thanks to the actual success of part 1.

In part 2, Quixote and Sancho are recognized by a duke and

duchess who have read part 1. These "real" aristocrats now invite this "fictional" pair to their "real" castle, where their theatrically minded majordomo physically creates the make-believe world of a chivalric novel. Quixote and Sancho's experience is analogous to modern celebrities who take part in reality television shows and appear trapped by the realization of a fiction over which they have lost control. In due course, in a remarkable anticipation of politicized twentieth-century literary theory, both rebel against having their stories usurped by their readers and do what most texts are unable to do in the real world: they get up and leave!

Two meals presented to Sancho Panza are at the heart of two scenes that articulate this central and defining episode of part 2. These meals introduce social decorum to the carnivalesque appointment of Sancho as governor of a make-believe "island" called Barataria. They also embody a personal process of disillusionment for Sancho: throughout the book, he has been encouraged by the dream of being made governor of an island because Quixote has suborned him by telling him such rewards are common in chivalric novels. Yet when he achieves that dream, despite being remarkably effective at administering local justice, he quickly rejects it, partly because he does not get enough to eat. He had imagined such an exalted role would be one long feast, but he also discovers that he prefers simple peasant fare and the concomitant lack of responsibility to the fancy foods of governors and aristocrats. This was a period that had inherited notions associated with medieval sumptuary laws, and considerable intellectual effort was exerted in establishing a range of conceptual links between foodstuffs, eating habits, and social hierarchy, which were even reflected in Spanish social policy. When Sancho is appointed governor, Quixote advises him not to eat garlic and onions, in case the smell gives him away as a peasant, and to eat and drink in moderation. Sancho's investiture is then marked by a banquet at which his zealous doctor denies him every dish, one by one: "A plate of fruit arrived, but hardly had [Sancho] taken a bite, but [the doctor] touched the plate with his wand and it was removed with great haste. The steward brought him another dish. Sancho went to try it, but, before he had touched or even tasted it, the wand had touched it, and a page picked it up as quickly as the fruit." An astonished Sancho is then denied pheasant, rabbits, a beef stew, and a mixed stew known as *olla podrida*, which was very popular with all social classes in Spain.[11] Eventually, he is allowed to eat some breadsticks and quince cheese (2:47). With the reader's heartfelt sympathy, Sancho dismisses the doctor, but immediately receives a letter warning of a plot to poison his food; he is forced to settle for bread and grapes.

With the joke over, he is in fact allowed "a *salpicón* of cow meat with onions and some cooked calves' hooves," which he eats "with greater gusto than if they had given him Milanese partridges, Roman pheasants, veal from Sorrento, partridges from Morón, or geese from Lavajos" (2:49).

Sancho's success as Barataria's judge is based on wisdom entirely derived from common sense and proverbs, and in this, it is intentionally comic as well as satirical. Thus, it is appropriate that the peasant governor should eat a peasant meal of cow meat and calves' hooves, rather than partridge, pheasant, or goose. In fact, in part 1, Sancho makes this very point when he and Quixote seek a meal with some goatherds and Quixote invites Sancho to eat at his side, to which Sancho replies: "If I have to eat well, then I'll eat all the better standing up on my own than sitting on a par with an emperor. . . . What I eat in my corner, without manners or decorum, tastes much better, even if it is bread and onions, than the peacock served at other tables where I would have to chew slowly, drink little, wash myself endlessly, and neither sneeze nor cough if I want to, nor do all the other things which solitary freedom allows (1:11)." These comments mark both Sancho's sense of independence from Quixote and also his personal sense of social decorum. He is a peasant and it is not appropriate that his food and manners should be those of his master's table.

Sancho and Quixote eventually tire of the charade organized around them for the amusement of the duke and duchess. Independently of one another, Sancho abdicates his governorship and Quixote abandons the castle. After a number of further episodes related to the duke and duchess, they eventually escape permanently and are together again on the roads of Spain, in search of adventure. Once again, we find them arriving at an inn, which Sancho is relieved to find that Quixote sees as an inn and not a castle: "Dinnertime arrived, they retired to their room, Sancho asked their host what he could give them to eat, to which the host replied that . . . he could ask for whatever he liked, for his inn was stocked with all the little birds of the air, the game on the ground, and all the fish in the sea." Sancho is offered a meal worthy of an imperial or ducal table, for the phrase "to ask for the little birds of the air" (*pedir las pajaritos del aire*), meant to ask for the choicest foodstuffs. But Sancho replies: "So much is not necessary . . . with a couple of roast chickens we'll have quite enough." However, it turns out that the innkeeper has no chickens. Sancho suggests a capon and, when that fails, he asks for veal, kid, eggs, or bacon, but the innkeeper has none of these either. Sancho is driven to ask what is really on the menu, to which the innkeeper replies: "What I really and truly have are two cow's hooves which look like veal hooves, or two veal hooves which look like cow's hooves; they are stewed with garbanzos, onions, and bacon; and right now they are saying: 'Eat me! Eat me!'" (2:59).

Sancho's governorship and the episodes at the castle highlight Cervantes's own ideas about what is permissible in fiction and above all his focus on verisimilitude. It is a carnivalesque episode in which the fictional world of *Don Quixote* is appropriated by the duke and duchess and turned upside down. Sancho cuts the classic ridiculous figure of the carnival who is elevated to the throne, while Quixote, with his ascetic, Lenten gravitas and misinformed idealism, is relentlessly made a figure of fun during his stay at the castle.[12] But Cervantes's carnival is also inverted, for Sancho finds himself denied the plethora of food that the carnival character always has on offer: he has boarded Quixote's ship of fools in search of the mythical land of plenty, Cockaigne, only to arrive and discover that he is not allowed to partake of the milk and honey; and more than that, he does not find it to his liking. At the castle, the roles of author and reader are reversed in similarly carnivalesque fashion as Don Quixote—who has styled himself as autobiographer ever since Quijano adopted his new persona—finds his narrative wrested from him. This struggle for control of the fiction emerges at the end of part 1, when Quixote is imprisoned on the back of an ox cart and forced to return to his village so that he can be cured of his madness (1:56). That struggle intensifies in part 2 with the castle episode as its centerpiece.

Sancho's first vanishing meal marks his deliberate separation from Quixote by the duke and duchess. The meal itself is presented as being really on the table, unlike the innkeeper's fictional menu, and Sancho is simply denied the chance to eat it. That image of a glutton who usually has to make do with a relatively limited amount of simple fare and this banquet that he cannot touch highlights the extent to which Sancho has become dislocated from his usual context. Sancho's long-standing, but literally quixotic ambition to become a governor has only been realized because he is a celebrity, a fictional character in part 1, who has been recognized and therefore patronized by the duchess. That, of course, can only happen in fiction, for Sancho is fictional, yet Cervantes uses the trick of relative verisimilitude to persuade the reader to perceive the duke and duchess as somehow real and Sancho as somehow realized within their theatrical reality. Briefly, we are allowed to see Sancho as a peasant realizing his dream of becoming a governor, just long enough for Sancho to become disillusioned with a governor's lot, before Cervantes reminds us that Sancho's governorship is a theatrical fiction anyway by making the banquet vanish as the doctor waves his wand like some wizard from chivalric fiction. The governor's banquet epitomizes the marvelous and quite unexpected moment when Sancho's dream is realized and then denied, while the innkeeper's subsequent claim to be able to offer Sancho whatever he might want draws attention to the endless possibilities of fiction: Cervantes draws attention to the fact that should he wish to do so, he can create an innkeeper whose larder is infinitely stocked. But while exquisite foods can plausibly appear on Sancho's dinner table at a ducal castle, were the same thing to happen at a seventeenth-century wayside inn, the fiction would become implausible. Such things only happen in romances of chivalry. Having suggested the possibility of a fantastical meal at the inn, Cervantes takes it away plate by plate, just as the doctor took Sancho's meal away from him, leaving Sancho and his readers with a plausible meal of bovine hooves. Those hooves are uncertainly identified as either calf or cow, reminding us that fiction often needs only to make a suggestion that leaves much of the work to readers' imaginations.

The innkeeper's meal of cow- or calf hooves marks the return of the narrative to the default state of the book: Quixote and Sancho are on the road again after their fantastic excursion into the world of the ducal castle and the apparent, but theatrical and illusionary, realization of their fictional identities. The reader is reminded that in "reality" they are a pair of eccentrics who anachronistically play the roles of a knight-errant and his squire by engaging with a recognizably contemporary landscape.

Cervantes quite deliberately returns Quixote, Sancho, and the reader to this familiar, default state, at this point. He needs his protagonists to be once again authors of their own adventures and his readers to be firmly in their armchairs, prohibited from engaging in any further quixotic attempts to recreate fiction in the real world. For, as the hooves are brought to the table, Quixote and Sancho overhear a conversation in the next-door room: two travelers are about to continue reading a "pirate" continuation of *Don Quixote*, a real work that was indeed published by some unknown author under the pseudonym Avellaneda, in 1614. As Quixote realizes what the travelers have been reading, he becomes outraged, as Cervantes must have been when the apocryphal sequel appeared. Until now, Quixote's stated goal in Cervantes's part 2 has been to take part in jousting at Saragossa, but that has also been his intention in the apocryphal part 2. Determined to regain control of the story, Quixote changes his plans and immediately announces that they are in fact going to go to Barcelona, denying the imposter authenticity, while Cervantes regains control of his own characters.

Even in the context of *Educated Tastes*, it is worth reminding ourselves that foodways have become so imbued with cultural symbolism that it is easy to forget that we are basically engaged in refueling when we choose a "seasonal ragout of quail and partridge cooked in a ginger and balsamic soy reduction, with soft-roast parsnip and garbanzo," because, as I carefully match it to a glass of Alsatian Gewurztraminer—having checked with the sommelier to make sure it has a crisp, dry edge to its slight floral sweetness—I am displaying my social sophistication as much as preparing the way to gastric delight. The dichotomy between moments of Panzaresque cow-hoof eating—now more likely to be ground into a cheap hamburger—and the elaborate fusion of flavors in a modern dish of "pajaritos del aire" remains symbolic today. But during the early modern period, Europeans frequently suffered severe local famines, which from time to time became widespread. Dearth was a reality in a way no longer familiar in the Western world, sharpening awareness of the importance of food and the symbolic meaning of foodways. References to and the depiction of food had even more capacity to make a mouth water then than they do today.

Cervantes's contemporary, the great court painter Diego Velázquez, launched his career in Seville, where, between 1615 and the early 1620s, he painted a number of genre works combining still-life elements and human figures engaged in everyday activities relating to the preparation and consumption of food and drink. Inspired by a Caravaggio-like chiaroscuro and subject matter drawn from Dutch painting, these works show intimate tavern or kitchen scenes in which a few figures are gathered around a table on which there is a limited amount of food. As viewers, we are seemingly invited to join the company at the table, our perspective that of another guest.

By the first decades of the seventeenth century, Spaniards were beginning to refer to this type of genre painting as a *bodegón*, a word that today encompasses both still life and genre painting. The word derives from *bodega*, a winery, and bodegón was first used to describe the food stalls that were once often set up near the entrance to wine shops, a traditional arrangement that has only disappeared from Seville in recent years and which had its origins in the widespread prohibition on the sale of food and alcohol in the same place across early modern Castile, ostensibly on moral grounds. By Velázquez's day, the word was used generally to describe the various eating houses and food stalls that were an essential public service in the cities of early modern Spain in general and Seville in particular.

In 1502, Seville had been granted a monopoly on trade with Spanish colonies in the New World, attracting a large number of merchants and adventurers to the city, from both Spain and elsewhere. A combination of this large transient population and wealth from America made inns, taverns, and public restaurants an affordable necessity. However, the very nature of such places and their clients caused regular moral outcry and there were frequent attempts to limit the bodegones and control what they could serve. The bodegón was a byword for iniquity and lax morality, but these establishments were also seen as a threat to the gastronomic hierarchy in much the same way as Sancho's banquet: in 1630, the city fathers of Seville (the *jurados*) petitioned for the "casas de gula" (literally "houses of gluttony") to be closed down because there were now in excess of thirty such places, "to which all the game and fish is taken, where it is sold at excessive prices, instead of being sold in the public markets, to the great detriment of the people."[13] In fact, the bylaws of Seville theoretically prohibited taverns and bodegones from selling "partridges, rabbit, pigeon, other game, kid, or any kind of game bird." These attempts to control what kind of foodstuffs might be sold in which kind of outlet were based on the same principle as medieval sumptuary laws and were intended to ensure that individuals consumed food that was appropriate to their social status.

As a result, Velázquez's genre paintings appear to have met with disapproval because of their subject matter. The influential artist and theorist Vicente Carducho complained about artists who were guilty of bringing intellectual paucity to "el generoso Arte," "as can be seen today in so many paintings of bodegones, lowly and vulgar in conception, others of drunkards, yet others of card sharps and similar subjects of no more wit nor purpose than the painter's whimsy . . . to the detriment of Art itself." Worse still—as far as Carducho was concerned—were similar "devotional works, painted with such profanity and inappropriateness that they are hardly recognizable for what they are. Recently, I saw a painting of that holy visit of Christ to [Mary and Marta], all surrounded by such a quantity of food . . . that it seemed more like a house of gluttony than a holy refuge; it was strangely well painted and I am astonished by the painter's lack of intelligence."[14]

Carducho was probably complaining about the kind of Dutch and Italian works by Aertsen, Snyders, or Carracci, which had influenced Velázquez, who knew them through engravings, in which background religious scenes were dominated by an implausible abundance and variety of foodstuffs, all represented very naturalistically. However, perhaps the best known of Velázquez's early bodegones is *Christ in the House of Martha and Mary* (London, National Gallery), clearly the kind of mixture of profane and religious subject matter that so offended Carducho.

Although Carducho had grafted religious orthodoxy onto his complaint about hierarchy, his objection was essentially classical, for Pliny had described such lowly art as rhyparography, "sordid subjects," in his *Natural History*. Art, it was felt, should be above the representation of such lowly subject matter as everyday food-stuffs and the people who ate them. They should be banished from the walls of aristocratic palaces just as Cervantes eventually removed Sancho Panza from the ducal palace and his comic, carni-valesque governorship. But others disagreed, and Velázquez had a more powerful advocate than Carducho to defend him: his father-in-law and teacher, Francisco Pacheco, was inspector of paintings for both the Inquisition and the city hall in Seville and was prob-ably the most influential Spanish art theorist of his day. He asks rhetorically whether bodegones are worthy of praise, to which he offers the following reply: "Clearly the answer is yes! If they are painted as my son-in-law paints them . . . they are worthy of great esteem, for it was through these beginnings and by painting por-traits . . . that he discovered true naturalism in his representation, giving great encouragement to others by that powerful example. . . . When the figures are strongly painted, well drawn and colored, and they seem alive, and they are as naturalistic as the other objects in such paintings . . . they bring great honor to our work."[15]

Pacheco was intensely proud of Velázquez's "invention of natu-ralistic portraiture," which brought his son-in-law quite excep-tional success as the official court artist. But Pacheco's standard explanation for his interest in figures was that he conceived of the duty of the artist as being to serve the post-Tridentine Catholic Church, which saw art as the "Bible of the illiterate," the most important function of which was the representation of Christ, the Madonna, the doctors of the Church, and the saints. By con-trast, with lifelike figure painting, Pacheco considered the realistic depiction of foodstuffs and other still-life objects to be easy. The real talent was to juxtapose such easily painted objects with figures, thereby highlighting the realism of the figures in two ways: first, by setting the figure in a familiar, everyday context; second, by ensuring that the difficult figures are as realistically executed as the easily painted pots and foods.

There is a remarkable parallel between the way Cervantes uses food as a means to verisimilitude, as a tool to apparently anchor his fictional characters in a realistic world, and Velázquez's use of mimesis—the artistic analogy of verisimilitude—in his representation of still-life elements, kitchen utensils and foodstuffs, in order to emphasize the realism or naturalistic representation of his figures. This representation of food and eating as a way of giving life to characters in fiction or to figures in two-dimensional paintings neatly parallels the way food is essential to our continued existence in the real world.

The early modern period in Spain is usually referred to as the Golden Age because of the extraordinarily rich cultural output in art, painting, sculpture, literature, poetry, and drama during the period. It is important to understand that this cultural flowering took place in cities and towns that were growing fast, where very large numbers of individuals were thrown together for the first time in European history. The structure of society was changing, old hierarchies ceased to function, and sumptuary laws were abandoned as eating habits changed. Writers, artists, their patrons, and anyone with a curious mind were all interested in what was happening around them. Without the reductive vision of hindsight, men like Cervantes and Velázquez observed and recreated those aspects of that changing world of which they had experience. *Don Quixote* and Velázquez's bodegones are signally representative of the secularization of subject matter in the cultural production of the period and the rise of humanistic interest in the interaction of people, their place in the world, and their everyday reality. Cervantes and Velázquez showed eating and the sharing of food as central elements in those interactions. Recognizing that food was both a necessity and a luxury—and increasingly simultaneously so—they were able to harness the realistic representation of food to ground their work, to achieve verisimilitude or mimesis, while using the actual social symbolism of the real foodways they represented to contextualize their work more broadly. So while their subject matter was increasingly secular, these works were created and understood within the context of contemporary moral theories. For Cervantes and Velázquez, at one level, verisimilitude and mimesis were ways of exercising and displaying their technical skills, but more importantly, realism had moral purpose. Velázquez's *Christ in the House of Martha and Mary* has been described as a "bodegón a lo divino," or a "moralizing bodegón" because the "sordid subject" of the foreground is glossed by a small religious caption in the top corner.[16] An older woman draws our attention to the focus of the painting, the figure of a young woman in the foreground who is using a pestle and mortar, a motif readily interpreted at the time as a reference to sexual intercourse. Fish, eggs, and garlic are on a table to one side, all ingredients associated with a meal of abstinence. In the top right, there is a view of Christ preaching to Martha and Mary. José Camón Aznar has suggested that the older woman, who is clearly the same model as Velázquez used in *An Old Woman Frying Eggs* (Edinburgh, National Gallery of Scotland), appears to be the same sitter as a woman in a painting identified as a self-portrait of Pacheco sitting with his wife (Seville, Museo de Bellas Artes).[17] In this context, it is useful to note that Martha is the patron saint of housewives, for the painting is dated 1618, the year in which Velázquez married Juana de Miranda, Pacheco's daughter, and so there is good reason to think that this is a painting of Velázquez's wife and mother-in-law. Without documentary proof, we will never know. However, the biblical scene indicates that the young woman is to be interpreted as a wife, whether representative of wives in general—of whom Martha is the patron—an actual wife, Juana, or both. She is preparing a meal suitable for a day of abstinence and the subject matter closely suits the way in which a woman should approach her role in the kitchen offered by the religious theorist Juan Luis Vives, in his *Formación de la mujer cristiana*: "Our maiden must learn the art of cooking: not sordid, tavern fare with its immoderate foodstuffs for the consumption of the many, as professional cooks do; nor refined foods for pleasure; nor to encourage gluttony; but instead that sober art of cooking—clean, measured, and frugal—with which she cooked for her parents and siblings during her maidenhood, and, later, once married, for her husband and children.[18] There has been considerable speculation about what this religious caption may be: is it a scene in a mirror, is it viewed through an opening in the wall, or is it a painting itself?

Pacheco drew heavily on Cicero's *De officiis* in establishing rules for decorum in painting, linking them closely to temperance and morality. But in understanding how we should interpret these religious captions in Velázquez's work, it is well to bear in mind that in a passage in which Pacheco is expressing his own views about decorum, he argues that paintings should be neither anachronistic nor geographically inaccurate.[19] Of course, we cannot be sure that Velázquez was adhering to his master's opinions about this aspect of decorum, but if he were, then the representation of Christ, Martha, and Mary alongside the characters in the foreground who wear early seventeenth-century dress is clearly an anachronism. It is striking that the perspective of the background religious scene is "wrong" and that the figures are painted with much less technical ability than the foreground. While the foreground is strikingly realistic, with its juxtaposition of naturalistically depicted foodstuffs and vivid portraiture, the moralizing captions are painted almost as though they are intended to represent a painting within a painting.

In these works, Velázquez's startlingly naturalistic depiction of the foodstuffs means they actually appeal to the viewer as though they were real foods. They are a form of trompe l'oeil. This sleight of hand engages the viewer's stomach as much as the mind, drawing us into the painting, blurring the distinction between what is real and what is represented. Once we have been transported inside the painting, as it were, Velázquez then draws attention to the nature of his representation by the lack of naturalism in the moralizing caption. The moral message is abstracted from the representation of reality that it glosses. In due course, the viewer will return to the real world, accompanied by the moral gloss experienced within the virtual world of the painting. Ernst Gombrich once described the simple mechanics of this process, which he described as an "experience most of us have had. We go to a picture gallery, and when we leave it after some time, the familiar scene outside, the road and the bustle, often look transformed and transfigured. Having seen so many pictures in terms of the world, we can now switch over and see the world in terms of pictures."[20]

Not everyone has Gombrich's keen eye for art, let alone the world. But for the educated seventeenth-century Spaniard viewing Velázquez's *Christ in the House of Martha and Mary*, fish, eggs, the people who prepare them, and their reaction to these foodstuffs in particular, and food in general, had all been imbued with moral meaning. Their superficial appearance had been stripped away within the realism of the painting, allowing their true, moral nature to be understood: the process of *desengaño* described above. This is akin to the way Cervantes shifts Quixote and Sancho between the verisimilar world of inns, salt cod, and cow's hooves, and the fantastical, chivalric world of Quixote's vision, drawing the reader into the text before, in due course, attracting attention to the fictional nature of the story. At the end of a collection of stories, the *Exemplary Novels*, in a scene set after a meal at an inn, one of Cervantes's characters closes the book from which he had been reading the postprandial story that we have just read and says to his companion: "Vámonos al Espolón a recrear los ojos del cuerpo, pues ya he recreado los del entendimiento."[21]

Notes

1. Manuel Fernández Nieto, "La comida del *Quijote*," *Edad de Oro* 25 (2006): 157–79; María Luz López Terrada, "La alimentación en *El Quijote*," in *La ciencia y "El Quijote*," ed. José Manuel Sánchez Ron (Barcelona: Crítica, 2005), 189–207; Carolyn A. Nadeau, "Critiquing

the Elite in the Barataria and 'Ricote' Food Episodes in *Don Quixote II*," *Hispanofilia* 146 (2006): 59–75. The current chapter is adapted from my own PhD thesis, *Food, Art, and Literature in Early Modern Spain* (University of London, 2001).

2. No satisfactory interpretation of the dish "*duelos y quebrantos*" has yet been established, despite almost as many opinions as commentators; there is a limited consensus that it involved eggs. References to *Don Quixote* are shown in parentheses within the text indicating part and chapter. The translations are my own.

3. B. W. Ife, *Don Quixote's Diet* (Bristol: Department of Hispanic Studies, 2000).

4. Javier Puerto, "La materia medicinal de Dioscórides, Andrés Laguna, y *El Quijote*," in *La ciencia y "El Quijote*," ed. José Manuel Sánchez Ron (Barcelona: Crítica, 2005), 141–54, 141, and 142; Puerto draws special attention to a reference in *Don Quixote* (1:18) to the *Pedacio Dioscórides Anazarbeo, acerca de la Materia Medicinal* (1555), by Andrés Laguna, which he argues is indication that Cervantes had read it.

5. See Francisco Rodríguez Marín, introduction to Cervantes's *La ilustre fregona* (Madrid: Revista de Archivos, Bibliotecas y Museos, 1916); Miguel Sabuco de Nantes [published in the name of his daughter, Oliva Sabuco de Nantes y Barrera], *Nueva filosofía de la naturaleza del hombre y otros escritos*, ed. Atilano Martínez Tomé (Madrid: Biblioteca de Visionarios, 1981; first published Madrid, 1587).

6. Juan de Aviñón, *Sevillana medicina*, ed. Alfonso Fernández (Seville: Bibliófilos Andaluces, 1885; reprinted Saragossa: Gráficos Navarro, 1995; first published Seville, 1545), 100–101, 59, 110–12.

7. De Aviñón, *Sevillana medicina*, 96; Arnaldo de Villanova, *Regimen Sanitatis*, facsimile ed. in *Historia de la Medicina*, ed. by Juan Antonio Paniagua (Saragossa: Cátedra, 1980), 76.

8. Enrique García Solana, *La cocina en "El Quijote"* (Albacete: Diputación de Albacete, 1984), 9–10.

9. Arthur Terry, "A Consuming Interest: Eating and Not Eating in Don Quixote," *New Comparison* 24 (Autumn 1997): 56.

10. Salvador de Madariaga, *Guia del lector del Quijote* (Buenos Aires: Sudamericana, 1947).

11. Nadeau, "Critiquing the Elite," 64.

12. Mikhail Bakhtin, *Rabelais and His World*, trans. Helene Iswolsky (Cambridge MA and London: MIT, 1968), 22.

13. José Gestoso y Pérez, *Curiosidades antiguas sevillanas*, 2nd ed., ed. Manuel Grosso Galván (Seville: Ayuntamiento de Sevilla, 1885), 311.

14. Vicente Carducho, *Diálogos de la pintura*, ed. Francisco Calvo Serraller (Madrid: Turner, 1979), 338–39 and 350–51.

15. Francisco Pacheco, *El arte de la pintura*, ed. Bonaventura Bassegoda i Hugas (Madrid: Cátedra, 1990), 519

16. Julián Gállego, *Visión y símbolos en la pintura española del Siglo de Oro* (Madrid: Aguilar, 1972), 310; Allan Braham, "A Second Dated *Bodegón* by Velázquez," *Burlington Magazine* 107 (1965): 362–65.

17. *Velázquez*, exhibition catalogue, ed. Antonio Domínguez Ortiz et al. (Madrid: Museo del Prado and Ministerio de Cultura, 1990), cat. 4, 74–77.

18. Juan Luis Vives, *Obras completas*, trans. Lorenzo Riber, 2 vols. (Madrid: Aguilar, 1947; reprinted 1992), 1:994.

19. Pacheco, *El arte de la pintura*, 291 and 296.

20. Ernst Gombrich, *Art and Illusion* (London: Phaidon, 1960), 258.

21. Miguel de Cervantes, *Novelas ejemplares*, ed. Harry Sieber, 2 vols. (Madrid: Cátedra, 1995), 2:359; which loosely translates as "Let's go to the main square [of Valladolid] and see what we can see with the eyes in our heads, now that I have given your mind's eye something to think about."

Nourishment, Body and Soul

Modern Performers, Diverse Tastes

COLIN LAWSON

Music and food enjoy each other's company to an enormous degree. In fact, having one without the other is, for some, unthinkable. They certainly attract a common vocabulary, with the word *taste* somewhere near the top of the list. One could easily substitute music for gastronomy in the recent claim that "taste (as discrimination of flavor) is a function of refinement; empirical tastes are determined and organized according to cultural meanings and usages."[1] Music and food coincide in Orsino's celebrated lines in Shakespeare's *Twelfth Night*, where he reflects that too much music might have the power to cure him of love in the same way that overeating might remove one's appetite:

> If music be the food of love, play on;
> Give me excess of it, that, surfeiting,
> The appetite may sicken and so die.

Unsurprisingly, parallels between the delights of culinary and musical tastes have been prominent in a variety of primary sources throughout history.

All matters relating to the senses are difficult to describe in words but often present some striking analogies. In the food industry, a common word to describe flavor is *note*, while *texture* is a popular term across both areas. C. P. E. Bach, in rejecting the music of his father's generation, compared its baroque ornamentation with cooking that has been overspiced. Erik Satie likened the ripe chromaticism of Wagner's music to sauerkraut and compared it unfavorably with the fresh flavor of French music. Prokofiev flinched at the cloyingly sweet berries he sampled on a visit to the country, an audible metaphor for what he calls Chopin's "effete" nocturnes.[2] A recent book humorously correlates the respective musical and culinary talents of composers living between 1350 and 2000. It also suggests ways for listeners to distinguish composers' styles by way of gastromusical association.[3] Author Ira Braus claims the dubious distinction of having coined the term *gastromusicology*, maintaining that "the gastromusical metaphor helps us to better digest the sounds, sensations, and structure of music." More conventional literature revolves around music, musicians, and recipes, such as Al Stankus's *Jazz Cooks* and June Lebell's *Kitchen Classics from the Philharmonic*.[4]

The history of music demonstrates that food can play a significant part in the creative process. The influence of food and drink on the professional lives of singers and players has been a regular feature of didactic treatises. Music teachers (at least in print) have tended to counsel a moderate lifestyle, advice that has never quite reflected the world of reality. In addressing the management of the physical demands of musical performance, a recent edited volume focusing on strategies and techniques to enhance performance identifies maintenance of a good diet as a key factor in preventing injury.[5] The book also addresses the various effects of drugs, ranging across alcohol, caffeine, nicotine, antidepressants, beta-blockers, tranquillizers, amphetamines, cannabis, cocaine, ecstasy, hallucinogens, and opiates. The authors' advice inevitably errs on the side of sensible consumption, with exercise and psychological treatment preferred to beta-blockers as a cure for bad performance anxiety.

Appropriate quality and quantity of food intake has often featured among advice for performers, though such generously proportioned and hugely successful singers as Jesse Norman and Luciano Pavarotti are hardly encouraging role models. Indeed, some of the stories surrounding the career of Pavarotti stretch the limits of credibility. Recounts Leone Magiera, who often conducted Pavarotti: "The lightning cracks outside the window were terrifying. We were on a tiny twelve-seater plane, from Romania back to Italy, and seemed to be flying straight into the middle of a storm. At one point the turbulence got so bad that our airhostess gripped her rosary and started praying. It was then, amid all this panic, that Luciano Pavarotti piped up. 'OK, there's nothing for it. If we're going to die, I want to die eating.' He promptly grabbed an unopened packet of chocolate biscuits and wolfed down the lot."[6] Nevertheless, private flights were definitely Pavarotti's preferred way of transport, so as to facilitate moving the mountains of food that traveled with him. "He was always devastated when he got to immigration—usually in America, for they had the tightest controls on imported goods—and his cured hams and pigs' trotters got confiscated."

On a two-week trip to China in the late 1980s, Magiera remembered him

> flying over five refrigerators' worth of pasta, pesto, parmesan, tomato sauce and olive oil, as well as two personal chefs from his beloved Zeffirino Restaurant in Genoa. Two of the rooms in our Beijing hotel were even turned into kitchens. In one sitting, Luciano could eat twelve people's dinners; fifteen if it was lasagne Bolognese, his favourite dish. He ate next to nothing during concerts, though. He just had water with lots of ice cubes in—many singers would disagree but Luciano swore that ice was good for the singing voice. After

the concert was invariably a different matter, as we usually had an official dinner to attend, with the rest of the orchestra, concert promoters, sponsors and city dignitaries such as the mayor. They knew Luciano was a real meat-lover, so they used to put out lavish spreads of cuts for him.[7]

In 2004 the 350-pound soprano Deborah Voigt was famously sacked from the title role in Strauss's *Ariadne* at Covent Garden when she could not fit into one of the costumes, a modest black cocktail dress. As Charlotte Higgins wrote in the *Guardian*, she was obese: the kind of extreme overweight where her features had disappeared into a pillowy anonymity and she would panic when given a chair with arms. "I didn't feel good. My knees were starting to hurt", she said. "I knew it would be only a matter of time before diabetic or hypertensive problems. I was out of the large-lady dress sizes; I was about a size 28 or 30 (UK size 30–32). I think back and I just can't believe it."[8]

By the end of the year, she had had gastric bypass surgery and two years later was a UK size 14–16 and just over 140 pounds. Her long-awaited *Ariadne* at Covent Garden eventually took place in 2008. This story is instructive; opera houses have increasingly begun to accept that singers have to be right for a role, both dramatically and physically. Hitherto, opera has, fairly or otherwise, become known for its fat ladies. In an art form that traditionally valued the quality of a voice above all things, it long seemed reasonable to cast fleshy divas, sometimes advanced in years, to play sex goddesses or consumptive teenagers. Looks were secondary. Audiences were used to suspending disbelief. Voigt confesses that she is still a food addict and enjoys occasional fast food, recalling an occasion while driving when she took a handful of fries and stuffed them in her mouth. She was so ill she had to pull off the road. "It was so ingrained."

Musical history resounds to tales relating to singers and food, including the creation at the Savoy Hotel of Melba toast and

Peach Melba by the French chef Georges-Auguste Escoffier. These were in honor of Australian soprano Nellie Melba, who sang regularly at nearby Covent Garden. Favorites of other stars included Luisa Tetrazzini's turkey and noodles and Enrico Caruso's chicken livers.[9] Among the opera community at large, food variously serves to calm nerves before the performance and to help deal with the elation and exhaustion after a show.

Lessons from History: Some Practical and Philosophical Sources

There is indeed a long tradition of performance advice from which to draw inspiration. For example, J. F. Agricola observed in his *Anleitung der Singkunst* (Berlin, 1757) that the castrato Farinelli before going on stage was in the habit of eating one uncooked anchovy. Agricola's more general dietary recommendation for singers was a healthy diet of pheasant, lark, and trout. He observed that

> a good lifestyle and diet . . . are the best means for maintaining the health of the voice as long as possible, thereby necessitating very little medication. . . . A singer must generally avoid excesses in eating and drinking; if this is his usual pattern, once in a while it will not harm him to eat something very greasy or very salty. It does, however, do harm to the voice constantly to eat those things that make the lungs slimy or caustic or those that cause gluey, viscous phlegm, which would indeed do the voice no good. The old teachers specifically prohibited herring. . . . They forbade sour foods and foods cooked with lemon; experience teaches over and over again, however, that a spoonful of vinegar or a little lemon juice with zwieback is very useful in preventing or cleansing the throat of mucus, which is most harmful to the voice. On the other hand, many sweet baked goods and other sweets do exactly the opposite.[10]

Mattheson tells us that Bimmler, the former *Kapellmeister* from Ansbach, and a considerable phonologist, before an evening performance refused both tea and noonday meal, drinking only a warm drink with fennel from time to time, as he sang his part easily and gently at the keyboard.[11]

By contrast, the celebrated (and corpulent) composer Handel is now believed to have been the victim of a pathological condition that compelled him to binge eat. This in turn resulted in chronic lead poisoning from the quantity of adulterated wine he imbibed. Symptoms were stomach colic, pain, creeping paralysis, confusion, and eventually blindness. The poisoning may have contributed to his legendary bad temper and must surely have influenced the character of his music. On one occasion, Handel famously invited his friend Joseph Goupy to his house in Brook Street, Mayfair, for dinner, warning that the food would be plain. After the meal, Handel excused himself from the table and was absent for quite some time. Goupy eventually found his host in the next-door room, stuffing himself with delicacies. Furious, Goupy (a painter and set designer whose patron was the Prince of Wales) wreaked revenge in a published caricature, which showed Handel with a pig's head seated at the organ on a barrel of wine, a brace of fowl hanging from the pipes, and further food supplies in evidence.[12] Inevitably, the picture ended their friendship. Obese musicians were relatively rare in the eighteenth century, though among Mozart's near contemporaries Jan Ladislav Dussek (1761–1812) was notably rotund, as evidenced by a painting (1795) by Henri Pierre Danloux in the collection of London's Royal College of Music.

It need hardly be emphasized that any historical evidence must be interpreted in the spirit of the times. In 1811, when health was still a relatively fragile affair, Joseph Fröhlich's *Vollständige theoretisch-praktische Musikschule* (Bonn, 1810–11) recommended for wind players a moderate lifestyle and the avoidance of anything that could damage the chest, such as running, horseback riding, and the excessive consumption of hot drinks. One should not practice after a meal, so the afternoon was best avoided; furthermore, one should not drink immediately after practicing if the lungs were still warm, since this had been the cause of many early deaths. In the case of dry lips—very bad for the embouchure—the mouth should be rinsed with an alcoholic beverage to give the lips new strength.[13] Moderation seems not to have been a characteristic of one of the greatest wind players of that era. Weber's clarinetist, Heinrich Baermann, became markedly stout as a result of his love of food, in stark contrast to the emaciated figure cut by his composer friend.

Some fifty years later, in contrast to Fröhlich's supremely practical advice, Baudelaire provides heady praise for the salutary effects of wine and how it might relate to music. Allen Weiss has noted that "a taste for infinity" was crucial to the Romantics' art. He adds, "to these transfigurations of paradise [through drugs and wine] Baudelaire added the complexities of synaesthetic correspondences."[14] Baudelaire's light-hearted celebration of wine illustrates the system of correspondences created by his intoxicants: "I open the Kreisleriana of the divine Hoffmann, and I read a curious recommendation. The conscientious musician must partake of Champagne in order to compose a comic opera. He shall find a frothy gayness therein. Religious music necessitates wines of the Rhine or Jurançon. They contain an inebriating bitterness, as in the depths of profound ideas; but heroic music cannot do without burgundies. They contain the serious fire and the drive of patriotism."[15] Contemporary with this passage is his observation on Wagner's *Tannhäuser* and *Lohengrin* that "these profound harmonies appear to resemble those stimulants that accelerate the pulse of the imagination."[16] He went on to claim of *Tannhäuser* that "it sometimes seems, while listening to this ardent and despotic music, that one rediscovers the vertiginous conceptions of opium, painted on a background of shadows and torn apart by reverie."[17]

Traditions of Music and Feasting

Music was closely woven into the society of early civilizations; it maintained a close relationship with the pleasures of the table. Scholars have increasingly recognized the importance of music to the Greeks, which pervaded every aspect of their private and social existence. Sophisticated poets composed well-crafted songs for such daily events as dances of young girls and fighting men, weddings, funerals, processions, wars, drinking bouts, love songs, and political outbursts. A celebrated coming together of music and intoxication in fifth-century BC Athens was Euripides' Bacchae, whose singing and dancing ripped apart Pentheus in wine-filled ecstasy. The link between music and feasting had already been firmly evidenced by Homer, who in the *Odyssey* speaks of "singing and dancing, the ornaments of a feast."[18] In the *Iliad*, Homer describes a shield made for Achilles by Hephaestus: "On the shield he made two cities of mortal men. In one of them weddings and banquets were in progress: they were leading the brides from their houses through the town with blazing torches, and a loud wedding-song rose up. Young men whirled in the dance, while among them wind and stringed instruments gave out their cry; and the women stood in their doorways admiring the sight."[19] A fundamental relationship of music and food is again eloquently expressed at the beginning of book 9 of the *Odyssey*, where Odysseus remarks: "For myself, I would say that no accomplishment is more delightful than when good cheer reigns throughout the people, and banqueters sit next to one another in a house listening to a singer, while beside them are tables covered with bread and meat, and a wine-server draws wine from the mixing-bowl and carries it round to pour into the cups. This, I think, is the finest thing of all."[20]

Roman sources are similarly full of indications of the role of music in everyday life, which increased during the course of the empire.[21] Music was everywhere, whether a little light music after dinner at Pliny's villa or a noisy trumpet playing at Trimalchio's dinner party. Significantly, Martial remarked that the best entertainment was where there was no piper to drown the conversation, a seeming rarity. Ceremonial music achieved consistent prominence and maintained an intimate interaction with the culinary delights.

No chronicler of music and food can afford to ignore the year 1454 AD, when Philip the Good, Duke of Burgundy, as part of his promotional push for a planned crusade to Turkey, invited the cream of knightly society to attend his "Feast of the Pheasant," an event of unsurpassed extravagance. Little did guests suspect that when a giant meat pie was rolled into the hall on the largest of three tables, out of the crust would burst twenty-eight musicians—possibly the origin of the four and twenty blackbirds of the nursery rhyme. They accompanied the interludes of the choir that was housed within a church on one of the other tables. In addition, the towers of a castle squirted orange punch into its moat. With no expense spared, leading composers Binchois, Frye, and Dufay were all recruited to write music for Philip's extraordinary feast (whose associated crusade never did take place). Music included chansons and motets, the occasion enlivened by a bagpiper and trumpet fanfares. The main entertainment included an assortment of musical numbers and acrobatic acts, interspersed with three scenes of a play relating the story of Jason.[22]

European court society bears witness to an intimate, ongoing relationship of food and music. At the coronation banquet of the gourmet composer Henry VIII, for example, "there was a stage on which there were some boys, some of whom sang and others played the flute, rebeck, and harpsichord."[23] During his reign, Henry presided over a large increase in the number of court musicians, including a significant number of foreigners. The great seventeenth-century festivals at Versailles combined ballet, theater, music, feasts, fireworks, waterworks, and illuminations into a dazzling whole. André Félibien describes the first such event under

Louis XIV on July 18, 1668, a "light" meal of great visual impact composed upon five grand tables.[24] Significantly, the evening also included a musical comedy by Molière and Lully, *Fêtes d'Amour et de Bacchus*, in praise of love and drink.

Tafelmusik

From the sixteenth century, the term *Tafelmusik* was used to denote the musical fare at feasts and banquets and it occurs as a title for printed and manuscript anthologies. Although there are written and pictorial accounts of compositions and performances at table from the Middle Ages, it was only in the mid-sixteenth century that the genre became equivalent in stature to sacred or chamber music. Major sources include Michael Praetorius, whose *Syntagma musicum* of 1619 reported that vocal and instrumental music was performed at feasts as at intermezzos. In 1617 Samuel Schein published his *Banchetto musicale*, and other variants of the term included Isaac Posch's *Musicalische Tafelfreudt* and Thomas Simpson's *Tafelfreudt* (both 1621). In 1733 Telemann published three sets of *Musique de Table*, each comprising an overture and suite, a quartet, a concerto, a trio sonata, a solo sonata, and a finale. As the genre gradually transformed into the Divertimento, other titles began to appear, such as *Musicalische Blumenlese*, *Musikalisches Magazin*, and *Musikalischer Blumenkranz*. After 1800 *Liedertafel* maintained the tradition, latterly through the medium of male-voice choral societies.[25]

One remarkable Baroque case study and commentary on prevalent social mores falls outside the genre of Tafelmusik. Bach's so-called *Coffee Cantata* (1732–34), is essentially a miniature comic opera, though originally written for concert performance. "Schweigt stille, plaudert nicht" (Be still, stop chattering) BWV 211 focuses upon an addiction to coffee, a significant social problem in eighteenth-century Leipzig. Zimmerman's Coffee House hosted the première by the Collegium Musicum, which Telemann had founded in 1702. The text has the father Schendrian threatening to take away his daughter Lieschen's meals, clothes, and other pleasures if she refuses to give up coffee. She protests that without three bowls of coffee a day she will shrivel up like a piece of roast goat. To her, coffee is sweeter than a thousand kisses, mellower than a Muscat wine. Schendrian threatens to prevent her marrying, but she secretly tells possible suitors that she must be allowed to drink coffee. Finally, the two characters are joined by the narrator in a final trio: "A cat won't stop from catching mice, and maidens remain faithful to their coffee. The mother holds her coffee dear. The grandmother drank it also. Who can thus rebuke the daughter?" Contemporary with the *Coffee Cantata* are a host of operatic examples from other composers, prominent among which are Handel's *Balthazar* and *Alexander's Feast*, where culinary delights occupy center stage.

During the classical period, music and the table remained inextricably linked. Wind bands were a popular source of musical entertainment in the eighteenth and early nineteenth centuries. At first *Harmoniemusik* was developed as an outdoor entertainment, particularly for warm summer evenings. That is the true meaning of "serenade" (*sera*, Italian "evening," the serene time), and Mozart actually described his C Minor Serenade K. 388 as *Nachtmusik* (night music). But the principal function of *Harmonien* was to provide colorful background music for dinners, court, and social functions; although they also performed at public and private concerts, they were not always listened to with rapt attention. From the 1760s, Haydn, Mozart, J. C. Bach and many others were composing dinner music especially for the oboe and clarinet sextets (with pairs of horns and bassoons) employed by the aristocracy of central Europe, England, and France. The Duke of Orléans, the Prince of Condé, and the Prince of Monaco retained three of the best-known ensembles. In England public performances were given at Ranelagh Gardens, while in the 1780s the Prince of Wales employed a Tafelmusik. Dinner music was written by Mozart for the Archbishop of Salzburg in the mid-1770s, and a wind band played such music in Albert's tavern in Munich in 1777.

An important development came in 1782, when Emperor Joseph II and several Viennese aristocrats, such as Prince Esterházy and Prince Liechtenstein, gathered together full Harmonien—octets including both oboes and clarinets—an inspired combination of first-class professional musicians (rather than liveried servants), which brought forth some of the most sublime chamber music ever written. Arrangements of famous operas and symphonies, used mainly for dinner music, gave a wide public the opportunity to enjoy their favorite pieces outside the concert hall. It was normal for opera transcriptions to contain twelve or more near-complete movements. All Mozart's mature operas were transcribed, a task normally undertaken by the director of the Harmonien that played it, though in the case of *Die Entführung aus dem Serail*, written by the composer. The repertory also included operas by Beethoven, Weber, Rossini, Bellini, Donizetti, and a host of others.[26] Roger Hellyer has remarked that the privations caused by the Napoleonic wars were a major influence on most of the Viennese aristocracy discontinuing patronage of their Harmonien, though those of the emperor and Prince Liechtenstein survived intact into the 1830s. In Germany, the Duke of Sondershausen retained his until 1835, when it was replaced by a full orchestra.

Mozart himself brought the wind band center stage during his opera *Don Giovanni*, where food and drink play a central role in the lifestyle of the vile seducer, and refreshment forms a central backdrop to the opera-buffa elements within the drama, such as the wedding preparations of Masetto and Zerlina. Don Giovanni's so-called Champagne aria "Fin Ch'an dal Vino" is something of a manifesto, though the specified items on the menu for his elaborate party at the end of act 1 amount only to coffee, chocolate, lemonade, and biscuits. It is during the extravagances of act 2 that an off-stage Harmonie plays extracts from Martin y Soler's *Una Cosa Rara* and Sarti's *I due Litiganti*, chosen perhaps primarily for their popularity. Significantly the third tune is "Non Più Andrai" from Mozart's own *Figaro*. In terms of on-stage parties (though in a very different dramatic context), act 2 of Johann Strauss's *Die Fledermaus* is a true successor to Mozart, since singing in praise of champagne enlivens the atmosphere of dancing and supping. The ultimate musical gourmet was probably Gioacchino Rossini (1792–1868). His *Péchés de Vieillesse* (Sins of Old Age) include a collection of piano pieces collectively called "Hors d'oeuvre" (radishes, gherkins, anchovies, butter) and four dry fruit desserts (figs, raisins, almonds, hazelnuts). They reflected a lifetime in which the composer's own love of food was manifested in his operas. Apart from some early letters, the bulk of information about Rossini's active career derives from Stendhal's brilliant and witty but erratic *Vie de Rossini* (Paris, 1824), which the composer never read. Rossini certainly produced the most amusing eating scene in opera in *L'Italiana in Algeri*, in which the Italian Isabella feeds copious amounts of spaghetti to Mustafà, to distract him as she engineers her escape. As she runs to a ship in the harbor, Mustafà is dutifully twirling his pasta as he has been instructed. Gastronomical scenes appear frequently in other operas such as *La Cambiale di Matrimonio*, *Il Viaggio a Reims*, and *Ciro in Babilonia*. From Stendhal comes the information that the popular aria in *Tancredi*, "Di Tanti Palpiti," was composed while Rossini waited for his rice to cook one day in Venice. "Nacqui all'Affanno e al Pianto" in *Cinderella* was said to have taken little more than fifteen minutes of Rossini's time in a tavern in Rome.

Recipes named after the composer continue to this day, notably Tournedos Rossini and Stuffed Turkey/Fillet of Sole alla Rossini. Cannelloni alla Rossini is stuffed with his favorite truffles and foie gras. A man of wide-ranging tastes in food and wine, Rossini's love of gastronomical and musical connection is reflected in Don Magnifico's dreams in the opera *Cinderella*. Anticipating the fruits of the marriage between the prince and his daughter, he sings that he will have lots of memories and petitions of hens and sturgeons, bottles and brocades, candles and marinades, buns and cakes, candied fruits and sweets, slabs and doubloons, vanilla and coffee.[27]

Grape and Grain On Stage and Off

Musical twists to the glories of the grain and the grape have continued to flourish on the operatic stage since Rossini's shining examples. Indeed, at times, culinary context contributes as much to the dramatic narrative as the music itself. Drinking songs abound, such as "O Vin, Dissipe la Tristesse" from *Hamlet*, by Ambroise Thomas, which assumes the suicidal imagery of "To be or not to be" in Shakespeare's original. Earlier in the nineteenth century, Berlioz's "dramatic legend" *The Damnation of Faust* yields four drinking songs and retains Goethe's "Song of the Rat" and "Song of the Flea." Unlike the *Faust* settings of Gounod and Boito, Berlioz gives us Auerbach's tavern as the first stop on Mephistopheles' tour. As a further example, veering toward political incorrectness, Offenbach's *La Péricole* has a tavern where, in act 1, a series of incidents takes place in which alcoholic beverages are poured into characters to get them to do things that they would not contemplate sober. The tavern sells the highest possible amount of low-cost drink to men in the mood for lots of liquor served by good-looking women; it sets the upbeat mood for the entire work. La Péricole is given food and drink so as to get her acquiescence to the role of court favorite, after which she sings, "What a wonderful meal and what excellent wines. I drank so much that I think I'm a bit muzzy. If you see me zigzagging about or notice that my speech is slurred, pretend not to notice." As James Hill has observed, "Sexual exploitation, degradation of women, and trivialization of substance abuse are treated as central parts of an entertainment. On the other hand, exactly parallel considerations faced Offenbach in the Paris of the 1860s. In fact Offenbach made his fortune by being a bit 'racy' and by 'pushing the envelope' of his times."[28]

Each of the acts of Verdi's *Falstaff* begins in the Garter Inn in

Windsor, where Falstaff has a guest room. Although the remains of breakfast are evident at the outset, drink is its primary attraction. But whereas this inn is subservient to Falstaff's character, the Café Momus in the second act of Puccini's *La Bohème* is one of the most celebrated taverns in the whole of opera. Located in the Latin Quarter of Paris, it is the backdrop for a meeting on Christmas Eve of the artistic yet impecunious characters at the center of the plot. In the restaurant we are introduced to the artistic environment and develop sympathies with the interacting characters. Their boisterousness raises the audience's spirits and sets the stage for the opera's rendezvous with poverty, domestic discord, and pulmonary tuberculosis. Street urchins, toy sellers, and marching bands enliven the scene. Street peddlers flog a variety of foodstuffs right up to the table. Oranges, dates, hot chestnuts, toffee, whipped cream, fruit pies, nougat, coconut milk, and plums are all available without buying them from the restaurant! As for the Café Momus, we hear beer and coffee being ordered, and Colline shouts for a sausage. The male characters order roast venison, turkey, and dressed lobster, along with table wines. Mimi settles for crème caramel, while Marcello acquires a plate of stew. The café is clearly a middle-of-the-road establishment.[29]

Away from opera itself there have been consistent connections of music and food, ranging from Schubert's song "Die Forelle" (The Trout) to Tchaikovsky's *Nutcracker* ballet, with its "Dance of the Sugar Plum Fairy." Aspects of nature and the fantastic are indeed subjects readily depicted in music and illuminated by references to the kitchen. Controversially Debussy's "Golliwog's Cakewalk," the finale to his *Children's Corner Suite*, commemorates the dance competition for a prize of cake, sponsored by a plantation owner and featuring his own slaves who were allowed to mock the airs of their masters. Minstrel shows idealized plantation life with white actors blacked up, an important influence on early American musical theater. Worthy of a smile rather than a stir are Erik Satie's "Three Pieces of Pear" for piano duet.[30]

None of these examples could be further from Mahler's inebriate enjoying the alcoholic joys of spring in *Das Lied von der Erde*. Songs 1 and 5 of the cycle, "Das Trinklied vom Jammer der Erde" (The Drinking Song of Earth's Sorrow) and "Der Trunkene im Frühling" (The Drunkard in Spring), take as their texts Hans Bethge's German translations of the ancient Chinese poet Li-Tai-Po. One of the most complex drinking songs imaginable, a recurrent theme in the "Trinklied" is that

> Dark is life, and so is death.
> The earth will long stand fast and blossom in spring.
> But thou, O man, for how long do you live?
> Not for a hundred years can you delight
> In all the rotten trash of this earth!
> . . . .
> Now take the wine! Now it is time, companions!
> Drain your golden goblets to the dregs!
> Dark is life, and so is death!

In analyzing Mahler's response to his challenging text, Donald Mitchell has drawn special attention to the fascinating relationship between the strophes—the contrasts, the developments, and truncations, together with their interfertilization. As Mitchell observes, Mahler "had to circumvent by compositional means the constraint of so bald a nihilistic statement if he were to create a work that was to extend beyond a simple, unadorned statement of despair." Among the composer's tactics and strategies is "the countering of the forward, depressive motion of the musical ideas associated with death and the poet's visions of the spirit laid waste, by the energetic, ascending musical ideas that embody that part of the drinking song's character that is a protest against the sentiments of the very poem that is being set. Life may be dark and worthless and not to be preferred to death, but while life and song remain, then so do creative vitality and creative will."[31]

Mahler seizes upon some very traditional aspects of the drinking song so as to generate contrasts and conflicts. These return in less extreme form in the later song, where spring intrudes on what Mitchell describes as "the drunkard's energetic dismissal of life," an intrusion that "almost convinces him that there is some reality to the fresh vision. All the more reason, then, hastily to suppress it, to return to the anodyne of the bottle."[32]

The Modern Age

The twentieth century has witnessed many new links between food and music, alongside those that maintain tangible links with the past. For example, oratorio has sometimes recalled with relish the excesses of earlier times. As colorfully relived in Walton's 1931 oratorio *Belshazzar's Feast*, the Babylonian king brazenly invites a thousand of his lords to drink wine with him using sacred silver and gold goblets taken from the temple in Jerusalem. In Orff's *Carmina Burana* the diners gather round as a strangulated swan describes what it is like to be roast on a spit and then served up on a large plate. The world of ballet encompasses Richard Strauss's rarely heard *Schlagobers* (Whipped Cream), which contains such numbers as "Dance of the Pralines." In Maxwell-Davies's extraordinary orchestral piece *Orkney Wedding, with Sunrise* the band can hardly be held together by its leader as the effects of the whiskey take hold.

Some 120 years ago, as recording began to be developed, concert life was still often relatively informal. A painting now in the archives of the Royal Opera House at Covent Garden shows the inaugural concert of London's Queen's Hall in 1893; conductor and orchestra are in full flight, yet conversation is also flowing freely in the front rows of the audience.[33] When the Promenade Concerts opened in the Hall two years later, eating, drinking, and smoking were permissible, though patrons were asked to refrain from striking matches during the vocal items. This is a world that would now seem deeply unfamiliar, since of course Brahms and his contemporaries heard music only when they were in the presence of someone performing it. The development of recording and the constant availability of music mean that nowadays our ears are often assaulted without permission. Restaurants and supermarkets choose to pipe music at their clients for a variety of reasons.

Different kinds of music and food nowadays permeate our lives in ways that would have been unthinkable a generation ago. A longer-term parallel development has been the parting of the ways between so-called classical and popular music. The more informal settings typical of pop music quite naturally encourage the simultaneous imbibing of music, food, and drink. As with classical music, pop lyrics are scarcely short of references to refreshment of various kinds. A famous example is George Harrison's "Savoy Truffle" that appeared on the Beatles' *White Album* recorded in 1968. A tribute to Harrison's friend Eric Clapton's chocolate addiction, the title and many of the lyrics were derived from a box of Mackintosh's Good News chocolates. The song includes a reference to needing to have one's teeth extracted after the deterioration caused by eating too many sweets.

In regretting the loss of elements of musical surprise in today's digital age, Robert Philip has recently observed that

in both food and music, there has been a limited reaction against the predictable perfection of modern products. People have begun to tire of the constantly available tomato, perfect and regular in appearance, but almost tasteless. So a market has developed for tomatoes "on the vine"—more expensive and with more taste. But these are still remarkably perfect fruit compared with the much more variable and irregular shapes and flavors of tomatoes forty years ago. Similarly, there has developed a market for so-called live recordings. It represents a response to a feeling that the highly edited studio recordings have . . . become a little predictable and dull. As with tomatoes, there are limits to the current state of this trend. Just as tomatoes on the vine are still expected to be perfect, so "live" recordings cannot have mistakes in them. Most recordings of concerts are corrected with editing, either from combining more than one concert, or by engaging the musicians for a "patching" session. To shift the metaphor slightly, we seem to want to have our cake and eat it: we want the excitement of the live event without any uncertainties.[34]

As this chapter has attempted to show, the culinary agenda has played a colorful role throughout the history of music. Food and drink continue to fuel the creativity of performers and composers, sometimes in very public ways and not always to advantage. They regularly contribute to characterization on the musical stage, complementing melodic and rhythmical dramatic elements contained within the score.

Meanwhile, as the position of music within society undergoes subtle changes from one generation to the next, propelled by the impetus of the digital age, there is an increasing desire to comprehend more scientifically its impact on the brain. Recent research has explored the neurological effect of musical consonance and dissonance, as well as the alleged benefits of the "Mozart effect" on the unborn child. Furthermore, during the last decade, research by Professor Adrian North of Heriot Watt University has established that playing a certain type of music can enhance the way wine actually tastes.[35] Commissioned by the Chilean winemaker Aurelio Montes, who customarily plays monastic chants to his maturing wines, North ascribes his results to "cognitive priming theory," where the music sets up the brain to respond to wines in a certain way. For example, his research has shown that Cabernet Sauvignon is most affected by powerful and heavy music and rather less so by mellow and fresh repertory. North's previous supermarket research suggests that people are five times more likely to buy French than German wine if accordion music is playing; if an oompah band is performing, the German product outsells the French by two to one. Here is evidence that harder key performance indicators are beginning to impinge upon the world of passion, fantasy, and drama with which music and victuals have been associated throughout the history that is charted within this chapter.

Notes

1. A. S. Weiss, *Feast and Folly: Cuisine, Intoxication, and the Poetics of the Sublime* (New York, 2002), 98.

2. "Is Classical Music an Acquired Taste?" an interview (March 1, 2007) with Ira Braus, author of *Classical Cooks*, in *Audiophile Audition*, web magazine for music, audio, and home theatre, www.audaud.com (accessed September 6, 2008).

3. I. Braus, *Classical Cooks: A Gastrohistory of Western Music* (Bloomington IN, 2007).

4. Bob Young, Al Stankus, and Deborah Feingold, *Jazz Cooks: Portraits and Recipes of the Greats* (New York: Stewart, Tabori, & Chang, 1992); June Lebell, *Kitchen Classics from the Philharmonic* (New York: Doubleday, 1992).

5. Aaron Williamon, ed., *Musical Excellence* (Oxford University Press, 2004), 56, 271–85.

6. Leone Magiera, "A Full Life of Passion and Pasta—My Friend Pavarotti," *Sunday Telegraph*, August 31 2008, published in advance of his book *Pavarotti Up Close* (London: Ricordi, 2008). Magiera, who conducted Pavarotti in more than a thousand concerts over fifty years, is the source for the material in this and the succeeding paragraph.

7. Magiera, "A Full Life."

8. Charlotte Higgins, "The Fat Lady Slims," *Guardian* (London), September 26, 2006.

9. See Fred Plotkin, *Opera 101: A Complete Guide to Learning and Loving Opera* (New York: Hyperion, 1994) and his article at www.answers.com/topic/food-in-opera. Among more recent singers, Plotkin notes Birgit Nilsson's liking for a beer at the side of the stage during performances.

10. J. A. Baird, trans. and ed., *Introduction to the Art of Singing by Johann Friedrich Agricola* (Cambridge University Press, 1995), 86–87.

11. Johann Mattheson, *Der Vollkommener Capellmeister*, part 2, chapter 1 (Hamburg 1739).

12. For further context (with illustrations), see I. Chrissochoidis, "Handel, Hogarth, Goupy: Artistic Intersections in Early Georgian England," *Early Music* 37 (2009): 577–96.

13. Translated in E. E. Rousseau, *Clarinet Instructional Materials from 1732 to ca. 1825* (PhD diss., University of Iowa, 1962), 161–64.

14. Weiss, *Feast and Folly*, 20.

15. Claude Baudelaire, *Les Paradis artificiels* (1860) in *Oeuvres complètes*, vol. 1, ed. Claude Pichois (Paris: Gallimard, 1975), 378.

16. Baudelaire, letter to Richard Wagner, February 17, 1860, in *L'Art romantique* (Paris: Garnier-Flammarion, 1968), 264.

17. Baudelaire, "Richard Wagner et *Tannhäuser* à Paris" in *L'Art romantique* (Paris: Garnier-Flammarion, 1968), 273.

18. Homer *Odyssey*, bk. 1, line 152. Greek translations are taken from Andrew Barker, *Greek Musical Writings*, vol. 1, *The Musician and His Art* (Cambridge: Cambridge University Press, 1984).

19. Homer *Iliad*, bk. 18, lines 490–96.

20. Homer *Odyssey*, bk. 9, lines 5–14.

21. Examples in this paragraph are taken from J. E. Scott, "Roman Music," in *New Oxford History of Music*, vol. 1, ed. E. Wellesz (Oxford: Oxford University Press, 1957), 415.

22. See J. E. Hurlbut, "From Functional Feast to Frivolous Funhouse: Two Ideals of Play in the Burgundian Court," in the Fifth Annual Indiana University Symposium on Medieval Studies: Work and Play in the Middle Ages, April 1992. See also the DC by the Orlando Consort, *Food, Wine & Song: Music and Feasting in Renaissance Europe*, music by Adam de la Halle, Machaut, Smert, Zachara da Teramo, Isaac, Dufay, Binchois, Compère, Ponce, del Encina, Greiter, and Senfl (Harmonia Mundi France, 2001).

23. From an account of 1517 by Nicolò Sagurdino, secretary to the Venetian ambassador to England.

24. A. Félibien, *Relation de la fête de Versailles* (Paris, 1668), cited by Weiss, *Feast and Folly*, 6, who identifies the garden as *Gesamtkunstwerk*, both spectacle and stage.

25. Hubert Unverricht, "Tafelmusik," *Grove Music Online* (accessed September 1, 2008).

26. Roger Hellyer, "Harmoniemusik," *Grove Music Online* (accessed September 1, 2008).

27. Translation from www.eat-online.net/Rossini_on_food, accessed September 8, 2008. This article includes the celebrated anecdote that "Rossini claims only to have wept three times in his life: the first time over the fiasco of his first opera, the second when he heard Nicolò Paganini play the violin, and finally, when the picnic lunch, a turkey stuffed with truffles, fell overboard on a day's outing on a boat."

28. See www.londonfoodfilmfiesta.co.uk/Musicum~1 (accessed September 3, 2008), from which information on operatic taverns in Berlioz, Offenbach, Verdi, Puccini, and Hahn is taken.

29. The article "Puccini" notes the accuracy with which Puccini recreated the atmosphere of Henry Murger's novel *Scènes de la vie de Bohème*. There are important differences in Murger's version of the food and drink; Musette drinks Champagne, Mimi Beaune (in a basket). Sardines with bread and butter and radishes with meat are also on the menu. If Puccini's Café Momus is a dramatic icon, then the Smoking Dog Café in Reynaldo Hahn's *Ciboulette* is a mere contrivance whereby the hero can be dumped by his girlfriend and can get drunk enough that he passes out on his future wife's cabbage cart. More prominent operatic culinary contexts include Turiddu enjoying a glass of wine between church and duel in Mascagni's *Cavalleria Rusticana*, Gilbert and Sullivan's sherry-drinking *Pirates of Penzance*, as well as rousing scenarios in the works of such diverse figures as Verdi, Janácek, and Britten.

30. Satie was known for his prodigious appetite. His death at the age of fifty-nine of sclerosis of the liver was at least partly caused by his heavy drinking.

31. Donald Mitchell, *Gustav Mahler: Songs and Symphonies of Life and Death* (London: Cambridge University Press, 1985), 182.

32. Mitchell, *Gustav Mahler*, 317.

33. Reproduced in Michael Forsyth, *Buildings for Music* (Cambridge MA: MIT Press, 1985), 229.

34. Robert Philip, *Performing Music in the Age of Recording* (New Haven CT: Yale University Press, 2004), 245–46.

35. See www.news.bbc.co.uk (accessed April 28, 2010).

Lionizing Taste

Toward an Ecology of Contemporary Connoisseurship

ROGER HADEN

In 1875 a special banquet was prepared at the famed restaurant Magny in Paris. Hosted by the editor of the hunters' journal *La Chasse Illustrée*, it featured two dishes that today may well strike the reader as bizarre if not horrifying: an estouffade of lion haunch à la Méridionale and the great beast's heart, prepared à la Castellane.[1] While hunters have traditionally viewed their prey much in the same way as headhunters have viewed theirs, as a trophy to be consumed in triumph, the final all-conquering act, gourmets, epicures, and connoisseurs have tended to appreciate food gastronomically; which is to say, solely on its culinary and gustatory merits. No doubt there were a few gastronomic connoisseurs present on that night, and apparently, again according to the reports, the dishes of lion were well enjoyed. As hard a concept as this may be to stomach, particularly for today's ethical eater, the consumption of lion and gourmandise are not mutually exclusive notions. To be reminded that this is the case we need only think of the predilections of those whose taste gravitates toward the farthest shores of gastronomy (in one current incarnation this goes by the name of "extreme cuisine"), and which underlines the more general point that humans can and do eat and enjoy almost anything that is not immediately toxic: insects, spiders, grubs, molds, intestines, the putrescent, the "high," the very old, the unborn, the fresh, the ripe, the rotten, the living and still moving, the savagely hot, the intensely bitter, and more.[2]

This anthropological omnivorousness is the theoretical ground zero of taste, although it has always been clear enough that human beings exercise their powers of taste in choosing only some foods from among many more available to them. This has been called the *omnivore's paradox*.[3] This essay considers the notion of gastronomic connoisseurship, a practice based on the exercise of discriminatory taste as it applies to gustatory taste. Omnivorousness sets a broad material limit for the exercise of both connoisseurship and taste, although the omnivore's paradox suggests there are many cultural factors that limit the gastronomic choices implied. Religion, ethics, health, personal experience, and food associations all at some point affect our personal taste for foods and drinks. This broadly cultural influence on taste certainly in part explains the more or less infinite range of preferences expressed in the name of taste. At the same time, however, the notion of (Western) gastronomic connoisseurship connotes a "higher" aesthetic, a refined sensory awareness of the qualities of food and drink (typically wine). Although, historically, connoisseurs certainly appear to have had their culturally imparted prejudices shaped by culturally specific tastes, nevertheless, the objective reading of aesthetic qualities was expected of the connoisseur. In spite of the obvious differences between individuals, and their taste, the acceptance of the idea of an objective discriminatory taste seems curious for other reasons; in particular, that popular sentiment appeared to follow the often-cited Scholastic dictum, *de gustibus non est disputandum*: there can be no disputing over matters of taste. The inference here was that taste could lay no claim to objective criteria upon which to base an aesthetic judgment because taste was too subjective. Why argue over what I, as opposed to you, like to eat? Liking and disliking speak for themselves.

A further complication was that this traditional logic appears to be totally contradicted in practice, at least in the modern West. Who could seriously deny that the social expression of taste—the choices we make about what to wear or listen to, what we drive, or what we choose to eat—is not at the same time the very means by which we express our *social* selves and thereby our class, our wealth, and cultural status? That this process involves the shared understanding of commonly used signs seems to undermine the sense in which taste might be construed as fundamentally subjective. Moreover, Pierre Bourdieu's efforts to document the modus operandi of "cultural capital" and its role in the performance of "good taste" surely reduce belief in the independence of personal taste relative to the power of class domination. Hence, one must conclude that there is in fact an incessant accounting for everything to do with taste, because taste is a fundamental tool of social differentiation. Whether person, group, or class, the exercise of "personal" taste distinguishes one from another. Bourdieu has comprehensively outlined the extent of the power and application of this social construction of taste.[4] Despite such efforts to reconsider the role of taste as an instrument of social regulation rather than as a purely personal faculty, the old notion of there being no accounting for taste persists.

There is, however, another possible connotation suggested by the saying *de gustibus non est disputandum*, one based on a total acceptance of the idea that the cultural power of taste is entirely relative and thus does not warrant or support logical disputation. This too becomes the reason for the injunction "This is not to my taste" and applies in all cases, due to cultural and individual differences of opinion. But crucially, the dictum also *implies* the opposite: that only some members of the community ever possess a "higher power" of aesthetic awareness, making discussion of "good taste" equally pointless with anyone other than the select few. Therefore, what begins as an appeal to logic ends with a deferral to morality: there *should* be no disputing over differences of taste because in the final analysis only some (will ever, and by their virtue) possess "refined" good taste. For the rest (the poor, uneducated, and "coarse"), discriminatory taste is irrelevant. Taste is socially constructed, as Bourdieu illustrates, and the historical justification given in tacit support of *de gustibus non est disputandum* is that one must be born (into a class) with taste or not have it at all.

Historically, the act of connoisseurship, often expressed as a public performance of discrimination, confirms how the social mechanism of taste operated according to this underlying logic. The archetypal connoisseur, conventionally satirized as a snob (one with pretension to superior knowledge and taste), might indeed possess great mental acuity and great organoleptic skill in aesthetic appreciation. Yet even such skills can easily be used with deference to conventional standards of good taste. The term *connoisseurship* (from the French *connais*, to know) denotes learning and knowledge, thereby underlining the relation between knowledge, power, and the cultural domain in which both circulate. The exercise of taste—as connoisseurship—has thereby served historically to maintain hierarchies of class. Importantly, connoisseurship also reinforces the moral virtue of "good taste" in contradistinction to "poor taste," distinguishing the snob, as someone prone to vulgar ostentation, from the truly refined "gentleman," and between those born with class and those without. Connoisseurship maintained the divide between good taste and vulgarity.

Would eating lion in the manner described above be regarded as vulgar ostentation in the contemporary West? While it would certainly be distasteful to some (and one imagines on a number of grounds), terms such as snob, vulgarity, ostentation, and also connoisseurship seem quaintly old-fashioned and almost irrelevant in a post-Bourdieu world in which class power and cultural capital is no longer defined by conventional aesthetic forms, whether haute cuisine, haute couture, or "fine art." We have seemingly moved on. Tastes have proliferated. Indeed, the term *omnivorousness* has also been applied to changing consumption patterns and to connoisseurship itself. While we have our gastronomic experts and professional judges of the aesthetic qualities of food and drink, the democratization of taste has given rise to aesthetic "omnivorousness": connoisseurship defined as openness to appreciating qualities in potentially any, but also in a lot more, things or experiences.[5] Apparently, eclecticism rather than elitism is the new direction. Equating lion (as the king of the beasts) with a "regal" banquet scene (historically, hunting was the preferred sport of kings) seems weirdly out of whack with such a democratization process. But we might also emphasize here that knowledge is part of this new economy of taste. So when it comes to eating lion, we now just simply know better, because more than ever before, readily accessible knowledge and information of all kinds informs choices, experiences, and levels of appreciation in a far more comprehensive if not necessarily more nuanced way.

Given these changes, the aim of this chapter is to map the historical roots of gastronomic connoisseurship in order to expose the culturally specific ecology of mutually affecting relationships between taste, knowledge, and experience as they have developed over the last two centuries. "Ecology," defined as a living and therefore changing set of relationships, acts here as a model for a discussion of a future connoisseurship, which, in order to be relevant, needs to take account of recent and current cultural change.[6] Having linked connoisseurship, gastronomy, and discriminatory taste, I want now to consider gustatory taste's role in such an ecology. Taste is, of course, indispensable to the very notion of gastronomic connoisseurship, but it is also taken for granted. As "a sense," taste's apparent physiological givenness has historically undermined inquiry into its social and cultural construction. Importantly, on closer examination the major historical forces that have shaped our understanding and definition of gustatory taste appear to have had a profound effect on how taste has been understood, and consequently, I would argue, on how it has been experienced. Put simply, to experience "Western taste" does not only infer a physiological activity; it is a culturally determined experience that is part of a broader ecology that this essay explores.

Taste and Connoisseurship

Given that we might generalize about something called Western sensory taste, what are the forces that have affected the understanding and experience of it? Scientific, philosophic, and moralistic discourse, the advance and application of techno-science, and the growth of the consumer economy have all played significant roles. Perhaps the most important point to stress initially, however, is the philosophic denigration of gustatory taste, because this has had a profound and lasting effect, which can be seen widely reflected in taste culture today. The refusal to acknowledge sensory taste as a legitimate and unique mode of knowing the world goes back at least to the writings of the pre-Socratic Greek philosophers.[7] Taste would come to be regarded as a "lower" sense, principally because, like smell, it was considered as a poor mode of access to the objective character of the world understood in material terms. This was not only because both sight and hearing seemed to offer much more reliable and comprehensible information about that world, but because any "reasoning" about the nature of things based on stimuli received via the "lower" senses was thought to be not only partial with regard to the account of "the world" so perceived, but also unreliable because compromised by physical desires like hunger and effects like pleasure. As a consequence, food and drink, the basis of taste and to some extent smell's grasp on the material world, pandered to the body's sensual appetites. Only the higher senses could rise above this carnal subjectivism and consider the world in a properly rational light.

This flawed but nonetheless pervasive and influential doctrine has arguably carried forward to this day. In brief, sensory taste is still regarded as the register of pleasure or displeasure, of flavors understood in terms of chemical stimuli and psycho-chemical responses, something experienced purely as an *effect*. Even our collective acknowledgement of a cuisine's "great dishes" suggests that this is so. These are after all the end products of what is a complex process (production, transportation, cookery) that is responsible for the food on a plate. But having been written out of philosophic discourse concerned with knowledge (epistemology), gustation was left, as it were, to modern sciences of chemistry, physiology, and biology, and later, to food science, which further inculcated the belief in a rudimentary causality applied to taste. This translated into an attitude that "flavored" much industrialized food innovation. The chemical causes and effects of taste and tasting became the building blocks for taste innovation and synthesis, at the same time serving to undermine consideration of taste as an active intellectual faculty engaged with the material and social worlds.

To understand how the low status accorded sensory taste transmuted into a scientific essentialism that largely went unchallenged, we need only consider how taste appears in the consumer culture of today, after nearly two hundred years of taste science. "Minimum work for absolutely maximum taste!!!" raves an online recipe reviewer, while Pepsi turns this sentiment into a mantra: "Pepsi: Maximum Taste No Sugar." Not surprisingly, taste is represented here as a "thing" that has been crudely quantified. Beginning with Michel Chevreul's reductionistic attribution of four essential tastes to the human tongue, in 1824, taste was subjected to rigorous analysis. The artificial synthesis of flavor was fully realized in the 1950s. Today the industrial-scale engineering of food products based on flavor and texture is the result of highly sophisticated technologies and processes, but the products themselves often lack all subtlety, because the limitations of the original scientific paradigm have been duplicated in the social consciousness. Consumers experience sensory effects via "foods" that are considered fun vehicles for specific taste *intensities*. Even the humble potato crisp has become a platform for multiple mixtures of flavors and sensations: "xtreme" taste highs (zinging, zesty, astringent) are bulked out with the standard industry triumvirate of fat (or low-fat substitutes that provide similar mouth-feel), salt, and sweetener—even though the crisp itself is all carbohydrate.

The results are horrifyingly similar across a range of products: from the pseudo-gourmet "Xtreme Taste Dill Ranch" dressing from Johnny's Foods, to "chili and sour cream" flavored corn snacks. By virtue of two centuries of reductionism (a type of fundamentalism), such taste hits represent the degree zero of the West's current ecology of taste. Whereas the concept of ecology potentially gives expression to a subtle "chemistry" of relations and relationships such as are expressed or facilitated by traditional cuisines, the "democratizing" of taste undermines complexity with banality. Even a basil plant grown on a back porch can connect you with the world in a real and personal way. Its fragrant, warm, reassuring aroma is a living part of an organic whole. It has the potential to focus us on knowing the world, ecologically. The deep-seated denigration of taste in the history of the West closes the door on all but taste effects, dislocated from earth, sun, sea, or sky; not through lack of attention but by virtue of overdetermination. A history of taste sensitive to such determination demands an appreciation of how particular forms of knowledge, discourse, and technology have shaped the corporeal experience of taste. The notion of connoisseurship as an engaged form of aesthetic appreciation and the contemporary form of taste just described seem oddly out of step. Connoisseurship is a kind of reasoned judgment, while sensory taste for many today is a brutalized sense register of effects. This disparity needs to be contextualized with reference to the cultural ecology of taste and connoisseurship past and present.

To some extent, it is true that taste and connoisseurship have been mutually defining. Gourmet culture, foodie-ism, gastronomy, restaurant culture, serious amateur food lovers, and cooks have together served to maintain or raise standards of quality and aspire to heights of gustatory appreciation that require taste to be considered a reflective and creative sense. The importance of this performative role of taste (sensory and discriminatory) has been recognized by contemporary theorists.[8] But this taste culture has also always been one made up of aficionados. Indeed, connoisseurship is represented by both professionals and eccentric amateurs. When this taste culture is contrasted with a history of denigration on one hand and a mainstream world of "xtreme taste" on the other, a much broader, mainstream division appears, and the conflict between taste and connoisseurship can be seen more clearly. How might the cultural education of sensory taste proceed, as expressed through discriminatory taste, in the act of connoisseurship, after two hundred years of philosophic denigration, essentializing counterintuitive science and the spread of a crass taste culture? The ecology of connoisseurship therefore implies more than food-focused activities like cooking and eating. It suggests relationships between the political and aesthetic, the personal and the environmental, the economic and the philosophic.

To lionize means to bestow a lot of public attention on a cause or a concern: to make a celebrity of such a concern. In its currently modish, media form, "taste" itself is a celebrity. Having inherited a cultural profile from a number of sources, "taste" has become a sign, a metaphor, a thing, and an effect. Flavors, textures, the idea of instant pleasures and sensational effects have all become objectified, commodified, and functionalized under the rubric of "taste," to the extent that all manner of disparate products can be represented as "tasty" in the same way as others are deemed to be "sexy." Apple computers and Volkswagen cars have both, in the past decade and a half, been advertised with explicit reference to various flavors. By conflating taste with literal consumption, catchphrases like "Taste Sydney" or "Taste Scotland" advertise place as taste and meccas of consumption at the same time. This is also a symptom of the trend toward omnivorousness, since the metaphoric utilization of terms like taste, as added values, perfectly encapsulates how the consumer system itself invents tastes and desires. Omnivores appear necessary in a world filled with many more options. They spread their taste around, often inventing criteria that are eclectic and individualized. Not surprisingly, some have argued omnivorous consumption to be an undistinguished form of connoisseurship.[9] Differentiation is perhaps the key concept here, in a world saturated with products that vie for space in an oversupplied market. How does one make a product distinct in such a market? Give it a "flavor." This has become a particularly popular trend in marketing because taste, for example, imputes a sense of the private, the personal, the internally satisfying and pleasurable—to *any* product—edible or not. This dissociative type of marketing has generally proved very effective. Without any logical connection between the marketing representation and the product's use or purpose, like that between computers and flavor, marketing as dissociation perfectly achieves its goal of making a product stand out in the crowded product market, disarming the consumer's knee-jerk interpretation of product specifications or to rationalize over value or suchlike.

Far more important, it appears, is the "emotional" bond that can be nurtured through clever marketing and design. As the so-called experience economy is showing us, developing relationships with products is proving to be a very good business strategy. Appeals to the senses immediately create this sense of personal bond. In a world where quality is assumed (if not always assured), the premise for purchase is that the "Apple" is cute, lemon-flavored, and that you like it, relieving the cashed-up but bored-with-technical-stuff consumer of having to think at all about whether the thing bought is going to do its job. A consequence of technological progress is that cars, computers, and kitchens are so well equipped with regard to reliability and quality that these things no longer make much difference. A television commercial from the chocolate makers Cadbury depicts a gorilla drumming to the hit Phil Collins's pop song *I Can Hear It Coming in the Air*

Tonight (Hold On).[10] Taste can seemingly migrate in or out of the postmodern marketing scene in order to enhance all manner of nonfood products, just as food commercials like this one can be divested of all reference to taste except by literal association with the product they advertise. Such culture mitigates against the practice of reasoned appreciation that I argue is the basis of (gastronomic) connoisseurship. Any attempt to lionize the latter approach to taste without careful articulation would presently be obscured in the shadows of a hyperactive global taste culture. But we have nonetheless come a long way since estouffade of lion haunch à la Méridionale was on the menu. The following discussion explores the tangled history of taste and connoisseurship with the aim of assessing what grounds there may be for a contemporary ecology of taste that does justice to sensory taste's powers.

Connoisseurship and Gastronomy

In the context of gastronomic connoisseurship, judging what might be described as the "beautiful" qualities of gourmet delicacies was not considered culturally acceptable until the early nineteenth century, when French gastronomy and the connoisseurship of cuisine emerged as part of the newly secular culture. France is of course crucial to this modern history of taste. It would lead the way in gastronomic connoisseurship throughout the nineteenth and for most of the twentieth century. While eighteenth-century philosophers had argued persuasively that "beauty" could not be appreciated objectively by taste, smell, or touch, and although the belief that the pleasure taken in eating and tasting was intrinsically sinful lingered on, gastronomy and connoisseurship emerged, nonetheless, as a new culture.

Championed by the likes of Grimod de La Reynière and Jean Anthelme Brillat-Savarin, gastronomy and connoisseurship were given crucial support and ultimately legitimacy via the gastronomic discourse that proliferated in the first three decades of the nineteenth century.[11] Gastronomy, literally meaning the rules pertaining to the stomach, found a ready stage when cultural and religious restrictions on the expression of taste began to break down, driven as this was by the desire for and availability of many new foods and flavors and consequently for the feelings and sensations that went with them. Dining culture (the rise of the restaurant), new culinary and communication technologies, and the democratization of art and science were all linked forces that shaped the emergence of gastronomy as a cultural field. Socially, it was the affluent middle classes who worked hardest at establishing their own cultural credibility, claiming aesthetic as well as moral and economic rights to govern the new consumer culture. In this instance, food was another medium through which class superiority might be expressed, and it proved to be extremely powerful and pervasive. Gastronomy made just such a claim as the first modern urban European dining culture took shape. Grimod wrote his gourmet guide to food shopping in Paris, aimed at the nouveaux riches: unschooled consumers of modern food and dining. Paris was a city in need of advice on what to eat and where to get the best of what was on offer. Suddenly there were many more people, many more restaurants, and more varieties of foods and wines available to all who could pay for them. Choices proliferated. In such an environment, "taste" became de rigueur. The role of the connoisseur seemed clear.

The tone of much of the gastronomic discourse was idealist, but also pragmatic, clearly articulating the moral virtues of gastronomy. The discourse provided models, guidelines, rules, and standards that served to publicly legitimize the new field.[12] The gastronomic connoisseur emerged as a champion of clearsighted moderation. The defense against criticism also entailed the embrace of "scientific method," further legitimizing the discourse. In the past, taste had been equated with physical pleasures and not therefore with learning, knowledge, or refined aesthetic appreciation. But gastronomy made taste the virtuous guide of a new science. There was of course a generalized interest and belief in science during the late Enlightenment, and so gastronomy's appeal to the sciences was simply good marketing. Advocating an interest in and devotion to "gastronomic science" (although there was definitely a sense in which the devotees of gastronomy aspired to a kind of secular spirituality) buffered the gastronomic connoisseurs from criticism. Subjects as diverse as art, philosophy, economy, politics, social organization, technology, agriculture, and industry also entered gastronomic discourse in a bid for cultural legitimacy. Brillat-Savarin boldly made the claim that the invention of a new dish brought more happiness to humankind than the discovery of a new star, and he defined gastronomy as "the reasoned comprehension of everything connected with the nourishment of man."[13] Such universalizing of the application and importance of humanity's relationship with food was profound. The gluttonous gourmand of old was thereby transformed into its newly modern counterpart, the gastronome, or "man of taste." "He" was now a man of learning and possessed the ability to discourse intelligently on the subject of cuisine and taste. "The gourmand only knows how to ingest; the gastronome moves from effects to causes, analyses, discusses, searches, pursues the useful and the agreeable, the beautiful and the good."[14] This was the distinction made in the *Encyclopédie* between gourmandism and gastronomy, one that would be reinforced by de La Reynière and Brillat-Savarin.

What gastronomy expressed in spirit and in the letter did not, however, describe the broader reality of foodways or attitudes in Paris, or anywhere else. Gastronomy arguably developed in just as rule-bound a way as had the classical French food culture of the *ancien régime*. The universalizing and idealizing of gastronomic discourse is fondly remembered and referred to endlessly by subsequent generations of food lovers, but a very narrow definition of "good taste"—based on the belief in an innate "sense"—led to (gastronomic) connoisseurship being more about social distinction than aesthetic appreciation. The figure of the gastronome was also stereotyped and lampooned. The idea of the glutton transformed into a "gourmet" seemed to cut both ways. Typically represented as a man of portly dimensions, wealthy, or very wealthy, the gastronome was something like the banker depicted by the French artist Grandville. Resembling a corpulent turkey, the banker reminds us of *dinde aux truffes* (truffled turkey), a gastronomic signature dish of wealth.[15] Gastronomic connoisseurship came to be seen as slightly eccentric and indulgent, if not indeed still sinful. The ideals and the reality parted company. At the same time, professional wine and food connoisseurship also developed, along with commercial cookery and proto-industrial food production, restaurant and public dining culture.

In this context of diversifying foodways and culture, gastronomy and connoisseurship arguably limited the extent to which sensory and discriminatory taste diversified and remained open to effects, change, and stimulus over time. As specialist fields, the underlying assumption was that taste was being well-served, but in fact, as modern French gastronomy developed as French cuisine, the aesthetic parameters ossified, restricting any sense in which taste could be innovative or experimental. As idealized by Grimod de La Reynière and Brillat-Savarin gastronomy would become a specialist, not a universalist, creed.

Connoisseurship, Taste, and Cuisine

Gastronomic culture evolved along elitist lines, as remains the case today. Nonetheless, the modern institutionalization of cooking and cuisine did turn gastronomy, broadly speaking, into a legitimate subject of academic attention and aesthetic appreciation. The latter, however, would be shaped by the established artistic standards already set by "the fine arts." The chef Marie-Antoine Carême famously proposed that confectionery was a branch of architecture, arguably so as to confer artistic credibility and thereby cultural legitimacy upon cookery. "Culinary art," as developed by Carême and his disciples, coincided with the new connoisseurship, which had also taken on the contours of a social art at a point when, as Norbert Elias notes, "savoir vivre, the correct attitude, assured taste—ceased to be imparted imperceptibly to each member of the social group concerned, and had to be taught to individuals by specialists."[16] Gastronomy and culinary art were new realms to be discovered, invented, and shaped by a new (bourgeois) elite of tastemakers. Grimod de La Reynière, the self-styled culinary sage of his day, influenced Parisian diners in an age when Beau Brummell and Carême gave sartorial and gastronomic advice, respectively, to the prince regent, across the channel in England. Seeking advice of this kind was an early sign of the democratization of taste and underscores the breakdown of established tastes (courtly fashions) in the face of a growing and diversifying culture of consumer goods that soon required the skills of tastemakers to interpret.

Cooking, cuisine, diet, and taste were all being reinvented at this time. So the cooking and eating of food and drink, the dining event, and the behavior deemed appropriate to dining were all aesthetically redefined, as at the same time they became the focus of rationalization within a new regime of knowledge. Again foreshadowed in the mid-eighteenth century by Diderot and D'Alembert's *Encyclopédie*, the codifying of knowledge—in this instance, related to the art and craft of food production—was set out with numerous references to food, taste, and cuisine. The *Encyclopédie* signaled the way forward insofar as all human arts and technologies would henceforward be subjected to rationalization. The rationalizing of cuisine also tied in with the establishment of French gastronomy and the ascendancy of French haute cuisine in the form of grande cuisine. Connoisseurship did not develop exploratively with regard to taste, but was principally employed performatively through recourse to what would become the enduring symbolic power of "French culinary art"—a gastronomic expression of nationalism and militarism rather than of (gustatory) taste. The connoisseur typically recognized an exemplary standard of culinary art in French cuisine, at the same time deferring to its cultural power. It is no coincidence that French haute cuisine became almost synonymous with empire. The standards of excellence and the aesthetic forms of this culinary-gastronomic system would dominate internationally for well over a hundred years.

Without wishing to belittle the enormous achievements of the pioneers of French gastronomy, their efforts were shaped by broader technical and ideological developments that are important to consider if we are to understand connoisseurship and taste in this, and subsequent, periods. Despite the obvious connection between gastronomy and sensory taste and connoisseurship, what active role did—or indeed could—taste play as an inquiring sensory mode within such a regimented and doctrinaire system of gastronomic values?

Carême's attempt to raise cuisine to the status of art took place against a backdrop of incipient industrial food production and processing. Gastronomic connoisseurship was therefore threatened almost immediately by a profusion of new and manufactured tastes. Grimod de La Reynière's self-styled role was to advise the nouveaux riches of the day on how to eat. But for the professional gastronomer like Grimod, wasn't it merely a kind of deductive taste that operated under such conditions? How reasonably can we claim that modern French gastronomy acted in the interests of taste as a mode of knowing? While gastronomic connoisseurship certainly aspired to raise the status of gustatory power to a "transcendental" form (the word appears in the subtitle of Brillat-Savarin's *Physiology of Taste*), the emergence of gastronomic culture was a complex and ongoing cultural process. Many forces were at work.[17]

The separation of something identified as "gastronomic culture" from other cultural fields in one sense confirms how rarefied and out of touch gastronomic culture was from the start. "Good taste" belonged to an elite. Indeed, gourmets as such would become the butt of ridicule and satire. Despite the modern relaxation of morals pertaining to "the pleasures of the table," pleasure for pleasure's sake was still equated, disparagingly, with this new "science of food" (the term itself seemed to invite ridicule in that it punned on "astronomy," a scientific field of inquiry whose legitimacy, by comparison, was presumably without question). A point to add here is that both Carême and Brillat-Savarin were focused on the science (as they saw it) of the kitchen, on the rationalization of culinary techniques and gastronomic values, rather than on taste and its potential as a mode of knowing. Although Brillat-Savarin's book reads less like a "physiology" than it does a cultural account of food culture in early nineteenth-century France, his aspiration was to organize and codify, to set the scene for gastronomy's acceptance into an orthodox field of knowledge. Similarly, beyond the popular image of being the chef-artist, the gastronomic connoisseur par excellence, Carême's claim that "French cuisine will remain the emblem of the beautiful in culinary art," betrays how "taste" in fact was made to bow to a rationalized aesthetic that Carême's cuisine would come to embody.[18] In this context, Rebecca Spang's comment that "the first restaurants brought science into the urban marketplace" makes perfect sense, especially if we consider, as Spang does, how the restaurant began its cultural ascent as a *maison de santé*, where carefully prepared broth (called *restaurant*) was served to health-conscious customers; an early modern form of medicalization related to food and diet.[19]

The science of chemistry also partly determined how taste would subsequently be understood and experienced. This knowledge could also be imparted in the culinary discourse. Recipes (cookbooks) were often simplified rationalizations of culinary lore frequently made in the image of the new sciences of chemistry and nutrition. As rations were to the meal, so the recipe was to culinary understanding. Leading chefs in the first half of the twentieth century recognized the importance of regarding cookery as a lived, sensory experience, rather than in terms of simplistic instructions. Chef X. Marcel Boulestin (1878–1943) warned that "the dangerous person in the kitchen is the one who goes rigidly by weights, measurements, thermometers and scales." He further remarked that "scientific implements are not of much use . . . there is nothing certain [in cookery], and the possibilities are infinite, since so many things have to be considered."[20] Similarly, Edouard Nignon (1865–1935) was "purposefully vague about quantities and cooking times."[21] In his *Plaisirs de la table* (1926), Nignon also extolled "meditation and patience," exclaiming: "Down with chemistry! Down with speed!"[22] But there was never any real hope of turning back the clock. Recipes and cookery would continue to be rationalizing, essentializing forces. Cooking is in many ways an intuitive art that develops as does cuisine and taste, slowly, over centuries, incorporating changes, new ingredients, meanings, technologies, and procedures. But food and taste culture are not governed by internal rules and formulas. Cookbooks, as texts, convey ideological messages. New technologies often come with a hidden or unacknowledged social agenda. Nutritionism became the very logic of cookbooks in the first half of the twentieth century, just as "modern kitchens" were being designed to facilitate a more rational cookery. Both texts and spaces can perform an ideological function. Leon Rappoport writes, for example, that nutritionism "as a matter of principle ignores all the qualities of food except those relevant to conveniently measurable nutrients needed to produce energy."[23] Similarly, the designers of the modern kitchen of the 1950s seemed to do so with the belief that they would only be used by women. One could easily list other ideological functions linked to food culture. Culinary fashions are often contrived to express "class," for example, while the cultural stereotyping of "the exotic other" seems to have continuing allure in numerous contexts.

One man who saw problems with the whole political, social, and economic system as it was emerging in the modern (European) world after the French Revolution was the utopian thinker

Charles Fourier.[24] Fourier has perhaps come closest to developing an ecology of taste and connoisseurship, one that challenged gastronomic orthodoxy. Gastrosophy, as Fourier named his alternative, was to be the principal driver of the whole social and material economy and the most *extensive* passion, while sexual love was conceived of as the most *intensive*. Fourier's "ecological" thinking is clearly at the heart of his system, where, in the words of Octavio Paz, "combinations are infinite, and pleasure . . . tends to diffuse and communicate itself (tastes and flavors)."[25] For Fourier, gastrosophy was a science corresponding to wisdom. Fourier therefore represents an opportunity to reconfigure taste and gastronomy as principal activities in a new ecology of connoisseurship.

Fourier's Gastrosophy: Of Old Hens and Passionate Attraction

Charles Fourier's radical attack on "civilization" was focused in part on then-current culinary fashions that he clearly set apart from his own philosophy of gastronomy and erotics. Fourier thought both these activities to embody the highest social values and so devoted himself to a utopian vision that would hold both and so constitute the very engine room of "harmony." Fourier's theory of "passionate attraction" (by Fourier's own account something akin to Newton's laws applied to social life) operated according to the law of the "series." In the realm of sensory taste— "the chief of the five material passions," asserts Fourier—the law of the "series" means the continual multiplication of the possibility of new combinations, just as the "combinative order" of the Fourierist phalanstery (autonomous social units comprising 1,600 persons) multiplies the possibilities for passionate attraction among the sexes. Series, which could be related to, say, apples or pears, are also interconnected by "ambiguous species," like the quince, for example. In society there are also transitions that are passional—"mixed tastes and unusual personalities" form a link between "societary series." Accommodating the maximum of variant individual tastes, the active engagement in promoting nuances of difference according to series offers the widest opportunities for pleasure across an entire spectrum of tastes, textures, and flavors.[26]

The appeal of this schematic understanding of taste is that it has nothing generically "cultural" about it at all; no references are made to styles of cuisine, past or present. Fourier was careful not to do this since he risked criticism for being inconsistent. His condemnation of "civilization," therefore, extended to gastronomy. "Civilization deteriorates incessantly in good living, owing to the spirit of trade, which alters the nature of all eatables, applies all the discoveries of modern chemistry to falsify and poison aliments, to multiply cheats and to multiply tricks of all kinds," Fourier contends.[27] Compared with meals in harmony, those of civilization appear to be the offerings of "gastronomically ignorant bumpkins."[28] Not only is the food of civilization limited but so are the social relations of the dining occasion. "[Guests] are so ill-matched that everyone would die of boredom if it were not for the food. But food alone is a boorish pleasure.... What a deluge of insipid nonsense you get at these civilized gatherings, even though no expense has been spared in their preparation and in the outlay on good food!"[29]

Importantly, "Taste and Touch, exert a colossal influence in material concerns, as well by necessity as by refinement," and by means of which "the pleasures of the senses are accordant with propriety and virtue, and become the springs of general equilibrium," writes Fourier.[30] The "equilibrium of the passions' transitions are what pins and joints are in carpentry," so that the play of free passions creates a stability by way of establishing series that link all tastes and emotions, providing for maximization of pleasure.[31] Accordingly, at the dinner table, as everywhere else, the "harmonians" need stimulants, which unite their hearts, minds and senses. Fourier's "Gormandism [sic]," he argues, "will be the magnetic needle of health and wisdom.... It will constitute the science named Gastrosophy." Moreover, "a clever gastrosopher...

will be revered as an oracle of supreme wisdom." Secondly, "as a "gastroculturist," he will be experienced in the laws of agriculture and the culinary preparations that a dish may require." Thirdly, as a "gastrohygienist," the gastrosopher will understand food in terms of health.[32] This approach ties the social scale of passionate attraction to the material scale of food and flavors, but through the widest ambit of knowledge pertaining to sense experience. That is to say, the pleasures of sense experience are potentially increased by knowledge of a food's provenance, for example, which is made explicit by Fourier in his reference to agriculture. Valuing the source of our food of course has its echo in contemporary tastes for produce that is organic, free-range, barn-laid, line-caught, vine-ripened, and so on. In Fourier's vision, the ties with the land and with the sensory world of appreciation were being stifled by civilization.

Using the example of "tough old hens" to make his case, Fourier explains that in the phalanstery a knowledge of poultry naturally extends to older birds, rather than exclusively being focused on young tender chickens (produced the same way as the modern battery bird). Fourier argues that passionate attraction dictates that all manner of chicken should be treated according to its relative culinary and gastronomic merits, which crucially extend to a knowledge of the creature's provenance and its "education." Fourier confesses that while his argument is offered in a light-hearted way, the fact that "certain people cannot stand tender poultry" serves to make a valid point. Tougher meats, he argues, have a good deal of flavor and can be made tasty by spices and sauces and tender by maceration and long slow cooking. If a guest wants to eat "a skinny old hen" then provision should be made because this can serve as the basis for the formation of a transitional group, which Fourier calls an ulterior transition. A lover of old hens attracts others with the same delectation, but the group of old-hen lovers also adds to the prestige of the cooks and to the group "which feeds [the chickens] in the henhouse."[33] Fourier concludes that "it serves to establish a passionate bond between these three groups of consumers, preparers, and producers," and that "the old hen creates as many discords in civilization as passionate bonds in Harmony."[34] Summing up his rationale in typical fashion, Fourier states: "The Apicius's of our capitals, who, with all their pretended delicacy, could not on eating a dish of poultry point out the errors committed in its education, nor rise to the rank of gastroculturists, still less to that of gastrohygienists."[35] Fourier's vision of gastronomy, and by inference, connoisseurship, is of an exalted sensory experience fed by a nexus of knowledge and understanding based on a full connection with food, from farm to plate. It is not the purpose of this essay to expound on Fourier's theories but rather to acknowledge his visionary gastronomy as a prototypical ecology of connoisseurship. Fourier provides a template for the consideration of sensory taste as a vital source of human happiness in the widest possible context.

Fourier presents us with an alternative vision of gastronomy and taste for which there have been no takers, although there have been attempts to make cookery less systematized, and thereby taste as well. How an ecology of connoisseurship might exist outside the systems that limit our understanding of gastronomic practice is described in *L'Amateur de Cuisine*, a "cookbook" published in France in 1999 by cardiologist Jean-Philippe Derenne. It caused something of a sensation because it deals not with dishes, styles, menus, or cuisines, but with heat and transformation. The book shows how thermal transformation itself can be understood as an organizing principle of taste relations, or more broadly, of the cultural ecology of taste. Instead of employing the customary form of a culinary-cultural genealogy of food and cookery styles, Derenne has made "an analysis of plants and animals and the chemistry of what happens when you apply different kinds of heat and cold to them before you eat them. . . . The glories of cuisine rise out of the limitless intersections of these two forces."[36] This is how commentator Adam Gopnik interprets Derenne's genealogical culinary system. In its eleven hundred pages, Derenne's book has "shown an underlying logic without attempting to make it logical," Gopnik suggests.[37] It appears that Derenne has been inspired by the notion that not only (the history of) cookery, but also taste, can be deconstructed, here in terms of thermal transformation. His gustatory intuitions begin from there. The title *L'Amateur de Cuisine* belies the rigid orthodoxy otherwise imputed to recipes and cookbooks, and that constitute a discourse that, as such, communicates on an ideological level. Derenne's explicit acknowledgment of the creative dynamic pairing of heat and cold serves to make taste relations contiguous, determined not by tradition or outward form, or brands, but framed only by the absolute physical parameters of human existence: incineration and absolute zero.

Connoisseurship Today

As a global phenomenon specific to every culture, irrespective of whether the notion of connoisseurship is conceived of on a conceptual level or not, a generic form of discernment can be thought to preexist (including in the prior instance, the right to eat lion) in the sense that consciousness itself depends on the ability to recognize difference. This is the fundamental principle of all choice making, a process extended on the basis of reflections, but primarily fueled by sensations. Taste, understood as discrimination, is universal in human culture. Without the freedom and ability to judge, discriminate, and to make choices on the basis of sensations, observations, beliefs, and reflection, human cultures remain limited in the degree to which they become self-reflexive. In today's world, where the proliferation of food types and styles, of eating experiences, of cultural commentary on food, of food-related theory, of food-related ethics and politics, continues to expand apace, expertise grows also. Perhaps it is important to rehabilitate the concept of connoisseurship so as to give shape to the individual's engagement with food on the broadest of levels. After all, connoisseurship at its most vital and life affirming still concerns the exercise of "taste," and in this particular register, to the exercise of taste as it relates to gustation and the choice of foods we eat.

Exploration, intuition, imagination, discovery, surprise, and pleasure are all fundamental to taste, as a mode of knowing, yet ironically, these values are only upheld by gastronomically marginal texts by thinkers such as Charles Fourier, or Jean-Philippe Derenne. Somewhat paradoxically, then, connoisseurship has, like gastronomy, been part of the problem with regard to taste, a sensory mode that has been overdetermined, marginalized, and subjected to commercial and scientific specialisms external to food culture per se; in being so it also ceased to figure as an actively engaged-with sense within Western culture. Indeed, in the case of branding, studies have shown that in a blind tasting, children find it hard to recognize the flavor of their favorite canned drinks, suggesting that brand power usurps taste in a world dominated by visual culture. "Taste today", as Alain-Claude Roudot argues, "is not considered the starting point, but rather the end result, of the chemical properties of food."[38] Taste is therefore experienced apathetically, with the sense of taste merely the receiver of heavily mediated "tastes." How might a culture reorient itself to taste as a lived sensory modality? I cannot claim that sensory taste has reached some perfect state at any time in the past, and that therefore, it has declined into the present time. The key assertion is that the overdetermination and shaping of the experience of taste by various cultural and material forces has seriously limited taste's potential as a reflective mode of knowing. One also need note that gastronomic culture and the culinary arts are flourishing and with them experiments in taste and a growing awareness of the sense's value in its own right. While this is encouraging, such developments are arguably taking place in a similar context to that which applied in Fourier's day, when gastronomy was in its modern infancy, diversifying and attracting attention as it does today. We need to be fascinated in the same way by taste, but also to respect its ecological wholeness rather than merely the effects of market drivers, professional ambition, and achievement.

In this context, the question arises as to what potential role, if any, might connoisseurship or epicureanism play in the rehabilitation of taste. While being long-since denigrated as forms of snobbery or rejected out of hand as hedonistic, both notions actually embody a consciously ethical approach to living that is striking a chord with many people who are seeking knowledge through their interaction with food and taste. The so-called experience economy, foodism, and gastronomic tourism are all exemplary signs of such interest. On closer examination of the classical discourse, the practice of connoisseurship also offers a way of making sense of food within aesthetic, ethical, and material contexts that are perhaps more relevant today than ever before: "The epicure abhors excess, and rises from his dinner as calm as a judge from the bench. . . . [He/she] is the antithesis of the glutton. . . . He is simply the moderate, cultivated man who knows what to eat, and how to eat it. He is to be found not only in great houses or West End clubs . . . but in very humble quarters indeed, living with refinement on some little pension."[39]

Moderation, refinement, and economy are part and parcel of the epicure's art, which is about making do, with dignity, as opposed to impressing with ostentatious display. The epicure seeks pleasure as a way of life that connects sensual pleasures with intellectual and ethical integrity. Conceptually, epicureanism and connoisseurship emphasize observation, discernment, judgment, and sensitivity of feeling: practices that in today's environment of proliferating (food) choices make a great deal of sense. Material (food) culture must be negotiated and what better way than through the cultivation of taste? While connoisseurship is historically suggestive of elitism and hierarchical gastronomic values, it can usefully be redefined so as to offer a means of mapping contemporary "tastescapes"; but more importantly, of plotting a way forward for the active involvement of gustatory taste as a mode of knowing: a form of inquiry. When knowledge coalesces into systems, it atrophies. Without the free play of desire and inspiration, taste also becomes fixed and inactive. Predictably, also, dictionary definitions of epicure often emphasize hedonism: "One who gives himself up to sensual pleasure" (*Oxford English Dictionary*; also *OED*). That pleasure should be defined in purely sensualist terms betrays the West's obsession with distinguishing between "mind" and "body," a strategy for the rational control of what Fourier understood as passions. The (Fourierist) epicure, it could be suggested, virtuously seeks pleasure as a way of life that integrates sensual pleasures with those of the mind and spirit.

But what of connoisseurship today? How has the term translated in terms of global food culture and the so-called democratization of taste. Theorists Richard A. Peterson and Roger M. Kern have traced medium to long-term changes in connoisseurship and marked a shift from "highbrow snobbishness" to omnivorousness, mentioned earlier, a shift that clearly results from democratization.[40] From another perspective, theorist Charlene Elliott describes a similar process occurring but looks at connoisseurship "in contemporary democratic culture" as being a "very specific practice of taste."[41] Both the examples Elliott includes (coffee and wine) are food-related, and both underline different dynamics between sensory and discriminatory taste. Setting parameters for how the latter functions as a faculty, Elliott draws on the late nineteenth-century work of Thorstein Veblen, who coined the now common expression "conspicuous consumption." Citing Veblen, an early observer of class taste, Elliot underlines his assertion that taste making requires "the aid of good friends and competitors." Taste is performative. The connoisseur publicly demonstrates his or her discriminatory skills. Elliott confirms that "taste is about surface, representation, and the advertising of self," and crucially, that "language is used to perform connoisseurship, so that the person of taste establishes his or her superiority." Moreover, "language is used to perform connoisseurship so that the person of taste is not mistaken for one with democratic tastes."

Elliott's intention here is to stress "the democratization of taste and connoisseurship."[42] She writes: "Two processes are [now] occurring simultaneously: One is the inscription of 'connoisseur' status upon objects previously outside the realm of connoisseurship [coffee]; and the second is the 'democratization' of objects previously located squarely within the realm of connoisseurship [wine]."[43] Taking the example of Starbucks as an instance of new connoisseurship, Elliott describes how the company provides its own consumer guide containing "thirty-eight key terms necessary to order coffee" and how it borrows the French notion of *terroir* in order to allow its customers to "use geography to illustrate both their knowledge and their taste preferences by ordering Sumatra, Kona," and so on. The Starbucks coffee connoisseur "orders a place in a cup."[44] With reference to her second example, Elliott writes that "while Starbucks busily creates a mystique around coffee, popular 'wine events' and 'wine education' courses emphasize that the veil can be lifted: The world of varietals and secrets of French terroir can be unearthed in one or six or twelve sessions (with a little side buzz to boot)."[45] According to Elliott, this two-pronged democratization of taste and connoisseurship bears out the key points of Veblen's theory of conspicuous consumption: "consumption for status purposes, the witnessing of taste, specialization or discrimination in goods consumed, and the cultivation of a particular language to negotiate the terrain." Elliott adds, however, that this form of consumption leads "to a certain hollowing out of what connoisseurship means, so that the performance is grander, the knowledge is smaller, and the language more of a game."[46] Elliott's study appears to support the idea that taste's role as a mode of knowing has been incrementally eroded. Indeed, both omnivorous choice making and Starbucks' discrimination undermine and trivialize. Moreover, if a "grander performance" is called for, look no further than "extreme connoisseurship":

The rarer the species, the more obscure the ingredients, the more peculiar the preparation, the more rewarding the meal, say the extreme connoisseurs. Treats include octopus eaten live (the tentacles cling to your mouth and teeth), ram's testicles pickled in their own urine before being moulded into cakes, the maggot-filled cheese Casu Marzu and ortolan, an endangered bird which is force-fed, then drowned in Armagnac and eaten whole. As coffee beans which have been excreted by civets in Sumatra make it on to the shelves of posh food halls . . . extreme connoisseurs are beginning to travel to experience these bizarre dishes in their places of origin, such as having a deep-fried cow brain sandwich in Indiana.[47]

Here the concept of connoisseurship certainly alludes to a form of omnivorous hyperconsumer, someone for whom differentiation and neophilia are paramount. Whereas competition, as Veblen well recognized, is fundamental to connoisseurship, extreme connoisseurship demands financial sacrifice as well:

As men begin to connect with the kitchen, the more engaged are becoming "extreme connoisseurs." These men see food connoisseurship as an indicator of virility, believing that cooking involves concepts such as (in their own words) science, technology, chemistry, rhythm and design. They refer to dishes being "done to plan" or "built" properly. They will smoke trout and venison in their own smoke-house (or garden shed) and make sausages from scratch. Extreme connoisseurs search for specialized food shops that only sell chilies, complete sausage making kits or bread tins.[48]

In the wake of the 2008 world financial crisis, Australian Prime Minister Kevin Rudd announced that "extreme capitalism" was the cause of the "global credit crunch."[49] If the term he chose has any resonance in the current context, it is to remind us that "extreme" connoisseurship of the kind we have been discussing (perhaps the food-related feats of *The Guinness Book of Records* are an early example of this culture) is but one sign (as are extreme sport and extreme politics) of the functional effects of consumer culture. Personal taste flexing its muscle as a survival mechanism in an aggressive market turns connoisseurship into an ultimately enervating struggle for self-definition. What space exists here for (the sensitivity of) sensory and discriminatory taste? How are they to be configured meaningfully in the current cultural context? How do, or might, they exercise their powers in such an environment? Extreme connoisseurship is one option, but this phenomenon is perhaps more a symptom of what happens when desires are overstimulated and oversupplied. The present wave of foodie-ism is no less a form of extreme connoisseurship: obsessional, but also an endemic feature of the culture of the West.

While there have been a number of contemporary theorists working on the above questions in an attempt to configure taste in the present cultural milieu, the prognoses are not all that positive.[50] As taste-culture theorist Pierluigi Basso Fosalli bluntly states: "The formation of a personal taste is no longer one of the priorities of a postmodern individual. . . . Advertising . . . provides taste for people who have none."[51] When we consider taste culture, whether from "high" or democratic angles, as humble or extreme, indications are that taste will be swallowed up in the rigorous application of marketing that inevitably shapes attitudes, and thereby, consumption patterns. Even by following the lead of gastronomy (the designated leader in taste culture) Fosalli suggests that all we do is "end up accepting the logic of fashion."[52] As argued earlier, both gastronomy and classic connoisseurship were historically more about the appropriation of cultural capital than skills or inquiry. Being a connoisseur today is equally problematic but principally because an ability to judge based on sensitivity of feeling rather than on knowledge or information is perpetually undermined by predetermined manufactured "tastes" of the type Fosalli identifies. Indeed, these are what appear to determine taste. Accepting the premise of theorist Kent Bach, that "being a connoisseur doesn't require more knowledge—it requires appreciation," we perhaps need now to explore in more detail what it means to exercise taste beyond the geography in a cup of Starbucks, the machinations of the extreme connoisseurs, the obsessive foodism of the gastronomic tourist, or celebrity chef fandom.[53] At this point, to conceive of a contemporary connoisseurship, we need first to consider the *tastescape*.

Configuring Taste

If the contemporary connoisseur is to fall back on taste itself as an exploratory and extracultural agency, unlimited in its scope for appreciation, he or she must first confront and negotiate the manner in which taste is culturally presented (and represented) in the everyday. As we have already seen, taste has been culturally configured in relation to gastronomy, science, and philosophy. But what might it look like today as a product still of that history? To begin with, then, an anecdote:

> An Italian family meets for an annual celebration. One of the nephews and his wife have come from the city, traveling to the small country town where their relatives have catered for a big family lunch. With them they bring some special wines, including a bottle of the world famous Barolo. The family duly assembles and is seated at the single, long table. The wines are displayed in front of them. But the hosts refuse to drink the expensive wines during the course of the meal; deigning only to taste them, they express their dislike. They prefer their local wines, of poorer quality, objectively speaking, but which, more importantly, celebrate a shared sensibility: "the power or faculty of feeling, [the] capacity of sensation and emotion as distinguished from cognition and will" (*OED*). The locals respond to the wine in terms of

feeling and emotion, it speaks to them intelligibly of who and where they are. The wine roots them to their locality and confirms their place within it. Barolo is a "fine wine" but it does not belong in this tastescape.

A question is raised here about judgment, of taste in relation to wine—a substance associated with professionalized taste and connoisseurship—but in an everyday, domestic, and clearly non-professional context: a family meal, at which, as it turns out, "good taste" matters less than true feeling. This distinction of course goes to the heart of the historical debates about taste mentioned earlier. We could well imagine the connoisseur's taste being for Barolo, but if we consider Fosalli's astute reconfiguring of taste, this expectation changes: "taste . . . entails a mixture of substances, a permeability of one's own/other qualities with a 'space of communion' . . . a coupling of subject/object."[54] Remembering that taste describes two separate experiences, sensory tasting and discrimination, there is cause here to reflect on the prerogative of the visitors and their Barolo, since it is they who are immersed in a global tastescape, one that delivers for a price both professionally endorsed "good taste," and accordingly, one that interpolates them as "connoisseurs." There is much that can be learned from the connoisseur, but what does one learn of oneself at the same time, of one's relationship with taste, of taste relations that go beyond the recognized, orthodox qualities of wine per se? I submit that these connoisseurs inhabit a world of taste premised on verifying subjects and well-defined objects, whereas taste, the sense of fluid relations, knows no such distinction. The local wine is part of the scene. It belongs. It is not an "object" in the sense implied, a thing that is acknowledged by others as having particular identifiable properties. It is relational, a pure element of conviviality.

Here Fosalli's notion of "system ecology" proves useful, since it is a concept that stresses the cultural and organic relations that create any tastescape. A world of taste created through an ecology of inclusion and relationship between culture and nature is best navigated by a culturally unfettered taste, by a local wine without a label. Secondly, Fosalli stresses "training and taste" as being "antidotes" to contemporary taste culture, in the sense that "taste education [can] drive the subject back towards recognition."[55] Reminiscent of Plato's belief that knowledge was always in fact recollection (how can one *know* unless there is already recognition, and so a rediscovery of something already known), Fosalli's abstraction posits an antithesis, described as a "pure consumerism [that] refuses reinterpretations of the consumer simulacrum." And therefore, "as a result, any system ecology remains unperceived," by which is meant that consumerism (and "taste" as a function of it) is a structurally closed system that functions according to its own internal logic.[56] Although the system can incorporate new tastes, to be admitted these must be related to the preassigned categories that give the system its structure. This is very close to Baudrillard's notion of a play of signs, one which constitutes a hyperreal world, no longer determined by actual events but by the manipulation of meaning. I can make no apology here for the degree of abstraction in the analysis since it is perfectly clear how much taste has already been abstracted, both in terms of it being "a sense" and as a "mental faculty" of discrimination. For many decades, the West could only "think" sensory taste in terms of there being four basic taste groups. This highly abstracted version of taste was determined by the modern sciences of physiology and chemistry that supported it. This simplistic structuring has stymied taste education ever since, much in the same way as nineteenth-century plant chemistry, having discovered the four basic chemical nutrients of plants, initiated the production of artificial fertilizers that over time render soil lifeless. More importantly, it also serves to reproduce that tastelessness already implicit in the modern abstracted version of taste adopted by science, in foods themselves, and consequently, in the experience of tasting. The latter is not only shaped by the ideology of "the four basic tastes" but by the techno-science that reproduces such logic in practice, undermining sensory acuity as it denies the full potential of the physiological dimension of the tastescape. Tastescapes are thus products of physiological, cultural, and technological forces. Reconfiguring taste, as Fosalli attempts to do, means coming to terms with what French philosopher Henri Lefebvre associates with sensory life:

> [A]t the body's center is a kernel resistant to . . . efforts to reduce it, a "something" which is not truly differential but which is nevertheless neither irrelevant nor completely undifferentiated: it is within this primitive space that the intimate link persists between smells and tastes. . . . The way for physical space, for the practico-sensory realm, to restore or reconstitute itself is therefore by struggling against the ex post facto projections of an accomplished intellect, against the reductionism to which knowledge is prone.[57]

More recently, in a moving evocation of taste, C. Nadia Serematakis has echoed this understanding: "Although the senses are a social and collective institution like language they *are not* reducible to it."[58]

Cutting back to the abstract, ideological principles that have been discursively applied to taste means revisiting the question of how taste might function "outside" these parameters. "Culture must be promoted," remarks Fosalli, "but bearing in mind that it is made up of processes and not of prepackaged categories of information, that knowledge is a heritage to be enjoyed and exercised, not a consistent encyclopedia of ideas deposited in an archive of knowledge."[59] If I interpret Fosalli correctly, the future ecology of taste relations begins with "training and taste." Fosalli explains, incorporating as he does so the terminology of sociologist Niklas Luhmann, "Training and taste are antidotes to [the] closed circuit of regulatory values typical of an identity communication that is well organized but indifferent to contents (not in the sense that it ignores them, but that it seeks a pure functional use designed to construct 'differentiation effects').["60] Fosalli believes in the actual, the sensory, that "resistant kernel" that is ever able to "reconstitute itself" (Lefebvre), aided in this instance by the gastronomically authentic (Italian culinary history and lore).

Differentiation effects, the distraction upon which consumerism ultimately relies, is precisely what leads to the kind of reductionism that has determined the fate of taste over two centuries. The supermarkets groan with a huge variety of bread, yet all these *brands* (the semiotic motor of differentiation effects) identify products remarkably similar in taste and texture. As an activity of engaged sensory awareness, "training and taste" vies with "identity communication." Brillat-Savarin put it simply enough when he coyly challenged: Tell me what you eat and I will tell you what you are (the gastronomer's riposte to *de gustibus non est disputandum*). Today foods and taste exhibit difference as superficial effects, visual cues on packaging and in advertising that have little to do with any reasoned use of sensory taste. Or, if present, they are, as famously suggested by gangster Vincent Vega, during the infamous "hamburger scene" of Quentin Tarantino's film *Pulp Fiction*, only "little differences"; no less important for being so since everyone has very particular taste. But the differences alluded to in the film, between fast food in Europe and in America, are entirely superficial, given the generic similarity of these highly processed products. For fast-food consumers, it is the image of the food as much as the "little differences" that matter. As Brillat-Savarin's prescient claim underlines, taste is to be understood as a popular, communicable sign of one's identity.

Theorizing Taste: Tastescapes

To return at this point to the concept of a contemporary connoisseurship means recognizing the historical limitations of taste discussed above, since connoisseurship has suffered from similar determinisms. This suggests that what is required is to engage with taste as a sensory modality equipped for aesthetic duties—for sensing, rather than merely being configured within a predetermined set of taste relations. Connoisseurship also suggests ascribing a locus for this activity. The home can be considered central to a contemporary form of connoisseurship that reengages with the notion of taste as a comprehensive form of knowledge that encompasses food production (garden), preparation (kitchen), and dining. It provides a locus where the wisdom in Epicurus's philosophy of "sober reasoning which tracks down the causes of every choice and avoidance" might also come into play.[61] Moreover, the home presents itself as a nodal point of global interconnectivity between any number of contemporary "scapes" (Arjun Appadurai's famous conceptualization includes ethno-, media-, techno-, finance-, and ideoscapes), cultural fields that are formed and maintained through media interconnectivity.[62]

The immediate challenges that confront grassroots taste education come into focus when we contextualize domestic foodscapes and tastescapes (amalgamations of material, ideological, and technological elements) within this broader global cultural economy, connected by media, serviced by car and supermarket, as it is by local and global food provision systems. Here the notion of taste relations suggests the ongoing intertwining and production of tastes within domestic spaces that no longer only correspond to actual places, times, or tastes. This is a "deterritorialized" space where tastes flow in various directions and form according to different orders of taste relations. The connoisseur at home is therefore an observer who takes it all in and digests different sorts of information before acting. A specific play of forces here creates tastes. Foodies are fond of singing the praises of cultural-culinary diversity, of the local, of authenticity, of difference and specificity in relation to food qualities. But this food culture depends absolutely on globalizing forces, including "glocalization," whereby global tastes are transformed at the local level, creating two-way traffic between the local and global. Tastescapes are not reducible to the foods and tastes themselves but only to the relations that give rise to them. As products become part of a global retail market, the impression or image they create puts pressure on amateur cooks and gardeners to compete in terms of quality and availability. We can therefore lose our taste for any real variety in flavor in the onrush of "real" products that are often in fact divested of any gustatory distinctiveness by a standardization that affects everything from extra-virgin olive oil and spices to "organic" meat, fruit, and vegetables. The hypothetical home connoisseur is aware that taste relations are shaped by global trends and "tastes" but also stays in touch with the garden, the season, the locality, region, and increasingly with politics, ethics, health science, and economy.

Connoisseurship today is being remade without much attention being paid to the process even though ethical food choices are being made, gastronomic ideals and values are being shared and lived by, and intercultural explorations of food culture have certainly raised awareness. Too often, however, what begins in earnest ends in the banality of commercialization or rigid orthodoxy. Classic connoisseurship went in both directions: democratization and elitism. A moment taken to reflect (what the archetypal connoisseur calls appreciation) also means to conceive of the "lines of flight" that connect taste to the earth, the sun, and the stars, and to the culinary-cultural histories that already make sense of it. As theorist Rick Dolphijn recognizes in his Deleuzian reading of global food culture, "it is only within the event, within the way relations are being shaped, that entities are created."[63] The organic structure of taste relations, are also rediscovered, as commentator Michael Pollan suggests: "What would happen if we were to start thinking about food as less of a thing and more of a relationship? . . . Relationships among species in systems we call food chains, or food webs, that reach all the way down to the soil."[64] Tastes are events, entities insofar as they represent, at the same time as they embody, a deep connectedness between the physiological act of tasting and the global event of which they are a part, insofar as taste remains simultaneously connected to the earth, to the global food system and to the expression of cultural "tastes."

Tastes always bring the outside inside, creating tastescapes that are not made up of material or chemical "facts," but that are constructed from the moveable feast of relations that develop at any given moment. A flavor reaches out to the world, to *a* world at least; it creates that world, as Marcel Proust so well understood. Mathew Latkiewicz writes of tasting: "I am interested in the reality of that space/moment—that horribly elusive union of intellect and sensation; external and internal; space and time."[65] Dolphijn encompasses the same idea about the convergence of space, time, and taste when he reflects on the shift from the dining room to meals consumed in front of the TV: "It is in the relation that time and space are created."[66] Within this domestic foodscape, it is easy to see how food, entertainment, and taste collapse into each other. The first TV dinners even came in a box that looked like a TV. You watched what you ate because the new food products were advertised on TV as you ate what you watched. This conflation is a contemporary addition to the dynamics of the domestic tastescape, one already overdetermined by the creation of flavors and products (seventeen thousand new ones each year in the United States), by philosophic and scientific discourse, and by cultural prejudice combined. This configuration of forces collectively wages a sort of war against the living agency of taste.

Theorizing the interconnectedness of taste-nature-culture requires adopting a kind of fluid model of flow and exchange. Such a model of flow and exchange already exists in sensory taste itself. Taste must not only be regarded as flavor (or texture, and so on), but also as a mode of engagement. Needless to say, the commercially driven strategy to sell products using sensory marketing techniques has to some extent picked up on the recent academic interest being taken in the senses. Sensory education, which has been creating connections and establishing relationships in the school system, with "kitchen-garden" programs now running in many Western countries, has also been taken seriously by media and advertising, who have developed strategies that use the cross-identification of sensory experiences as marketing tools. Represented by a metaphorical model of synesthesia, and typical of what theorist David Howes has dubbed "the sensory logic of late capitalism," such strategies turn the senses and sense experience into commodities.[67] Here one sense takes on the attributes of another within the advertising context, for example.[68] In this way, mass media representations of taste and the savvy marketing ethos that drive them, serve to reconfigure the sensorium, at the same time as they build on long-held prejudices and conceptions of taste (and of the other senses) deeply embedded in cultural life. The denigration of (gustatory) pleasure, as sinful, for example, although a moral position seemingly no longer recognized by our pleasure-seeking society, nonetheless appeals, subliminally, in the sense that the pleasures of taste are represented as being experienced as isolated effects, experienced without any super-ego interjection from the conscience. No ethics are required or responsibility taken. This historical decontextualization of taste has a huge shaping influence on taste's potential as a mode of knowing. As I have been arguing, taste relations (always) include ethical, intellectual, emotional, perceptual, as well as "sensational" elements that can, if recognized, contribute to pleasure-as-knowledge in the experience of taste. To conceive of taste only as pleasure in a purely hedonistic sense paradoxically exposes the Western world's perverse refusal to acknowledge taste's deep connectedness to the natural world, something that, as a culture, the West has been distancing itself from more and more. Nowhere is this distancing from nature more pronounced than when regarding food culture.

This sensory logic is literally capitalized on as it confirms how much is actually already understood and implemented with regard to taste relations. Taste is operationalized as a feeling of proximity (closeness) by being conflated with instant gratification, thus foreclosing on any sense in which the broader cultural context figures in the individual's experience of taste at all.[69] Taste relations in this instance remain undisclosed, internalized within the immediacy of the moment, and conditioned by the expectation of instantaneous thrills. Added values, from "instant" and "fat-free" to "authenticity" and "organic," preseason taste experience by creating expectation and the promise of gratifying desires for these "values," but by symbolically refusing to separate the proximate world of literal consumption from the generalized world of consumption as such, food advertising always tends to collapse the social outside into the sensational inside. Taste and pleasure therefore tend more and more to be experienced as transient, internalized effects that bear no real relation to social reality. This trend is perfectly in step with the growth of individualized eating patterns that create the point of entry for the promotion of this type of no-frills, guilt-free hedonism, equated as it is with the maximization of intense feelings and sensations—sensation as opposed to perception. Current food-related trends do illustrate how food and taste can be reconnected to agriculture, ethics, politics, economy, and ecology, adding meaning, creating knowledge through pleasure, also potentially increasing quality, variety, and nuances of taste, as in dialectical fashion, the influence of taste-as-knowledge grows. But given the inimitable gusto with which marketing executives apply their methodological insights to the workings of consumer desire, taste has some way to go before it can be extricated from the sensory logic of late capitalism.

Taste has also been taken out of all culinary contexts and reified as a modus operandi in marketing. Citing proto-capitalist Benjamin Franklin to begin his recent book, *Brand Sense: Build Powerful Brands Through Touch, Taste, Smell, Sight and Sound*, "brand futurist" Martin Lindstrom selects the following lines: "Tell me and I'll forget, show me and I might remember, involve me and I'll understand."[70] Apparently enamored of "stimulation" with regard to sensory life, Lindstrom understands involvement to mean sensory immersion, an approach that translates into one chapter heading as "Stimulate, Enhance, Bond." His how-to-enhance handbook therefore stresses "sensory consistency," advising, "If you've defined your consistent tactile, aroma, and visual expression, don't tamper with it—let it become mandatory in your brand platform."[71] The book goes to some pains, with typically evangelical zeal, to stress that the senses are marketing tools to be exploited. That this relatively recent, but already widely instrumentalized, approach will involve ever more sophisticated knowledge and constantly diversifying forms of hyperstimulation of the consumer's aesthetic experience may prove to be increasingly wearying. Keeping up with food fashions will henceforth extend to sensations themselves and "shopping till you drop" may soon become merely an additional side effect of sensory overload. Lindstrom indicates the kind of change underlined, eerily corroborating Jean Baudrillard's submission that the real recedes as it makes way for the simulated, although one should say, in Lindstrom's case, the stimulated: "Sensory authenticity" requires that "things have to feel credible, real, and genuine—even if coming from an artificial place. That's the paradox. People don't necessarily want to step into the Matrix, where everything is an illusion," meaning that sensory experience is always "real" even when it is being used to convey a false sense of the worth of a product or service.[72] The senses are appropriated, repackaged, and plugged back into daily experience as if nothing happened. Given that the sensorium is a system providing integrated aesthetic awareness, it only seems reasonable to expect that every measure will be taken to simulate/stimulate the sensorium, by whatever means. Shopping, like living, is now being seen as a seamless sensory adventure, as Lindstrom, like many others working in this field today, fully understands.

This presents another aspect of the cultural grid within which taste is now shaped, a grid ruled to a great extent by representations that can, for example, happily trade on culinary tradition, like "peasant cuisine," without fear of arousing any public sense of irony. Peasant food can scale the heights of fashion in a world almost devoid of peasants because representing peasant food as authentic (ethnically pure, honest, simple, or healthy), as well as tasty, is representative of a broader process whereby (food) fashion continually recycles a seemingly inexhaustible number of (culinary) traditions, linked as these are to the generalized desire for nostalgia, tradition, and authenticity. Dishes like risotto, for example, became iconic in the 1990s among neophilic urban communities of diners. But given the conditions of overexposure that must develop in our media-saturated age, as soon as they appear, dishes like risotto can never remain true to any origins, whether real or imagined. Like pizza before it, risotto soon became just another concocted dish, trading on its apparent authenticity, while simultaneously being a handy excuse for adding any old assortment of ingredients to a base of Arborio rice. "A simple dish," turned vehicle for hybrid experimentation and fusion, risotto perfectly suited the vicarious and omnivorous taste of customers.

While taste certainly has a past, one that remains perennially appealing (in the form of dishes like risotto), the recycling of that past in the present results in a multiplication of styles that collectively represents the fundamental influence on taste of the media, not the past. Mobilized within the global economy of consumption, such a tastescape perfectly illustrates the simultaneously global and local (glocal) nature of taste relations, which apply across time and space, whether as tradition reinvented in the present (risotto) or as a conflation of globally sourced ingredients within a single hybrid dish.

Any potential connoisseurship is clearly going to be challenged by what the foregoing describes. But I do not want to dwell any longer on what, somewhat depressingly, appears to be the all too logical development of consumerism, because along with these clearly negative developments are the positive countermoves taking shape to redress the role of taste in our lives. Firstly, the current "sensory turn" should be regarded as a welcome change: an analytical approach to the role of the sensorium and to the ways in which sense experience is culturally constructed. Studying taste in this way also means understanding culture as a dynamic process, one that configures conceptual, corporeal, and material worlds. Reflecting this understanding, significant political, ecological, and ethical strategies that implicate taste in positive ways have been in place for some years. Examples include the Slow Food organization, the surge in collaborative gastronomic tourism (that has the potential, through developing foodways, to reinvest local communities with identity, purpose, and economic benefits), and educational food- and taste-related programs. Added to these efforts are growing interest from academic and theoretical perspectives, like Fosalli and his colleagues, who publish through the University of Gastronomic Sciences (which, like Slow Food, is based in Italy). Such action is cause for thinking positively about the fate of taste and connoisseurship. Put simply, to know more about one's food, where it comes from, how it is produced, and what it tastes like as the result of numerous processes, both natural and cultural, means to potentially increase knowledge. This translates into pleasure taken in the taste of things known. Pleasure as knowledge.

The kind of connoisseurship implied here is already in evidence. Culinary superstar Jamie Oliver, for example, who has waged a very public one-man battle against what he describes as the "poverty" of food culture in the United Kingdom, has over the last ten years expanded his own personal tastescape, incorporating philosophy and ethics into a perspective that now encompasses the provenance of food, from the ground up. Following Oliver's career, which has largely been lived in front of a television camera, his audience has watched and no doubt appreciated how he has invested so much time, effort, and money into projects designed to help educate the British public about good food. His school-dinners program and Fifteen (the group of charity restaurants in which he takes fifteen disadvantaged young people and gives them a chance to become chefs) were direct interventions. More recently he has "gone country" in his kitchen garden program, filmed at his rural home where he waxes lyrical about the freshness and wholesomeness of home-grown foods. In 2008 he tried to get the entire city of Rotherham to take part in learning how to cook, enlisting council and locals in a drive dubbed "Pass it On," the nerve center of which was a centrally located kitchen-administration base called Jamie's Ministry of Food. This tele-history gives a palpable sense of the personal journey Oliver has taken from celebrity chef, to thinking, philosophizing social activist. Oliver represents one aspect of what contemporary connoisseurship might look like: an intelligent, ethically aware cook, with a social conscience, and, not forgetting, a desire for tasty food. Oliver is philanthropic in the same way as his illustrious nineteenth-century counterpart Alexis Soyer, who shared a desire to please, to nurture, to help, and educate. In this sense, connoisseurship is not by nature about consumption at all, but about conceiving of taste as the consummation of everything that leads to and away from it—to the social, that is the commensal aspect of food and eating; to discourse and the literal communication of ideas; and to philosophy (the symposium). These are not grandiose ideals so much as practical realities to be explored.

Other notable "connoisseurs," not directly involved in any hands-on way in cooking or producing, nonetheless reconnect taste to the world and therefore to the knowledge that feeds into it. Michael Pollan, whose two food books to date track the influence of scientific discourse, applied science, industry, big business and governmental agency on food culture and taste, could be counted among them. Pollan also takes pains to underline the ecology of taste (not his phrase), all the natural links that are created in the complexity of food chains that exist in the natural world; how these elements create taste; and how important it is to be aware of these links. Notwithstanding the efforts of people like Oliver and Pollan, food culture cannot very well change under the influence of a few good men and women. The Slow Food Movement is growing, along with the numbers of consumers who actively support farmers' markets and local production, and who involve their children in kitchen gardens at school and cooking at home. But connoisseurship also requires a very personal reappraisal of sensory life.

Urban and Domestic Tastescapes: From Lion Estouffade to All the Bits of the Boar

Tastes are an active constituent of contemporary imagined worlds, of individual tastescapes. We have noted the sensualization of products that is currently taking place. One might say that this is possible because of deterritorialization. The deterritorializing of taste also means that it too creates events. Taste, as a force, as a particular event, enters the greater global culture, igniting interest, inviting sensory engagement, and sharpening intellectual appetites. I want to finish here with an example of how taste-as-event can make a difference. In a brief but pertinent piece called "What a City Could Taste Like," entrepreneurs Katie Rabinowicz and Andea Winkler (in a move that recalls Michel de Certeau's strategies for "walkers" reclaiming the space of the city on their own terms) call for the reincorporation, rather than increasing outlawing and marginalization, of street food vendors.[73] This ground-up approach to the production of taste does not necessarily fall within the regime of food culture as it is managed by the media and food empires or sensory marketers. Street food vending circumvents the superhighways, to take the byways of taste, where flavors, aromas, and eating experiences provide the opportunity to connect with cooks who vie for business on the merits of their skill.

It is not product design or packaging that matters most here, but "preserving a wide array of cultural traits including traditional professions, a characteristic urban infrastructure, and consumption of food items that have their roots deep in the history of the region," write Matalas and Yannokoulia, in describing street food vending in Greece.[74] Fancy venues, marketing spin, and fashionability are undermined by the fragrance of foods that appeal on their own terms. The paradoxical outcome of progress in Western domestic food provision is that in terms of the now-global trend away from cooking at home, eating out regularly has become the norm. Historically, street foods "exhibit a diurnal pattern that follows people's activities and food habits," currently reflected in a range of nearly a thousand different food types being sold on the bustling city streets of the Asian continent, in India, Japan, Indonesia, and the Philippines.[75] But the streets of the West are rapidly losing their traditions of street food, a natural and egalitarian ally of an inquiring taste. Although the West's ethnic diversity of cuisine must be acknowledged here, ethnic cuisine can also become *represented* as merely one among other styles (or stylizations); the foods offered often being travesties of culinary tradition. Street foods serve to maintain and reintroduce gustatory dynamics and surprising new tastes to inspire the spirit of inquiry that the education of taste depends on. That street food vending is actively being discouraged in Western cities represents a missed opportunity to encourage unrestricted diversity and so too to enter the tastescape as an adventurer in taste, something that the archetypal gourmand Grimod de La Reynière emphasized when he called for an "enlightened sense of taste . . . developed through extensive experience."[76]

For me, sensory taste, and following from that, discriminatory taste, are intersubjective and intercultural modes that rely ultimately on the relations that take the fluid form of a tastescape: a subjectively oriented taste that must be negotiated, for example, through simultaneous engagement with the global foodscape, the domestic foodscape, and the street tastescape. One irony of capitalism is that those critical endeavors to redress its iniquities or shortcomings may in time become commercialized as well. Rethinking taste can also mean reflecting on the system's own capacity for survival. New York's Central Park has recently become home to the Brooklyn Flea, a group committed to offering the public "quality, affordable, and locally made" foods with an "ecological" profile: coarse-ground pork sausages and wood-fire pizza.[77] These street foods help revive the individual's tastescape because potentially they open the consumer to provenance and production, communicating and connecting as they provide nourishment and pleasure. Again, ironically, it is the most cosmopolitan of cultures that cyclically "return" to food and taste basics, even while remaining quintessentially urban.

Thinking abstractly in this way is a first step in addressing the problems that confront taste. After all, abstract thinking has done a great deal to historically construct taste and our attitude to it. It has been "the rigid historical criticism of taste" that has "organized our whole [Western] experience . . . even the contemporary 'reevaluation' of taste and smell," writes Nicolla Perullo.[78] The notion of connoisseurship has provided an historical reference point for the discussion of the issues presented here and highlights that while sensory taste's role in knowledge creation and experience has been undermined, undervalued, and overdetermined, the notion that "the act of tasting, the taste experience itself, does not require knowledge," remains a constant.[79] It is the singular prerequisite that confirms taste's role in defining culture, since it presents the hope of creating individualized tastescapes that can redress the historical forces that continue to shape the experience of taste to this day.

The antisystem of street food vending, while raising the hackles of health authorities, also affirms at least the notional usefulness of the Fourierist series. Here "passionate attraction," led by the sense of taste and smell, seems at present to drive a new dimension of social engagement that is not limited by the restaurant or other culinary formalisms that result in thematizing, codification, and stereotypical dishes. As Rebecca Spang suggests, in a paper that addresses our conventional understanding of the historical role of the restaurant, street foods represent a "visibility" that equates with social reality, whereas the restaurant serves—as it in fact always has—as a façade that during the period of the restaurant's "invention" (Spang's term) served to reinforce class and social divisions made to look uncomfortably vulnerable in the years following the revolution.[80] For most of the nineteenth century, cooks were confined to belowground kitchens where they were made to endure horrific conditions for little pay. Whereas diners, to quote Spang, "retreat to the comfortingly familiar and invisible food production characteristic of a 'proper' restaurant" (original emphasis).[81] Taste, as a mode of knowing, can only benefit where the exchange of culinary and gastronomic determinants works freely. I am not arguing that championing street food is the answer to any future gastronomy, or gastrosophy (as Fourier called it), but rather that it signals where a fundamental difference exists between the singular, directed path modern taste's development has taken compared to how culinary and gastronomic cultures can develop organically. That is, without being limited by abstract divisions like that between consumption and production; historically, the restaurant reproduced the division between the old aristocracy and the (new) servant class (including the cooks) who served them. Separating restaurant kitchens from dining rooms further achieved social segregation and so legitimization for the capitalist middle classes, whose interests were served by any façade that obscured their connection to production, be it kitchens or otherwise. As Marx argued, the success of the ongoing control of the labor of others rested in part on obscuring their working lives. Out of sight, out of mind. To some extent the restaurant smoothed the passage of bourgeois revolution, as its invented interiors, themed on opulence and grandeur, posed emblematically as civilization and progress—the sophistry of cuisine being enough to permanently distract its occupants from any interest in the provenance of their food or the plight of those who provided it.

It is therefore no surprise that in the present climate of experimentation and consumer-led economics—where the value of culture as an added spice to one's eating experience involves knowing more and more about food (where it comes from, who has made it, how it is made, according to which tradition, and so on)—we should note a new phenomenon, called "the anti-restaurant."[82] This is a place of a new breed of gourmand, less interested in the language of food (gastronomy), in the formality of dining, or in the prescriptive form of knowledge of that which would have once singled out the connoisseur from the "lower orders." The anti-restaurant is reportedly an "underground" (as in guerrilla) restaurant, where evenings themed for example around "exploring and cherishing an entire wild boar" involve hands-on engagement from "diners" willing to pay eighty dollars to take part. A growing phenomenon, such events have been staged by "passionate enthusiasts" who, in recent years, have "opened dozens of unlicensed restaurants in apartments" but "do not generally aspire to become traditional restaurateurs. . . . They are not in it for the money . . . but for the community and the creative freedom." By "stringing together the farm-to-table movement and a bloggy kind of interactivity," the passionate enthusiasts prefer "intimate and casual to grand and ceremonial, and are open to meeting people and building connections in new ways." With names like New York Bite Club; A Razor, A Shiny Knife; Homeslice West; and Eat with your Hands!, such groups resemble nucleic phalansteries where "opinion on local versus organic" (that is, ethics) combines in a free association of impulse, intrigue, and a touch of danger.[83] Fourier would, I think, be excited by the prospect. The connoisseur no longer lingers over lion. Instead, a new breed of connoisseur is being forged outside of the conformism that has dogged the history of cuisine and served to overdetermine taste for over two centuries.

Beyond the scope of this discussion are a number of converging food-related cultures that focus on reconfiguring taste at the center of daily life and self-actualization. These include hospitality studies, Slow Food, popularized food ethics and politics, children's food-education programs; academic disciplines from ethics and agriculture to food studies and gastronomy; gastronomic tourism (at best a form of social change) and the media representation of cookery, food, and celebrity chefs. These cultural trends reflect a desire to act on a number of levels. To lionize the value of taste and its role in our lives now suggests a pluralistic multileveled activity no longer aimed at expressing status, satisfying hedonism, or fashionable to the extent that it creates and communicates "identity." Connoisseurship must be founded on taste understood as a mode of knowing that informs choice, and that has been reclaimed from a history not of its making.

Notes

1. Fin-Bec [pseudonym of William Blanchard Jerrold, 1826–84], *The Book of Menus 1876* (London: Grant, 1876), 297–98. Jerrold's account also describes the preparation of both dishes.

2. See, for example, Jerry Hopkins, *Extreme Cuisine: The Weird and Wonderful Foods That People Eat* (New York: Tuttle Publishing, 2004).

3. Paul Rozin, "The Selection of Foods by Rats, Humans, and Other Animals," in *Advances in the Study of Behavior*, vol. 6, ed. D. Lehrman, R. A. Hinde, and E. Shaw (New York: Academic Press, 1976), 21–76.

4. Pierre Bourdieu, *Distinction: A Social Critique of the Judgment of Taste* (Cambridge MA: Harvard University Press, 1984).

5. For recent examples, see, Josée Johnston and Shyon Baumann, "Democracy versus Distinction: A Study of Omnivorousness in Gourmet Food Writing," *American Journal of Sociology* 113, no. 1 (July 2007): 165–204; also Alan Warde, David Wright, and Modesto Gayo-Cal, "Understanding Cultural Omnivorousness: Or, the Myth of the Cultural Omnivore," *Cultural Sociology* 1, no. 2 (2007): 143–64.

6. Anthropologist Gregory Bateson described culture as a mutually interdependent world in which individual relationships are shaped by shared meanings at the same time as these collective meanings inform

the individual's understanding of their actions. See Gregory Bateson, *Steps to an Ecology of Mind* (Chicago: University of Chicago Press, 1999).

7. See Carolyn Korsmeyer, *Making Sense of Taste: Food and Philosophy* (Ithaca NY: Cornell University Press, 1999).

8. See Geneviève Teil and Antoine Hennion, "Discovering Quality or Performing Taste? A Sociology of the Amateur," in *Qualities of Food*, ed. Mark Harvey, Andrew McMeekin, and Alan Warde (Manchester University Press, 2004).

9. Warde et al., "Understanding Cultural Omnivorousness," 161.

10. See http://www.aglassandahalffullproductions.com/#/gorilla/, accessed October 10, 2008.

11. See Jean-Anthelme Brillat-Savarin, *The Physiology of Taste*, trans. Anne Drayton (Harmondsworth: Penguin, 1970); and excerpts by Alexandre Balthazar Laurent Grimod de La Reynière in *Gusto: Essential Writings in Nineteenth-century Gastronomy*, trans. Michael D. Garval, ed. Denise Gigante (New York: Routledge, 2005), 1–55.

12. I refer to the term used by Priscilla Pankhurst Ferguson in her theoretical essay on French gastronomy during this period, "A Cultural Field in the Making: Gastronomy in Nineteenth-Century France," *American Journal of Sociology* 104, no. 3 (1998): 597–641.

13. Brillat-Savarin, *Physiology of Taste*, 52.

14. Cited in Ferguson, "Cultural Field," 609.

15. *Financier* was the gastronomic appellation ascribed to dishes that were "rich," and survives today as a butter-rich cake, known as *financier*. For Granville's banker, see Robert Courtine, *The Hundred Glories of French Cooking*, (New York: Farrar, Straus, Giroux, 1973), 209.

16. Norbert Elias, "The Kitsch Style and the Age of Kitsch," in *The Norbert Elias Reader: A Biographical Selection*, ed. Johan Goudsblom and Stephen Mennell (Cambridge UK: Blackwell, 1998), 31.

17. Jean-Anthelme Brillat-Savarin, *Physiologie du goût ou Méditations de gastronomie transcendente; œuvrage théorique, historique et a l'order du jour...* (Paris: A. Sautelet, 1826).

18. Brillat-Savarin titled his book *The Physiology of Taste* and frequently uses scientific terms in his discussion as a way of legitimizing

his discourse. On Carême's scientism, see Alf Rehn, "Anachronism and Innovation: A Case of Hybrid Economies in the Early Nineteenth Century," *Management and Organizational History* 2, no. 1 (2006): 71–86.

19. Rebecca Spang, "All the World's a Restaurant," in *Food in Global History*, ed. Raymond Grew (Boulder CO: Westview Press, 1999), 80.

20. X. Marcel Boulestin, *What Shall We Have Today?* (London: William Heinemann, 1931), 23.

21. Ann Barr and Paul Levy, *The Official Foodie Handbook* (London: Ebury Press, 1984), 136.

22. Cited in Julia Csergo, "The Emergence of Regional Cuisines," in *Food: A Culinary History from Antiquity to the Present*, ed. Jean-Louis Flandrin, Massimo Montanari, and Albert Sonnenfeld (New York: Columbia University Press, 1999), 507.

23. Leon Rappoport, *How We Eat: Appetite, Culture, and the Psychology of Food* (Toronto: ECW Press, 2003), 115.

24. On Fourier's works in English, see Charles Fourier, *The Passions of the Human Soul*, vol. 1, trans. John Reynell Morell (London: Hippolyte Bailliere, 1851 [online facsimile]); Jonathan Beecher and Richard Bienvenu, eds., *The Utopian Vision of Charles Fourier: Selected Texts on Work, Love, and Passionate Attraction* (Boston: Beacon Press, 1971); Charles Fourier, *The Theory of the Four Movements*, ed. Gareth Stedman Jones and Ian Patterson (Cambridge: Cambridge University Press, 1996).

25. Octavio Paz, "At Table and in Bed," in *Convergences: Essays on Literature and Art* (London: Bloomsbury, 1990), 72.

26. Fourier, *Passions*, 29.

27. Fourier, *Passions*, 49.

28. Fourier, *Theory of the Four Movements*, 159.

29. Fourier, *Theory of the Four Movements*, 169.

30. Fourier, *Passions*, 31, 32.

31. Fourier, *Utopian Vision*, 267.

32. Fourier, *Passions*, 33.

33. Fourier, *Utopian Vision*, 269.

34. Fourier, *Utopian Vision*, 269.

35. Fourier, *Passions*, 34–35.

36. Jean-Philippe Derenne, cited in Adam Gopnik, *Paris to the Moon: A Family in France* (New York: Vintage, 2001), 163.

37. Gopnik, *Paris to the Moon*, 162.

38. Alain-Claude Roudot, "Food Science and Consumer Taste," *Gastronomica* 4, no. 1 (2004): 41–46, 45.

39. Fin-Bec, *Book of Menus*, 1–3.

40. Richard A. Peterson and Roger M. Kern, "Changing Highbrow Taste: From Snob to Omnivore," *American Sociological Review* 61, no. 5 (1996): 900–907.

41. Charlene Elliott, "Considering the Connoisseur: Probing the Language of Taste," *Canadian Review of American Studies* 36, no. 2 (2006): 230.

42. Elliott, "Considering the Connoisseur," 232.

43. Elliott, "Considering the Connoisseur," 233.

44. Elliot, "Considering the Connoisseur," 233.

45. Elliott, "Considering the Connoisseur," 234.

46. Elliott, "Considering the Connoisseur," 235.

47. "Trendwatch," *The Independent on Sunday*, July 2, 2006, http://findarticles.com/p/articles/mi_qn4159/is_/ai_n16514177?tag=artBody;col1, accessed September 18, 2008.

48. *Independent.uk*, August 20, 2005, http://www.independent.co.uk/news/science/the-future-now-10-lifestyle-trends-502288.html, accessed June 15, 2008.

49. Phillip Coorey (chief political correspondent), "Greed is bad," *Sydney Morning Herald*, October 16, 2008. Available online: http://www.smh.com.au/articles/2008/10/15/1223750129771.html.

50. For an indication, see the journal *Gastronomic Sciences*; also discussion, below.

51. Pierluigi Basso Fosalli, "The Consumption of Taste: Lifestyle and the Ecology of Communication," *Gastronomic Sciences* 1, no. 2 (2007): 26.

52. Fosalli, "Consumption of Taste," 29.

53. Kent Bach, "Knowledge, Wine, and Taste: What Good is Knowledge (in Enjoying Wine?)," in *Questions of Taste: The Philosophy of Wine*, ed. Barry C. Smith (Oxford: Signal Books, 2007), 33.

54. Fosalli, "Consumption of Taste," 26.

55. Fosalli, "Consumption of Taste," 26.

56. Fosalli, "Consumption of Taste," 30.

57. Henri Lefebvre, *The Production of Space*, trans. Donald Nicholson-Smith (Cambridge UK: Blackwell, 1991 [1974]), 200–201.

58. C. Nadia Seremetakis, ed., *The Senses Still* (Chicago: University of Chicago Press, 1994), 6.

59. Fosalli, "Consumption of Taste," 30.

60. Fosalli, "Consumption of Taste," 30.

61. Epicurus, *Letter to Menoiceus*; Diogenes Laertius X, in *The Hellenistic Philosophers*, vol. 1, trans. and ed. A. A. Long and D. N. Sedley (Cambridge: Cambridge University Press, 1987), 131.

62. See Arjun Appadurai, "Global Ethnoscapes: Notes and Queries for a Transnational Anthropology," in *Interventions: Anthropologies of the Present*, ed. R. G. Fox (Santa Fe: School of American Research, 1991), 191–210. In this paper I additionally draw on the conceptualization of Rick Dolphijn, whose use of the term *foodscape* not only provides much food for thought but a rich vein of theoretical possibility for further research. Rick Dolphijn, *Foodscapes: Towards a Deleuzian Ethics of Consumption* (Delft: Eburon, 2004).

63. Dolphijn, *Foodscapes*, 16.

64. Michael Pollan, *In Defense of Food: An Eater's Manifesto* (New York: Penguin Group, 2008), 102.

65. Matthew Latkiewicz, "Notes from a Wine-Tasting, Being an Inquiry into Sensation," *Gastronomica* 3, no. 4 (2003): 45.

66. Dolphijn, *Foodscapes*, 19.

67. David Howes, "Hyperaesthesia, or, The Sensual Logic of Late Capitalism," in *Empire of the Senses: The Sensual Culture Reader*, ed. David Howes (New York: Berg, 2005), 287.

68. For a brief discussion of this phenomenon, see Roger Haden, "Taste in the Age of Convenience," in *The Taste Culture Reader*, ed. Carolyn Korsmeyer (New York: Berg, 2005), 344–58.

69. "Proxemic" is a term often used to describe the chemical, close-range senses of touch, taste, and smell.

70. Martin Lindstrom, *Brand Sense: Build Powerful Brands Through Touch, Taste, Smell, Sight, and Sound* (New York: Free Press, 2005).

71. Lindstrom, *Brand Sense*, 155.

72. Lindstrom, *Brand Sense*, 155.

73. Katie Rabinowicz and Andea Winkler, "What a City Could Taste Like," in *Food*, ed. John Knechtel (Cambridge MA: MIT Press, 2008), 272–77.

74. Antonia-Leda Matalas and Mary Yannokoulia, "Greek Street Food Vending: An Old Habit Turned New," in *Street Foods*, ed. A. P. Simopoulos and B. V. Bhat (New York: Karger, 2000), 22.

75. Ramesh V. Bhat and Kavita Waghray, "Profile of Street Foods Sold in Asian Countries," in *Street Foods*, ed. A. P. Simopoulos and B. V. Bhat (New York: Karger, 2000), 67.

76. De La Reynière, in *Gusto*, 12.

77. Pete Wells, "Brooklyn Flea Curates Central Park Food Vendors," *New York Times*, March 23, 2010.

78. Nicola Perullo, "The Inexpressible Nature of Taste," *Gastronomic Sciences* 1, no. 2 (2007): 20.

79. Perullo, "Nature of Taste," 20.

80. Rebecca Spang, *The Invention of the Restaurant: Paris and Modern Gastronomic Culture* (Cambridge MA: Harvard University Press, 2000).

81. Spang, "All the World's a Restaurant," 88.

82. Melena Ryzik, "The Anti-Restaurants," *New York Times*, August 27, 2008, F1.

83. Ryzik, "Anti-Restaurants," F1.

Contributors

JOHN DUCKER worked for many years as an actor. He is now a tutor for the Wine & Spirit Education Trust and also teaches for The Wine Education Service Ltd.

ROBERT GOODWIN is Visiting Research Fellow at University College London. He is the author of *A Taste of Spain* and *Crossing the Continent, 1527–1540: The Story of the First African-American Explorer of the American South.*

JUKKA GRONOW is Professor of Sociology at the University of Uppsala, Sweden, and a docent at the University of Helsinki, Finland. He is the author of *The Sociology of Taste* and editor, with Alan Warde, of *Ordinary Consumption.*

ROGER HADEN is Manager of Educational Leadership with Le Cordon Bleu. Between 2004 and 2009 he was Lecturer in Gastronomy and Director of the Research Centre for the History of Food and Drink at the University of Adelaide. He is author of *Food Culture in the Pacific Islands.*

LISA HARPER is adjunct Professor of Writing in the MFA program at the University of San Francisco. She has published in *Gastronomica* and is coeditor of *Learning to Eat.*

LISA HELDKE is Professor of Philosophy and Sponberg Chair in Ethics at Gustavus Adolphus College, Minnesota. She is the author of *Exotic Appetites: Ruminations of a Food Adventurer* and coeditor of

Cooking, Eating, Thinking: Transformative Philosophies of Food. She is coeditor of the journal *Food, Culture, and Society.*

MATTHEW HIBBERD is Deputy Head, Department of Film, Media, and Journalism, University of Stirling, Scotland. He is Visiting Professor of Communication Theory at the Libera Università Internazionale per gli Studi Sociali (LUISS) and Visiting Professor of Journalism at the Interdisciplinary Centre for Social Communications (CICS), Pontifical Gregorian University, both in Rome.

COLIN LAWSON is Director of The Royal College of Music, London. He has an international profile as a period clarinettist and is the author of numerous books and articles, including *The Cambridge Companion to the Orchestra.*

JEREMY STRONG is Head of Higher Education at Writtle College, Essex, and Chair of the Association of Adaptation Studies. He has published in *Gastronomica, Literature/Film Quarterly,* and *Paragraph.* He is editor, with Garin Dowd and Lesley Stevenson, of *Genre Matters: Essays in Theory and Criticism.*

TIM WATERMAN is a landscape architect, urbanist, and former restaurateur. His current research is concerned with issues of taste and everyday practice at the intersection of home, community, civic life, and landscape. He is the author of *The Fundamentals of Landscape Architecture* and, with Ed Wall, of *Basics of Landscape Architecture: Urban Design.* He teaches in the School of Design at Writtle College.

SERGEY ZHURAVLEV is a leading researcher at the Institute of Russian History of the Russian Academy of Sciences in Moscow and a member of the *Slavic Review* editorial board. He is the author of "Malen'kie liudi" i" bol'shaya istoriya" and other books on Soviet history.

In the AT TABLE SERIES

To order or obtain more information on these or other University
of Nebraska Press titles, visit
www.nebraskapress.unl.edu.

Trocaire Libraries

CPSIA information can be obtained at www.ICGtesting.com
Printed in the USA
BVOW051612080911

270691BV00004B/8/P